MORAL MACHINES

Moral Machines

Teaching Robots Right from Wrong

WENDELL WALLACH
COLIN ALLEN

OXFORD
UNIVERSITY PRESS

2009

OXFORD
UNIVERSITY PRESS

Oxford University Press, Inc., publishes works that further
Oxford University's objective of excellence
in research, scholarship, and education.

Oxford   New York
Auckland   Cape Town   Dar es Salaam   Hong Kong   Karachi
Kuala Lumpur   Madrid   Melbourne   Mexico City   Nairobi
New Delhi   Shanghai   Taipei   Toronto

With offices in
Argentina   Austria   Brazil   Chile   Czech Republic   France   Greece
Guatemala   Hungary   Italy   Japan   Poland   Portugal   Singapore
South Korea   Switzerland   Thailand   Turkey   Ukraine   Vietnam

Copyright © 2009 by Oxford University Press, Inc.

Published by Oxford University Press, Inc.
198 Madison Avenue, New York, NY 10016

www.oup.com

Oxford is a registered trademark of Oxford University Press

Library of Congress Cataloging-in-Publication Data
Wallach, Wendell, 1946–
Moral machines : teaching robots right from wrong
/ Wendell Wallach and Colin Allen.
p.   cm.
Includes bibliographical references and index.
ISBN 978-0-19-537404-9
1. Robotics.   2. Computers—Social aspects.
3. Computers—Moral and ethical aspects.   I. Allen, Colin.   II. Title.
TJ211.W36 2009
629.8'92—dc22
2008011800

9 8 7 6 5 4 3 2 1

Printed in the United States of America
on acid-free paper

Dedicated to all whose work inspired our thinking,
and especially to our colleague Iva Smit

CONTENTS

ACKNOWLEDGMENTS

We owe much to many for the genesis and production of this book. First and foremost, we'd like to thank our colleague Dr. Iva Smit, with whom we coauthored several articles on moral machines. We have drawn extensively on those articles in writing this book. No doubt many of the ideas and words in these pages originated with her, and we are particularly indebted for her contributions to chapter 6. Iva also played a significant role in helping us develop an outline for the book. Her influence on the field is broader than this, however. By organizing a series of symposia from 2002 through 2005 that brought together scholars interested in machine morality, she has made a lasting contribution to this emerging field of study. Indeed, we might not have met each other had Iva not invited us both to the first of these symposia in Baden-Baden, Germany, in 2002. Her warmth and graciousness bound together a small community of scholars, whose names appear among those that follow. A key motivation for Iva is the need to raise awareness among business and government leaders of the dangers posed by autonomous systems. Because we elected to focus on the technological aspects of developing artificial moral agents, this may not be the book she would have written. Nevertheless, we hope to have conveyed some of her sense of the dangers of ethically blind systems.

The four symposia organized by Dr. Smit with the title "Cognitive, Emotive and Ethical Aspects of Decision Making in Humans and in Artificial Intelligence" took place under the auspices of the International Institute for Advanced Studies in Systems Research and Cybernetics, headed by George Lasker. We would like to thank Professor Lasker as well as the other participants in these symposia. In more recent years, a number of workshops on machine morality have contributed to our deeper understanding of the subject, and we want to thank the organizers and participants in those workshops.

Colin Allen's initial foray into the field began back in 1999, when he was invited by Varol Akman to write an article for the *Journal of Experimental and Theoretical Artificial Intelligence*. A chance remark led to the realization that the question of how to build artificial moral agents was unexplored philosophical territory. Gary Varner supplied expertise in ethics, and Jason Zinser, a graduate student, provided the enthusiasm and hard work that made it possible for a jointly authored article to be published in 2000. We have drawn on that article in writing this book.

Wendell Wallach taught an undergraduate seminar at Yale University in 2004 and 2005 titled "Robot Morals and Human Ethics." He would like to thank his students for their insights and enthusiasm, which contributed significantly to the development of his ideas. One of the students, Jonathan Hartman, proposed an original idea we discuss in chapter 7. Wendell's discussions with Professor Stan Franklin were especially important to chapter 11. Stan helped us write that chapter, in which we apply his learning intelligent distribution agent (LIDA) model for artificial general intelligence to the problem of building artificial moral agents. He should be credited as a coauthor of that chapter.

Various other colleagues' and students' comments and suggestions have found their way into the book. We would particularly like to mention Michael and Susan Anderson, Kent Babcock, David Calverly, Ron Chrisley, Peter Danielson, Simon Davidson, Luciano Floridi, Owen Holland, James Hughes, Elton Joe, Peter Kahn, Bonnie Kaplan, Gary Koff, Patrick Lin, Karl MacDorman, Willard Miranker, Rosalind Picard, Tom Powers, Phil Rubin, Brian Scasselati, Wim Smit, Christina Spiesel, Steve Torrance, and Vincent Wiegel.

Special thanks are reserved for those who provided detailed comments on various chapters. Candice Andalia and Joel Marks both commented on several chapters, while Fred Allen and Tony Beavers deserve the greatest credit for having commented on the entire manuscript. Their insights have immeasurably improved the book.

In August 2007, we spent a delightful week in central Pennsylvania hammering out a nearly complete manuscript of the book. Our hosts were Carol and Rowland Miller, at the Quill Haven bed and breakfast. Carol's sumptuous breakfasts, Rowland's enthusiastic responses to the first couple of chapters, and the plentiful supply of coffee, tea, and cookies fueled our efforts in every sense.

Stan Wakefield gave us sound advice on developing our book proposal. Joshua Smart at Indiana University proved an extremely able assistant during final editing and preparation of the manuscript. He provided numerous helpful edits that improved clarity and readability, as well as contributing significantly to collecting the chapter notes at the end of the book.

Peter Ohlin, Joellyn Ausanka, and Molly Wagener at Oxford University Press were very helpful, and we are grateful for their thoughtful suggestions and the care with which they guided the manuscript to publication. The subtitle "Teaching Robots Right from Wrong" was suggested by Peter. We want to express special thanks to Martha Ramsey, whose excellent editing of the manuscript certainly contributed significantly to its readability.

Wendell Wallach would also like to thank the staff at Yale University's Interdisciplinary Center for Bioethics for their wonderful support over the past four years. Carol Pollard, the Center's Associate Director and her assistants Brooke Crockett and Jon Moser have been particularly helpful to Wendell in so many ways.

Finally, we could not have done this without the patience, love, and forbearance of our spouses, Nancy Wallach and Lynn Allen. There's nothing artificial about their virtues.

Wendell Wallach, Bloomfield, Connecticut
Colin Allen, Bloomington, Indiana
February 2008

MORAL MACHINES

INTRODUCTION

In the Affective Computing Laboratory at the Massachusetts Institute of Technology (MIT), scientists are designing computers that can read human emotions. Financial institutions have implemented worldwide computer networks that evaluate and approve or reject millions of transactions every minute. Roboticists in Japan, Europe, and the United States are developing service robots to care for the elderly and disabled. Japanese scientists are also working to make androids appear indistinguishable from humans. The government of South Korea has announced its goal to put a robot in every home by the year 2020. It is also developing weapons-carrying robots in conjunction with Samsung to help guard its border with North Korea. Meanwhile, human activity is being facilitated, monitored, and analyzed by computer chips in every conceivable device, from automobiles to garbage cans, and by software "bots" in every conceivable virtual environment, from web surfing to online shopping. The data collected by these (ro)bots—a term we'll use to encompass both physical robots and software agents—is being used for commercial, governmental, and medical purposes.

All of these developments are converging on the creation of (ro)bots whose independence from direct human oversight, and whose potential impact on human well-being, are the stuff of science fiction. Isaac Asimov, more than fifty years ago, foresaw the need for ethical rules to guide the behavior of robots. His Three Laws of Robotics are what people think of first when they think of machine morality.

> 1. A robot may not injure a human being or, through inaction, allow a human being to come to harm.

2. A robot must obey orders given it by human beings except where such orders would conflict with the First Law.
3. A robot must protect its own existence as long as such protection does not conflict with the First or Second Law.

Asimov, however, was writing stories. He was not confronting the challenge that faces today's engineers: to ensure that the systems they build are beneficial to humanity and don't cause harm to people. Whether Asimov's Three Laws are truly helpful for ensuring that (ro)bots will act morally is one of the questions we'll consider in this book.

Within the next few years, we predict there will be a catastrophic incident brought about by a computer system making a decision independent of human oversight. Already, in October 2007, a semiautonomous robotic cannon deployed by the South African army malfunctioned, killing 9 soldiers and wounding 14 others—although early reports conflicted about whether it was a software or hardware malfunction. The potential for an even bigger disaster will increase as such machines become more fully autonomous. Even if the coming calamity does not kill as many people as the terrorist acts of 9/11, it will provoke a comparably broad range of political responses. These responses will range from calls for more to be spent on improving the technology, to calls for an outright ban on the technology (if not an outright "war against robots").

A concern for safety and societal benefits has always been at the forefront of engineering. But today's systems are approaching a level of complexity that, we argue, requires the systems themselves to make moral decisions—to be programmed with "ethical subroutines," to borrow a phrase from *Star Trek*. This will expand the circle of moral agents beyond humans to artificially intelligent systems, which we will call artificial moral agents (AMAs).

We don't know exactly how a catastrophic incident will unfold, but the following tale may give some idea.

Monday, July 23, 2012, starts like any ordinary day. A little on the warm side in much of the United States perhaps, with peak electricity demand expected to be high, but not at a record level. Energy costs are rising in the United States, and speculators have been driving up the price of futures, as well as the spot price of oil, which stands close to $300 per barrel. Some slightly unusual automated trading activity in the energy derivatives markets over past weeks has caught the eye of the federal Securities and Exchange Commission (SEC), but the banks have assured the regulators that their programs are operating within normal parameters.

At 10:15 a.m. on the East Coast, the price of oil drops slightly in response to news of the discovery of large new reserves in the Bahamas. Software at the investment division of Orange and Nassau Bank computes that it can a turn a profit by emailing a quarter of its customers with a buy recommendation for oil futures, temporarily shoring up the spot market prices, as dealers stockpile supplies to meet the future demand, and then selling futures short to the rest of its customers. This plan essentially plays one sector of the customer base off against the rest, which is completely unethical, of course. But the bank's software has not been programmed to consider such niceties. In fact, the money-making scenario autonomously planned by the computer is an unintended consequence of many individually sound principles. The computer's ability to concoct this scheme could not easily have been anticipated by the programmers.

Unfortunately, the "buy" email that the computer sends directly to the customers works too well. Investors, who are used to seeing the price of oil climb and climb, jump enthusiastically on the bandwagon, and the spot price of oil suddenly climbs well beyond $300 and shows no sign of slowing down. It's now 11:30 a.m. on the East Coast, and temperatures are climbing more rapidly than predicted. Software controlling New Jersey's power grid computes that it can meet the unexpected demand while keeping the cost of energy down by using its coal-fired plants in preference to its oil-fired generators. However, one of the coal-burning generators suffers an explosion while running at peak capacity, and before anyone can act, cascading blackouts take out the power supply for half the East Coast. Wall Street is affected, but not before SEC regulators notice that the rise in oil future prices was a computer-driven shell game between automatically traded accounts of Orange and Nassau Bank. As the news spreads, and investors plan to shore up their positions, it is clear that the prices will fall dramatically as soon as the markets reopen and millions of dollars will be lost. In the meantime, the blackouts have spread far enough that many people are unable to get essential medical treatment, and many more are stranded far from home.

Detecting the spreading blackouts as a possible terrorist action, security screening software at Reagan National Airport automatically sets itself to the highest security level and applies biometric matching criteria that make it more likely than usual for people to be flagged as suspicious. The software, which has no mechanism for weighing the benefits of preventing a terrorist attack against the inconvenience its actions will cause for tens of thousands of people in the airport, identifies a cluster of five passengers, all waiting for Flight 231 to London, as potential terrorists. This large concentration of "suspects" on a single flight causes the program to trigger a lock down of the airport, and the dispatch of a Homeland Security response team to the terminal. Because passengers are already upset and nervous, the situation at the gate for Flight 231 spins out of control, and shots are fired.

An alert sent from the Department of Homeland Security to the airlines that a terrorist attack may be under way leads many carriers to implement measures to land their fleets. In the confusion caused by large numbers of planes trying to land at Chicago's O'Hare Airport, an executive jet collides with a Boeing 777, killing 157 passengers and crew. Seven more people die when debris lands on the Chicago suburb of Arlington Heights and starts a fire in a block of homes.

Meanwhile, robotic machine guns installed on the U.S.-Mexican border receive a signal that places them on red alert. They are programmed to act autonomously in code red conditions, enabling the detection and elimination of potentially hostile targets without direct human oversight. One of these robots fires on a Hummer returning from an off-road trip near Nogales, Arizona, destroying the vehicle and killing three U.S. citizens.

By the time power is restored to the East Coast and the markets reopen days later, hundreds of deaths and the loss of billions of dollars can be attributed to the separately programmed decisions of these multiple interacting systems. The effects continue to be felt for months.

Time may prove us poor prophets of disaster. Our intent in predicting such a catastrophe is not to be sensational or to instill fear. This is not a book about the horrors of technology. Our goal is to frame discussion in a way that constructively guides the engineering task of designing AMAs. The purpose of our prediction is to draw attention to the need for work on moral machines to begin now, not twenty to a hundred years from now when technology has caught up with science fiction.

The field of machine morality extends the field of computer ethics beyond concern for what people do with their computers to questions about what the machines do by themselves. (In this book we will use the terms *ethics* and *morality* interchangeably.) We are discussing the technological issues involved in making computers themselves into explicit moral reasoners. As artificial intelligence (AI) expands the scope of autonomous agents, the challenge of how to design these agents so that they honor the broader set of values and laws humans demand of human moral agents becomes increasingly urgent.

Does humanity really want computers making morally important decisions? Many philosophers of technology have warned about humans abdicating responsibility to machines. Movies and magazines are filled with futuristic fantasies about the dangers of advanced forms of artificial intelligence. Emerging technologies are always easier to modify before they become entrenched. However, it is not often possible to predict accurately the impact of a new technology on society until well after it has been widely adopted. Some critics think, therefore, that humans should err on the side of caution and relinquish the development of potentially dangerous technologies. We believe, however, that market and political forces will prevail and will demand the benefits that these technologies can provide. Thus, it is incumbent on anyone with a stake in this technology to address head-on the task of implementing moral decision making in computers, robots, and virtual "bots" within computer networks.

As noted, this book is not about the horrors of technology. Yes, the machines are coming. Yes, their existence will have unintended effects on human lives and welfare, not all of them good. But no, we do not believe that increasing reliance on autonomous systems will undermine people's basic humanity. Neither, in our view, will advanced robots enslave or exterminate humanity, as in the best traditions of science fiction. Humans have always adapted to their technological products, and the benefits to people of having autonomous machines around them will most likely outweigh the costs.

However, this optimism does not come for free. It is not possible to just sit back and hope that things will turn out for the best. If humanity is to avoid the consequences of bad autonomous artificial agents, people must be prepared to think hard about what it will take to make such agents good.

In proposing to build moral decision-making machines, are we still immersed in the realm of science fiction—or, perhaps worse, in that brand of science fantasy often associated with artificial intelligence? The charge might be justified if we were making bold predictions about the dawn of AMAs or claiming that "it's just a matter of time" before walking, talking machines will replace the human beings to whom people now turn for moral guidance. We are not futurists, however, and we do not know whether the apparent technological barriers to artificial intelligence are real or illusory. Nor are we interested in speculating about what life will be like when your counselor is a robot, or even in predicting whether this will ever come to pass. Rather, we are interested in the incremental steps arising from present technologies that suggest a need for ethical decision-making capabilities. Perhaps small steps will eventually lead to full-blown artificial intelligence—hopefully a less murderous counterpart to HAL in *2001: A Space Odyssey*—but even if fully intelligent systems will remain beyond reach, we think there is a real issue facing engineers that cannot be addressed by engineers alone.

Is it too early to be broaching this topic? We don't think so. Industrial robots engaged in repetitive mechanical tasks have caused injury and even death. The demand for home and service robots is projected to create a worldwide market double that of industrial robots by 2010, and four times bigger by 2025. With the advent of home and service robots, robots are no longer confined to controlled industrial environments where only trained workers come into contact with them. Small robot pets, for example Sony's AIBO, are the harbinger of larger robot appliances. Millions of robot vacuum cleaners, for example iRobot's "Roomba," have been purchased. Rudimentary robot couriers in hospitals and robot guides in museums have already appeared. Considerable attention is being directed at the development of service robots that will perform basic household tasks and assist the elderly and the home-bound. Computer programs initiate millions of financial transactions with an efficiency that humans can't duplicate. Software decisions to buy and then resell stocks, commodities, and currencies are made within seconds, exploiting potentials for profit that no human is capable of detecting in real time, and representing a significant percentage of the activity on world markets.

Automated financial systems, robotic pets, and robotic vacuum cleaners are still a long way short of the science fiction scenarios of fully autonomous machines making decisions that radically affect human welfare. Although 2001 has passed, Arthur C. Clarke's HAL remains a fiction, and it is a safe bet that the doomsday scenario of *The Terminator* will not be realized before its sell-by date of 2029. It is perhaps not quite as safe to bet against the Matrix being realized by 2199. However, humans are already at a point where engineered systems make decisions that can affect humans' lives and that have ethical ramifications. In the worst cases, they have profound negative effect.

Is it possible to build AMAs? Fully conscious artificial systems with complete human moral capacities may perhaps remain forever in the realm of science fiction. Nevertheless, we believe that more limited systems will soon be built. Such systems will have some capacity to evaluate the ethical ramifications of their actions—for example, whether they have no option but to violate a property right to protect a privacy right.

The task of designing AMAs requires a serious look at ethical theory, which originates from a human-centered perspective. The values and concerns expressed in the world's religious and philosophical traditions are not easily applied to machines. Rule-based ethical systems, for example the Ten Commandments or Asimov's Three Laws for Robots, might appear somewhat easier to embed in a computer, but as Asimov's many robot stories show, even three simple rules (later four) can give rise to many ethical dilemmas. Aristotle's ethics emphasized character over rules: good actions flowed from good character, and the aim of a flourishing human being was to develop a virtuous character. It is, of course, hard enough for humans to develop their own virtues, let alone developing appropriate virtues for computers or robots. Facing the engineering challenge entailed in going from Aristotle to Asimov and beyond will require looking at the origins of human morality as viewed in the fields of evolution, learning and development, neuropsychology, and philosophy.

Machine morality is just as much about human decision making as about the philosophical and practical issues of implementing AMAs. Reflection about and experimentation in building AMAs forces one to think deeply about how humans function, which human abilities can be implemented in the machines humans design, and what characteristics truly distinguish humans from animals or from new forms of intelligence that humans create.

Just as AI has stimulated new lines of enquiry in the philosophy of mind, machine morality has the potential to stimulate new lines of enquiry in ethics. Robotics and AI laboratories could become experimental centers for testing theories of moral decision making in artificial systems.

Three questions emerge naturally from the discussion so far. Does the world need AMAs? Do people want computers making moral decisions? And if people believe that computers making moral decisions are necessary or inevitable, how should engineers and philosophers proceed to design AMAs?

Chapters 1 and 2 are concerned with the first question, why humans need AMAs. In chapter 1, we discuss the inevitability of AMAs and give examples of current and innovative technologies that are converging on sophisticated systems that will require some capacity for moral decision making. We discuss how such capacities will initially be quite rudimentary but nonetheless present real challenges. Not the least of these challenges is to specify what the goals should be for the designers of such systems—that is, what do we mean by a "good" AMA?

In chapter 2, we will offer a framework for understanding the trajectories of increasingly sophisticated AMAs by emphasizing two dimensions, those of autonomy and of sensitivity to morally relevant facts. Systems at the low end of these dimensions have only what we call "operational morality"—that is, their moral significance is entirely in the hands of designers and users. As machines become more sophisticated, a kind of "functional morality" is technologically possible such that the machines themselves have the capacity for assessing and responding to moral challenges. However, the creators of functional morality in machines face many constraints due to the limits of present technology.

The nature of ethics places a different set of constraints on the acceptability of computers making ethical decisions. Thus we are led naturally to the question addressed in chapter 3: whether people want computers making moral decisions. Worries about AMAs are a specific case of more general concerns about the effects of technology on human culture. Therefore, we begin by reviewing the relevant portions of philosophy of technology to provide a context for the more specific concerns raised by AMAs. Some concerns, for example whether AMAs will lead humans to abrogate responsibility to machines, seem particularly pressing. Other concerns, for example the prospect of humans becoming literally enslaved to machines, seem to us highly speculative. The unsolved problem of technology risk assessment is how seriously to weigh catastrophic possibilities against the obvious advantages provided by new technologies.

How close could artificial agents come to being considered moral agents if they lack human qualities, for example consciousness and emotions? In chapter 4, we begin by discussing the issue of whether a "mere" machine can be a moral agent. We take the instrumental approach that while full-blown moral agency may be beyond the current or future technology, there is nevertheless much space between operational morality and "genuine" moral agency. This is the niche we identified as functional morality in chapter 2. The goal of chapter 4 is to address the suitability of current work in AI for specifying the features required to produce AMAs for various applications.

Having dealt with these general AI issues, we turn our attention to the specific implementation of moral decision making. Chapter 5 outlines what philosophers and engineers have to offer each other, and describes a basic framework for top-down and bottom-up or developmental approaches to the design of AMAs. Chapters 6 and 7, respectively, describe the top-down and bottom-up approaches in detail. In chapter 6, we discuss the computability and practicability of rule- and duty-based conceptions of ethics, as well as the possibility of computing the net effect of an action as required by consequentialist approaches to ethics. In chapter 7, we consider bottom-up approaches, which apply methods of learning, development, or evolution with the goal of having moral capacities emerge from general aspects of intelligence. There are limitations regarding the computability of both the top-down and bottom-up approaches, which we describe in these chapters. The new field of machine morality must consider these limitations, explore the strengths and weaknesses of the various approaches to programming AMAs, and then lay the groundwork for engineering AMAs in a philosophically and cognitively sophisticated way.

What emerges from our discussion in chapters 6 and 7 is that the original distinction between top-down and bottom-up approaches is too simplistic to cover all the challenges that the designers of AMAs will face. This is true at the level of both engineering design and, we think, ethical theory. Engineers will need to combine top-down and bottom-up methods to build workable systems. The difficulties of applying general moral theories in a top-down fashion also motivate a discussion of a very different conception of morality that can be traced to Aristotle, namely, virtue ethics. Virtues are a hybrid between top-down and bottom-up approaches, in that the virtues themselves can be explicitly described, but their acquisition as character traits seems essentially to be a bottom-up process. We discuss virtue ethics for AMAs in chapter 8.

Our goal in writing this book is not just to raise a lot of questions but to provide a resource for further development of these themes. In chapter 9, we survey the software tools that are being exploited for the development of computer moral decision making.

The top-down and bottom-up approaches emphasize the importance in ethics of the ability to reason. However, much of the recent empirical literature on moral psychology emphasizes faculties besides rationality. Emotions, sociability, semantic understanding, and consciousness are all important to human moral decision making, but it remains an open question whether these will be essential to AMAs, and if so, whether they can be implemented in machines. In chapter 10, we discuss recent, cutting-edge, scientific investigations aimed at providing computers and robots with such suprarational capacities, and in chapter 11 we present a specific framework in which the rational and the suprarational might be combined in a single machine.

In chapter 12, we come back to our second guiding question concerning the desirability of computers making moral decisions, but this time with a view to making recommendations about how to monitor and manage the dangers through public policy or mechanisms of social and business liability management.

Finally, in the epilogue, we briefly discuss how the project of designing AMAs feeds back into humans' understanding of themselves as moral agents, and of the nature of ethical theory itself. The limitations we see in current ethical theory concerning such theories' usefulness for guiding AMAs highlights deep questions about their purpose and value.

Some basic moral decisions may be quite easy to implement in computers, while skill at tackling more difficult moral dilemmas is well beyond present technology. Regardless of how quickly or how far humans progress in developing AMAs, in the process of addressing this challenge, humans will make significant strides in understanding what truly remarkable creatures they are. The exercise of thinking through the way moral decisions are made with the granularity necessary to begin implementing similar faculties into (ro)bots is thus an exercise in self-understanding. We cannot hope to do full justice to these issues, or indeed to all of the issues raised throughout the book. However, it is our sincere hope that by raising them in this form we will inspire others to pick up where we have left off, and take the next steps toward moving this project from theory to practice, from philosophy to engineering, and on to a deeper understanding of the field of ethics itself.

Chapter 1

WHY MACHINE MORALITY?

Trolley Car Drivers and Robot Engineers

A runaway trolley is approaching a fork in the tracks. If the trolley is allowed to run on its current track, a work crew of five will be killed. If the driver steers the train down the other branch, a lone worker will be killed. If you were driving this trolley what would you do? What would a computer or robot driving this trolley do?

Trolley cases, first introduced by the philosopher Philippa Foot in 1967, are a staple of introductory ethics courses. In the past four decades, trolley cases have multiplied. What if it is a bystander, rather than the driver, who has the power to throw a switch and change the trolley's course? What if there is no switch, but the bystander could stop the train from plowing into the five workers by toppling a very large man from a bridge onto the tracks, sending him to his death? These variants evoke different intuitive responses. Some people take drivers to have different responsibilities than bystanders, obligating them to act, even though bystanders would have no such obligation. Many people find the idea of toppling the large man onto the track—what has come to be known as the "fat man" version of the dilemma—far more objectionable than altering the switch, even though the body count is the same.

Trolley cases have also become the subject of investigation by psychologists and neuroscientists. Joshua Greene and his colleagues conducted a brain-imaging study showing that the "fat man" version evokes a much greater response in emotional processing centers of the brain than does the "switching tracks" version. Scientific investigation of people's responses to trolley cases does not answer the underlying philosophical questions about right and wrong. But such investigations do point to the complexity of human responses to ethical questions.

Given the advent of modern "driverless" train systems—already common at airports and beginning to appear in more complicated situations, for example the London Underground and the Paris and Copenhagen metro systems—could trolley cases be one of the first frontiers for artificial morality? Driverless systems put machines in the position of making split-second decisions that could have life or death implications. As the complexity of the rail network increases, the likelihood of dilemmas that are similar to the basic trolley case also goes up. How, for example, should automated systems compute where to steer a train that is out of control?

Engineers, of course, insist that the systems are safe—safer than human drivers, in fact. But the public has always been skeptical. The London Underground first tested driverless trains more than four decades ago, in April 1964. Back then, driverless trains faced political resistance from rail workers who believed their jobs were threatened and from passengers who were not entirely convinced of the safety claims. For these reasons, London Transport continued to give human drivers responsibility for driving the trains through the stations. Attitudes change, however, and Central Line trains in London are now being driven through stations by computers, even though human drivers remain in the cab in a "supervisory" role. Most passengers likely believe that human drivers are more flexible and able to deal with emergencies than the computerized controllers are. But this may be human hubris. Morten Sondergaard, in charge of safety for the Copenhagen metro, asserts that "automatic trains are safe and more flexible in fall-back situations because of the speed with which timetables can be changed."

Nevertheless, despite advances in technology, passengers remain skeptical. Parisian metro planners have claimed that the only problems with driverless trains are "political, not technical." No doubt, some of the resistance can be overcome simply by installing driverless trains and establishing a safety record. However, we feel sure that most passengers would still think that there are crisis situations beyond the scope of any programming, where human judgment would be preferred. In some of those situations, the relevant judgment would involve ethical considerations, but the driverless trains of today are, of course, oblivious to ethics. Can and should software engineers attempt to enhance their software systems to explicitly represent ethical dimensions? We think that this question can't be properly answered without better understanding what is possible in the domain of artificial morality.

It is easy to argue from a position of ignorance that the goal of artificial moral agency is impossible to achieve. But precisely what are the challenges and obstacles for implementing artificial morality? There is a need for serious discussion of this question. The computer revolution is continuing to promote reliance on automation, and autonomous systems are increasingly in charge of a variety of decisions that have ethical ramifications. How comfortable should one be about placing one's life and well-being in the hands of ethically ignorant systems?

Driverless trains are here. Much more remote technologically are (ro)bots capable of perceiving that heaving a large man onto the tracks could save five lives and of physically carrying out such an action. Meanwhile, the threat of a terrorist attack has lead to an increase in remote surveillance, of not only train switches but also bridges, tunnels, and unattended stretches of track. Airport surveillance systems that scan the faces of passengers and try to match these to a database of known terrorists are under development. Ostensibly, these systems are designed to alert supervisors when unusual activity occurs. But one can easily imagine an emergency in which a system might act automatically to redirect a train or close down part of an airport terminal when not enough time is available for a supervisor to review and counter the action.

Suppose the driverless train is able to identify that the five individuals on one track are railroad workers and the one on the other track is a child. Should the system factor this information into its decision? As the information available to automated systems gets richer, the moral dilemmas it confronts will also grow more complex. Imagine a computer that recognizes that the lone individual on one track is not a railroad worker, but a prominent citizen on whom the well-being and livelihood of a large number of families depends. How deeply would people want their computers to consider the ramifications of the actions they are considering?

Trolley cases aside, engineers often think that if a (ro)bot encounters a difficult situation, it should just stop and wait for a human to resolve the problem. Joe Engelberger, the "father" of industrial robotics, has been among those interested in developing service robots capable of facilitating the needs of the elderly and others in the home. Wendell Wallach asked him whether a service robot in the home would need moral decision-making faculties. Wouldn't the robot need to discern whether an obstacle in its pathway is a child, a pet, or something like an empty paper bag and select an action on the basis of its evaluation? Engelberger felt that such a system would not need a capacity to reflect on its actions. "If there is something in the way it just stops," he said. Of course, this kind of inaction could also be problematic, interfering with the duties or tasks defined for the service robot, for example delivering medications every few hours to the individual being served.

For an engineer thinking about his or her own liability, inaction might seem the more prudent course. There is a long tradition in ethics of regarding actions as being more blameworthy than inactions. (Think about the Roman Catholic distinction between "sins of omission" and the more serious "sins of commission," for instance.) We'll return to the issues of responsibility and liability at the end of the book, but the main point for now is that even if there were a moral distinction between action and inaction, a designer of AMAs could not simply choose inaction as a substitute for good action.

Good and Bad Artificial Agents?

Autonomous systems are coming whether people like it or not. Will they be ethical? Will they be good?

What do we mean by "good" in this context? It is not just a matter of being instrumentally good—good relative to a specific purpose. Deep Blue is a good chess-playing computer because it wins chess games, but this is not the sense we mean. Nor do we mean the sense in which good vacuum cleaners get the floors clean, even if they are robotic and do it with a minimum of human supervision. These "goods" are measured against the specific purposes designers and users have. The kind of good behavior that may be required of autonomous systems cannot be so easily specified. Should a good multi-purpose robot hold open a door for a stranger, even if this means a delay for the robot's owner? (Should this be an owner-specified setting?) Should a good autonomous agent alert a human overseer if it cannot take action without causing some harm to humans? (If so, is it sufficiently autonomous?) When we talk about good in this sense, we enter the domain of ethics.

To bring artificial agents into the domain of ethics is not simply to say they may cause harm. Falling trees cause harm, but that doesn't put them into the domain of ethics. Moral agents monitor and regulate their behavior in light of the harms their actions may cause or the duties they may neglect. Humans should expect nothing less of AMAs. A good moral agent is one that can detect the possibility of harm or neglect of duty, and can take steps to avoid or minimize such undesirable outcomes. There are two routes to accomplishing this: First, the programmer may be able to anticipate the possible courses of action and provide rules that lead to the desired outcome in the range of circumstances in which the AMA is to be deployed. Alternatively, the programmer might build a more open-ended system that gathers information, attempts to predict the consequences of its actions, and customizes a response to the challenge. Such a system may even have the potential to surprise its programmers with apparently novel or creative solutions to ethical challenges.

Perhaps even the most sophisticated AMAs will never really be moral agents in the same sense that human beings are moral agents. But wherever one comes down on the question of whether a machine can be genuinely ethical (or even genuinely autonomous), an engineering challenge remains: how to get artificial agents to act as if they are moral agents. If multipurpose machines are to be trusted, operating untethered from their designers or owners and programmed to respond flexibly in real or virtual world environments, there must be confidence that their behavior satisfies appropriate norms. This goes beyond traditional product safety. Of course, robots that short-circuit and cause fires are no more tolerable than toasters that do so. However, if an autonomous system is to minimize harm, it must also be "cognizant" of possible harmful consequences of its actions, and it must select its actions in light of this "knowledge," even if such terms are only metaphorically applied to machines.

Present-Day Cases

Science fiction scenarios of computers or robots running amok might be entertaining, but these stories depend on technology that doesn't exist today, and may never exist. Trolley cases are nice thought experiments for college ethics courses, but they can also make ethical concerns seem rather remote from daily life—the likelihood that you will find yourself in a position to save lives by heaving a very large innocent bystander onto a railroad track is remote. Nevertheless, daily life is filled with mundane decisions that have ethical consequences. Even something as commonplace as holding open a door for a stranger is part of the ethical landscape, although the boundary between ethics and etiquette may not always be easy to determine.

There is an immediate need to think about the design of AMAs because autonomous systems have already entered the ethical landscape of daily activity. For example, a couple of years ago, when Colin Allen drove from Texas to California, he did not attempt to use a particular credit card until he approached the Pacific coast. When he tried to use this card for the first time to refuel his car, the credit card was rejected. Thinking there was something wrong with the pumps at that station, he drove to another and tried the card there. When he inserted the card in the pump, a message flashed instructing him to hand the card to a cashier inside the store. Not quite ready to hand over his card to a stranger, and always one to question computerized instructions, Colin instead telephoned the toll-free number on the back of the card. The credit card company's centralized computer had evaluated the use of the card almost 2,000 miles from home with no trail of purchases leading across the country as suspicious, and automatically flagged his account. The human agent at the credit card company listened to Colin's story and removed the flag that restricted the use of his card.

This incident was one in which an essentially autonomous computer initiated actions that were potentially helpful or harmful to humans.

However, this doesn't mean that the computer made a moral decision or used ethical judgment. The ethical significance of the action taken by this computer stemmed entirely from the values inherent in the rules programmed into it. Arguably, the values designed into the system justify the inconvenience to cardholders and business owners' occasional loss of sales. The credit card company wishes to minimize fraudulent transactions. Customers share the desire to be spared fraudulent charges. But customers might reasonably feel that the systems should be sensitive to more than the financial bottom line. If Colin had needed fuel for his car because of an emergency, it might not be so easy to assume that the inconvenience was worthwhile.

Autonomous systems can also cause very widespread inconvenience. In 2003, tens of millions of people and countless businesses in the eastern United States and Canada were affected by a power blackout. The blackout was caused by a power surge that occurred when an overheated electrical transmission line sagged into a tree just outside Cleveland. What surprised investigators was how quickly this incident cascaded into a chain of computer-initiated shutdowns at power plants in eight states and part of Canada. Once the power surge leaped beyond the control of Ohio's electrical company, software agents and control systems at the other power plants activated shutdown procedures, leaving almost no time for human intervention. Where humans were involved, they sometimes compounded the problems because of inadequate information or lack of effective communication. Days and sometimes weeks were required to restore electricity to customers throughout the northeastern power grid.

At the start of the blackout, Wendell Wallach was working at home in Connecticut. He and his neighbors lost electricity, but only for a few seconds. Apparently, technicians at his local utility company had realized what was happening, quickly overrode automated shutdown procedures, and disconnected the electrical service in southern New England from the power grid. However, this was a rare success. The sheer scale of the network makes effective human oversight impossible. The Finnish IT security company F-Secure investigated the malfunction. After going through the six-hundred-page transcript of conversations between operators of U.S. electrical grids in the moments leading up to the blackout, Mikko Hyppönen of the company's computer virus lab concluded that the computer worm Blaster played a major role. The transcripts indicate that operators did not receive correct information prior to the blackout, because their computers were malfunctioning. The computers and the sensors monitoring the power grid used the same communication channels through which Blaster was spreading. In Hyppönen's analysis, just one or two infected computers in the network could have kept the sensors from relaying real-time data to the power operators, which could have led to the operator error that was identified as the direct cause of the blackout.

In a perfect world, there would be no viruses, and control systems would be programmed to shut down only when doing so would minimize hardships for customers. However, in a world where operator error is a fact of life, and humans are unable to monitor the entire state of system software, the pressures for increased automation will continue to mount. With the increasing complexity of such systems, any evaluation of conflicts between values—for example, maintaining the flow of electricity to end users versus keeping computers virus free becomes increasingly problematic—it becomes harder and harder to predict whether upgrading software now or later is more or less likely to lead to future problems. In the face of such uncertainty, there is a need for autonomous systems to weigh risks against values.

The widespread use of autonomous systems makes it urgent to ask which values they can and should promote. Human safety and well-being represent core values about which there is widespread agreement. The relatively young field of computer ethics has also focused on specific issues—for example, maintaining privacy, property, and civil rights in the digital age; facilitating computer-based commerce; inhibiting hacking, worms and viruses, and other abuses of the technology; and developing guidelines for Net etiquette. New technologies have opened up venues for digital crime, eased the access of minors to hardcore pornography, and robbed people's time with unsolicited advertising and unwanted emails, but it has been extremely difficult to establish the values, governmental regulations, and procedures that will foster the goals of computer ethics. As new regulations and values emerge, people will of course want them to be honored by the AMAs they build. Machine morality extends the field of computer ethics by fostering a discussion of the technological issues involved in making computers themselves into explicit moral reasoners.

One significant issue at the intersection of machine morality and computer ethics concerns the data-mining bots that roam the Web, ferreting out information with little or no regard for privacy standards. The ease with which information can be copied using computers has undermined legal standards for intellectual property rights and forced a reevaluation of copyright law. Some of the privacy and property issues in computer ethics concern values that are not necessarily widely shared but often connect back to core values in interesting ways. The Internet Archive project has been storing snapshots of the Internet since 1996 and has been making those archives available via its Wayback Machine. These snapshots often include material that has since been deleted from the Internet. While there is a mechanism for requesting materials to be deleted from the archive, there have been several cases where the victims or perpetrators of crimes have left a trace on the

Wayback Machine, even though their original sites have been removed. At present, the data-gathering bots used by the Internet Archive are incapable of assessing the moral significance of the materials they gather.

Ethical Killing Machines?

If the foregoing examples leave you unconvinced that there is an immediate need to think about moral reasoning in (ro)bots, consider this. Remotely operated vehicles (ROVs) are already being deployed militarily. As of October 2007, Foster-Miller Inc. has sent to Iraq for deployment three remotely operated machine-gun-carrying robots using the special weapons observation remote direct-action system (SWORDS). Foster-Miller has also begun marketing a version of the weapons-carrying SWORDS to law enforcement departments in the United States. According to Foster-Miller, the SWORDS and its successor the MAARS (modular advanced armed robotic system) should not be considered autonomous, but are ROVs.

Another company, iRobot Corporation, whose Packbot has been deployed extensively in Iraq, has also announced the Warrior X700, a military robot that can carry weapons and will be available in the second half of 2008. However, robotic applications will not stop with ROVs. Semi-autonomous robotic systems, such as cruise missiles, already carry bombs. The military

Figure 1.1. MAARS ROV. Courtesy of Foster-Miller.

also uses semi-autonomous robots designed for bomb disposal and surveillance. The U.S. Congress ordered in 2000 that one-third of military ground vehicles and deep-strike aircraft be replaced by robotic vehicles. According to a *New York Times* story in 2005, the Pentagon has the goal of replacing soldiers with autonomous robots.

Some will think that humans should stop building robots altogether if they will be used for warfare. Worthy as that sentiment may be, it will be confronted by the rationale that such systems will save the lives of soldiers and law enforcement personnel. We don't know who will win this political argument, but we do know that if the proponents of fighting machines win the day, now will be the time to have begun thinking about the built-in ethical constraints that will be needed for these and all (ro)botic applications. Indeed, Ronald Arkin, a roboticist at Georgia Institute of Technology, received funding from the U.S. Army in 2007 to begin the development of hardware and software that will make robotic fighting machines capable of following the ethical standards of warfare. These rather extensive guidelines, honored by civilized nations, range from the rights of noncombatants to the rights of enemy soldiers trying to surrender. However, ensuring that robots follow the ethical standards of warfare is a formidable task that lags far behind the development of increasingly sophisticated robotic weapons systems for use in warfare.

Imminent Dangers

The possibility of a human disaster arising from the use of (ro)bots capable of lethal force is obvious, and humans can all hope that the designers of such systems build in adequate safeguards. However, as (ro)botic systems becoming increasingly embedded in nearly every facet of society, from finance to communications to public safety, the real potential for harm is most likely to emerge from an unanticipated combination of events.

In the wake of 9/11, experts noted the vulnerability of the U.S. power grid to an attack by terrorist hackers, especially given the grid's dependence on old software and hardware. It is a very real possibility that a large percentage of the power grid could be brought down for weeks and even months. To forestall this, much of the vulnerable software and hardware is being updated with more sophisticated automated systems. This makes the power grid increasingly dependent on the decisions made by computerized control systems. No one can fully predict how these decisions might play out in unforeseen circumstances. Insufficient coordination between systems operated by different utility companies increases the uncertainty.

The managers of the electrical grid must balance demands for power from industry and the general public against the need to maintain essential services. During brown-outs and surges, they decide who loses power. Decision makers, whether human or software, are faced with the competing values of protecting equipment from damage and minimizing the harm to end users. If equipment is damaged, harms can mount as the time to restore service is extended. These decisions involve value judgments. As the systems become increasingly autonomous, those judgments will no longer be in the hands of human operators. Systems that are blind to the relevant values that should guide decisions in uncertain conditions are a recipe for disaster.

Even today, the actions of computer systems can be individually quite small yet cumulatively very serious. Peter Norvig, director of research at Google, notes that

> today in the U.S. there are between 100 and 200 deaths every day from medical error, and many of these medical errors have to do with computers. These are errors like giving the wrong drug, computing the wrong dosage, 100 to 200 deaths per day. I'm not sure exactly how many of those you want to attribute to computer error, but it's some proportion of them. It's safe to say that every two or three months we have the equivalent of a 9/11 in numbers of deaths due to computer error and medical processes.

The dangers posed by systems used in medical applications are far from the science fiction disasters posed by computer systems engaged in making explicit decisions that are harmful to humans. These systems are not HAL, out to kill the astronauts under his care. Nor is this the Matrix, with robots bent on enslaving unwitting humans. Arguably, most of the harms caused by today's (ro)bots can be attributed to faulty components or bad design. Preliminary reports indicate that a component failed in the semiautonomous cannon that killed nine South African soldiers in 2007. Other harms are attributed to designers' failure to build in adequate safeguards, consider all the contingencies the system will confront, or eliminate software bugs. Managers' desires to market or field-test systems whose safety is unproven also pose dangers to the public, as will faulty reliance on systems not up to the task of managing the complexity of unforeseen situations. However, the line between faulty components, insufficient design, inadequate systems, and the explicit evaluation of choices by computers will get more and more difficult to draw. As with human decision makers who make bad choices because they fail to attend to all the relevant information or consider all contingencies, humans may only discover the inadequacy of the (ro)bots they rely on after an unanticipated catastrophe.

Corporate executives are often concerned that ethical constraints will increase costs and hinder production. Public perception of new technologies can be hampered by undue fears regarding their risks. However, the capacity for moral decision making will allow AMAs to be deployed in contexts that might otherwise be considered too risky, open up applications, and lower the dangers posed by these technologies. Today's technologies—automated utility grids, automated financial systems, robotic pets, and robotic vacuum cleaners—are a long way from fully autonomous machines. But humanity is already at a point where engineered systems make decisions that can affect people's lives. As systems get more sophisticated and their ability to function autonomously in different contexts and environments expands, it will become more important for them to have their own ethical subroutines. The systems' choices should be sensitive to humans and to the things that are important to humans. Humanity will need these machines to be self-governing: capable of assessing the ethical acceptability of the options they face. Rosalind Picard, director of the Affective Computing Group at MIT, put it well when she wrote, "The greater the freedom of a machine, the more it will need moral standards."

Chapter 2

ENGINEERING MORALITY

An Engineering Imperative?

In the Code of Ethics of the National Society of Professional Engineers (NSPE), the first "fundamental canon" is that engineers shall "hold paramount the safety, health, and welfare of the public." If giving machines moral standards would improve public welfare and safety, then American engineers are obligated by their own code of ethics to make it happen.

Where might they start? The task seems overwhelming, but all engineering tasks are incremental, building on past technologies. In this chapter, we will provide a framework for understanding the pathways from current technology to sophisticated AMAs. Our framework has two dimensions: autonomy and sensitivity to values. These dimensions are independent, as the parent of any teenager knows. Increased autonomy is not always balanced by increased sensitivity to the values of others; this is as true of technology as it is of teenagers.

The simplest tools have neither autonomy nor sensitivity. Hammers do not get up and hammer nails on their own, nor are they sensitive to thumbs that get in the way. But even technologies near the low end of both dimensions in our framework can have a kind of "operational morality" to their design. A gun that has a childproof safety mechanism lacks autonomy and sensitivity, but its design embodies values that the NSPE Code of Ethics would endorse. One of the major accomplishments in the field of "engineering ethics" over the past twenty-five years has been the raising of engineers' awareness of the way their own values influence the design process and their sensitivity to the values of others during it. When the design process is undertaken with ethical values fully in view, this kind of "operational morality" is totally within the control of a tool's designers and users.

At the other theoretical extreme are systems with high autonomy and high sensitivity to values, capable of acting as trustworthy moral agents. That humanity does not have such technology is, of course, the central issue of this book. However, between "operational morality" and responsible moral agency lie many gradations of what we call "functional morality"—from systems that merely act within acceptable standards of behavior to intelligent systems capable of assessing some of the morally significant aspects of their own actions.

The realm of functional morality contains both systems that have significant autonomy but little ethical sensitivity and those that have low autonomy but high ethical sensitivity. Autopilots are an example of the former. People trust them to fly complex aircraft in a wide variety of conditions, with minimal human supervision. They are relatively safe, and they have been engineered to respect other values, for example passenger comfort when executing maneuvers. The goals of safety and comfort are accomplished,

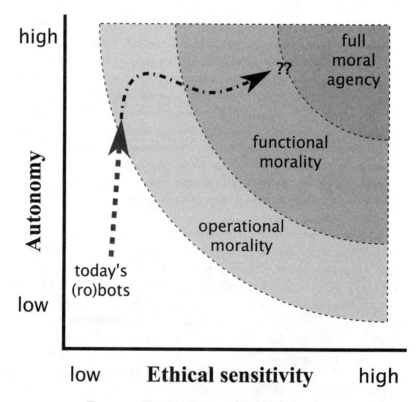

Figure 2.1. Two Dimensions of AMA Development.

however, in different ways. Safety is maintained by directly monitoring aircraft altitude and environmental conditions and continuously adjusting the wing flaps and other control surfaces of the aircraft to maintain the desired course. Passenger comfort is not directly monitored, and insofar as it is provided for, it is by precoding specific maneuvering limits into the operating parameters of the autopilot. The plane is capable of banking much more steeply than it does when executing a turn, but the autopilot is programmed not to turn so sharply as to upset passengers. Under normal operating conditions, the design of the autopilot keeps it operating within the limits of functional morality. Under unusual conditions, a human pilot who is aware of special passenger needs, for example a sick passenger, or special passenger desires, for example thrill-seeking joyriders, can adjust her flying accordingly. A significant amount of autonomy without any specific moral sensitivity puts autopilots somewhere up the left axis of figure 2.1.

One example of systems that have little autonomy but some degree of ethical sensitivity, falling on the right axis of figure 1, is an ethical decision support system, which provides decision makers with access to morally relevant information. Most of these systems that exist fall within the realm of operational rather than functional morality. Furthermore, when they deal with ethical issues, it is usually for educational purposes. The programs are structured to teach general principles, not to analyze new cases. For example, the software walks students through historically important or hypothetical cases. However, some programs help clinicians select ethically appropriate courses of action, for example MedEthEx, a medical ethics expert system designed by the husband-and-wife team of computer scientist Michael Anderson and philosopher Susan Anderson. In effect, MedEthEx engages in some rudimentary moral reasoning.

Suppose you are a doctor faced with a mentally competent patient who has refused a treatment you think represents her best hope of survival. Should you try again to persuade her (a possible violation of respect for the patient's autonomy) or should you accept her decision (a possible violation of your duty to provide the most beneficent care)? The MedEthEx prototype prompts a caregiver to answer a series of questions about the case. Then, on the basis of a model of expert judgment learned from similar cases, it delivers an opinion about the ethically appropriate way to proceed. We'll describe the ethical theory behind MedEthEx in more detail later. For now, the important point is that the Andersons' system has no autonomy and is not a full-blown AMA but has a kind of functional morality that provides a platform for further development.

It is important to understand that these examples are illustrative only. Each system is just a small distance along one of the axes of figure 1. Autopilots have autonomy only in a very circumscribed domain. The autopilot can't

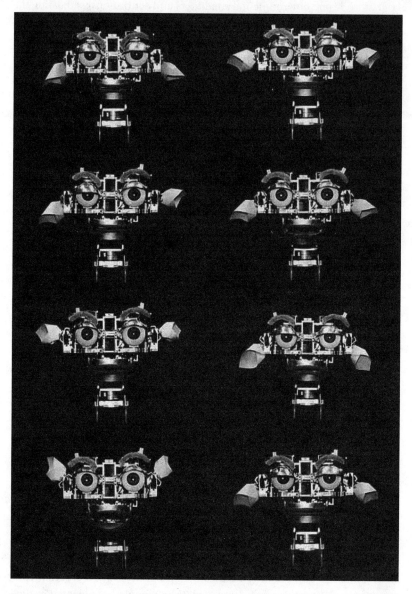

Figure 2.2. The many moods of Kismet: anger, calm, disgust, fear, interest, sadness, surprise, and tiredness. Courtesy MIT AI Lab.

leave the cockpit to comfort a distraught passenger. MedEthEx gives advice only within a very small range of cases. The software is entirely dependent on humans to provide the information relevant to its cases, and the practitioners must decide whether or not to follow its recommendations. Nevertheless, ethical issues arise even in these restricted domains, and the engineering side of machine morality will build on such basic beginnings.

These independent steps along each dimension are relevant for machine morality, and so are attempts to make progress in both dimensions simultaneously. One such project was Kismet, a robot developed by graduate students at MIT under the direction of Rodney Brooks and most closely identified with the work of Cynthia Breazeal. Kismet represents an attempt to combine emotional responsiveness with autonomous activity in a robot. Kismet's robotic head has cartoonish features typically associated with infants and young animals. By moving its head, ears, eyebrows, eyelids, and mouth it is able to display eight emotional states, including fear, surprise, interest, and sadness, as well as close its eyes and withdraw into a sleep-like pose. The actual emotional state the robot exhibits is determined by its analysis of the voice intonation of the speaker and other factors, for example whether the system is seeking stimulation or is overstimulated. Kismet can return a gaze and direct its attention to where an individual points.

Kismet is programmed to take turns, as it engages in what appears to be a conversation, waiting for a silent space before interjecting a response to human speech. While the apparent language Kismet speaks is gibberish, it can appear to be quite responsive to social cues—for example, the voice intonation of the speaker the robot is interacting with—even though the system has no actual comprehension of what the human thinks or is saying. For example, voice intonations that might be interpreted as scolding elicit the robot's looking downward with an expression of apparent shame.

Kismet, now retired and on display in the MIT Museum, was designed to read very basic social cues and respond with its own simple behavioral gestures. Among Kismet's capacities are reactions to the attention and proximity of a human being. For example, Kismet may pull back when a person leans too close. The extent to which it is acceptable for one person to be in another's face is perhaps nearer to etiquette than ethics, and varies from culture to culture. Nevertheless, Kismet's actions are an example of operational morality because the programmers have tapped into values that are important for the establishment of trust and cooperation. Kismet has no explicit representation of values and no capacity for reasoning about values. Despite these limitations, many people find their interactions with Kismet very compelling.

By placing Kismet in the realm of operational morality, close to the origin of the axes in figure 1, we aren't being dismissive. The field of artificial morality must build on existing platforms, and Kismet is the result of some significant ideas about how to make machines behave in ways that people find engaging. As an experiment in social robotics, Kismet was very successful in demonstrating how it is possible for robots to trigger natural and intuitive social responses in people.

Autopilots, decision support systems, and robots with basic capacities to engage in emotion-laden interactions all provide starting points for the field of artificial morality. Systems like these, which are within the domain of operational morality or very limited functional morality, are relatively direct extensions of their designers' values. The designers have to anticipate most of the circumstances in which their systems will operate, and the actions available in those circumstances are kept within tight limits. Written safety manuals attempt to offload the problem of appropriate, safe, and ethical use to the operators, but they are not always successful in doing so! As technology for autonomous decision making becomes more widespread, we envisage (ro)boticists realizing that their own professional code makes the development of AMAs an engineering imperative.

Some may wonder if we aren't trying to shoot the moon, when we ought to be concentrating on a few simpler tricks. The task of designing systems is hard enough without bringing in the ill-defined notion of values. Consider the systems approving credit card purchases. Shouldn't people be happy that these systems protect customers and banks from fraudulent purchases, even if sometimes customers are inconvenienced when their attempted purchases are denied? ("Computer says no...") The software that analyses activity for fraudulent patterns can always be improved, so why not concentrate on that without worrying about building explicit ethical reasoning into the system?

It's true, of course, that the pattern analysis can be improved, but only up to a limit. The software engineers and bankers who design and deploy the system cannot perfectly predict all the circumstances in which people will try to use their credit cards. Perfectly innocent purchases, and sometimes even emergency purchases, will be blocked because they are deemed "suspicious" by the bank's computers. From an engineer's (and a banker's) point of view, the problem is one of balancing an acceptable false positive rate (wrongly identifying innocent purchases as fraudulent) against an unacceptable false negative rate (wrongly failing to identify fraudulent activity). For the bankers, what's acceptable is primarily a matter of what costs they can afford to pass on to their customers. Most customers are willing to accept the occasional inconvenience (and embarrassment) of a denied purchase if it means they are protected against the financial losses and headaches that could be incurred from a stolen credit card. Some customers will worry about the implications for privacy that follow from the bank's ability to tie patterns of usage together. In this book, we're less concerned with the nefarious purposes of people who have access to such databases and more concerned with the capacities of the computers themselves to recognize when the ethical thing to do is extend credit even when the analysis suggest a higher risk for the bank. Because the existing approach to pattern analysis has inherent limits for protecting what people value, engineers are bound by their own ideals to pursue alternative approaches that promise to get beyond those limits.

Perhaps you think we are mistaken if we believe that engineering ideals should prevail over corporate objectives. Credit card companies, after all, are not contractually obligated to approve any purchase, so there is no ethical issue at all involved in the use of automated approval systems. But to accept this line of reasoning is already to take a position on a substantive moral question, namely, whether corporate morality is limited to contractual issues. Designers of autonomous systems who choose to ignore the broader consequences of the decisions made by their machines are implicitly embedding a particular set of values into these systems. Whether autonomous systems should consider only those factors relevant to the profitability of the corporations that employ them, and the contractual arrangements that exist between the corporations and their customers, is itself a question about ethics.

Perhaps you think us doubly naive if we believe that moral arguments can overrule the bottom line. We think, however, that increasingly sophisticated forms of functional morality, and eventually full-blown AMAs, will actually benefit companies financially.

One source of this benefit will be that these systems will make it possible to offer better service than the competition. The imperfect purchase authorization systems currently in use lead to customer frustration and sometimes defection to other companies. If you are lucky enough to get through to a human operator, as Colin was when his fuel purchase was denied in California, you may be able to have the problem fixed. But everyone has encountered situations with automated telephone systems where human intervention was unavailable. In the effort to enhance what we are calling the operational morality of these answering systems, large corporations are now trying to write software to detect frustrated (as well as "important") customers and route them quickly to a human agent. However, even when one does reach a human, he might be working within constraints set by a computer program and might lack sufficient autonomy to solve the problem. Frustrated customers are bad for business, while the bottom line drives corporations to incorporate more and more unsupervised decision making into the machines' programs. Software that is sensitive to customers' values and can make decisions approximating those of a morally good agent will help the bottom line, not hurt it.

The 2003 electrical blackout in the northeastern United States underscored the fact that electrical companies were dependent on obsolete technology. Upgrades to software and control systems will make them even more autonomous than the previous ones, which were implicated in the shutdown. The additional complexity will make the systems even less accessible to direct human monitoring, and this in turn will require a new level of self-monitoring. Because of operator errors and the inability of humans to monitor the entire state of system software, the pressures for increased automation will continue to mount. Even system upgrades and scheduled downtime for components of the grid might themselves be handled in an autonomous fashion by the computers' ongoing evaluation of a broad range of factors. This introduces a second level of decision making where the control system becomes self-supervising to a significant degree.

Such considerations indicate the need to move beyond simple control systems that ensure the network functions within safe parameters (operational morality) to systems capable of evaluating options at both the primary level of customer service and the secondary level of self-management. These systems will need to handle, at the speed of modern computing, complex situations in which choices are made and courses of action are taken that could not have been foreseen by the designers and software programmers.

With these examples, we have tried to make it plausible that existing technologies provide various starting points for progress toward AMAs. Incremental progress is often hard to see and difficult to predict. Even within our simplistic two-dimensional framework, there are multiple paths from current technologies to the full moral agency represented in the upper right corner of figure 2.1. In our approach to artificial morality, we take progress along the dimension of autonomy for granted—it is happening and will continue to happen. The challenge for the discipline of artificial morality is how to move in the direction specified by the other axis: sensitivity to moral considerations.

Decision support systems illustrate a trajectory in the development of intelligent systems by which technologies sensitive to moral considerations can develop independently from systems with increasing autonomy. This trajectory, which leaves decision making in the hands of humans, seems likely to move beyond external decision support systems to more intimate mergers of humans and technology. Thus, increased autonomy represents only one trajectory in the development of intelligent systems.

Perhaps one of the most memorable scenes in science fiction movies was the debut of ED-209, a large, ugly, metallic robot, in the 1987 hit film *Robocop*. The prototype for a robot police officer, ED-209 was programmed to shoot criminals who failed to drop their weapons after repeated warnings. In *Robocop*, Kinney, a young executive, eagerly volunteers to play the role of the criminal for the demonstration of the ED-209 to the board. The robot utters its warning in a standard computer-generated monotone voice, and Kinney drops his gun. The warning is repeated twice more. Then, the robot kills him with a stream of bullets.

ED-209 represents an autonomous, or at least semiautonomous, robot. In the movie, the failure of the ED-209 is a minor setback for Omni Consumer Products, as another team is already developing an alternative strategy for fighting crime—Robocop—a cyborg merging the brain of a slain officer with AI.

Many theorists believe that cyborgs will be the natural outgrowth of present research into IT, neuroprosthethics, neuropharmacology, nanotechnology, and gene therapy. The merging of humans with their technologies poses different ethical issues than the development of autonomous systems. Presumably the human component of a cyborg would provide sensitivity to moral considerations, although one ethical concern is that the implanted technology should not interfere with the autonomy and moral faculties of the human. This is a problem that arises in the emerging field of neuroethics. Issues in research ethics, social justice, and improving lives also arise when considering the increased intimacy humans are forging with their technologies. However, the larger social concern is whether the emergence of a cyborg culture is desirable.

Robocop and the ED-209 represent two different trajectories in the development of IT: AI under the direct control of humans, and autonomous systems capable of functioning independently. Here, the important thing to note is that advances in morally sensitive decision support technology and neuroprosthetics might be adapted for enhancing autonomous systems.

Moor's Categories of Ethical Agents

James Moor, a professor of philosophy at Dartmouth College, one of the founding figures in the field of computer ethics, has proposed a hierarchical schema for categorizing AMAs. At the lowest level is what he calls "ethical impact agents"—basically any machine that can be evaluated for its ethical consequences. Moor's own rather nice example is the replacement of young boys with robots in the dangerous occupation of camel jockey in Qatar. In fact, it seems to us that *all* (ro)bots have ethical impacts, although in some cases they may be harder to discern than others.

At the next level are what Moor calls "implicit ethical agents": machines whose designers have made an effort to design them so that they don't have negative ethical effects, by addressing safety and critical reliability concerns during the design process. Arguably, all (ro)bots should be engineered to be implicit ethical agents, insofar as designers are negligent if they fail to build in processes that assure safety and reliability.

Next come "explicit ethical agents": machines that reason about ethics using ethical categories as part of their internal programming, perhaps using various forms of "deontic" logic that have been developed for representing duties and obligations, or a variety of other techniques.

Beyond all these lie full ethical agents: those that can make explicit moral judgments and are generally quite competent in justifying such decisions. This level of performance is often presumed to require a capacity for consciousness, intentionality, and free will. If any of these three is lacking in a human context, then the person's moral agency and legal culpability comes into question.

While it is relatively easy to imagine artificial systems that are "ethical impact" or "implicit moral" agents, explicit moral agency poses more difficult challenges. Many philosophers (and some scientists) argue vigorously that it is impossible to have machines that are full ethical agents. These philosophers and scientists doubt that humans can build artificial agents with consciousness, intentionality, and free will, and maintain there is a bright line separating explicit moral agents from full moral agents.

Moor maintains that explicit ethical agents should be the goal of the emerging field of machine ethics. Whether it is even possible to do anything more, he argues, cannot be settled by philosophical argument or by engineering experiments in the near future. We agree with the strategy of taking small steps. While Moor's categories don't map directly onto our graph of autonomy and sensitivity to morally relevant features, we think they are useful for specifying the range of tasks confronting machine ethics. However, they don't do much to specify the *process* of building operational and functional moral agents. Is building implicit ethical agents a stepping-stone toward building explicit ethical agents? Moor doesn't tell us, and it's not really his concern to do so.

Our idea is that the development of technology lies in an interaction between increased autonomy and increasing sensitivity. As (ro)bots evolve incrementally toward becoming AMAs, it may not be possible to draw sharp lines to say when they have gone from being one kind of ethical agent to another in Moor's scheme. With increasing autonomy comes the need for engineers to address broader safety and reliability issues. Some of those needs may involve explicit representation of ethical categories and principles, and some may not. Our guess is that engineers will add these capacities in a piecemeal fashion. Increased autonomy for (ro)bots is a process that is already well under way. The challenge for the discipline of artificial morality is how to move in the direction specified by the other axis: sensitivity to moral considerations.

Sensitivity to moral considerations might mean several things for an AMA. A useful distinction is offered by Drew McDermott, Professor of Computer

Science at Yale University and an honorary fellow of the Association for the Advancement of Artificial Intelligence. McDermott argues that for the purposes of designing AMAs it is important to keep in mind the difference between ethical reasoners and ethical decision makers. Much of the initial thinking on how to build moral machines has not pursued moral decision making in McDermott's sense, but has instead focused on adapting the reasoning tools used in a wide range of expert systems for ethical reasoning.

For example, this is the approach proposed by Blay Whitby, a faculty member in Computer Science and Artificial Intelligence at the University of Sussex in Brighton, England. Whitby, who has been writing about the social and ethical dimensions of computing for over twenty years, includes a chapter on "The Computer Representation of Moral Reasoning" in his 1995 book *Reflections on AI*. He considers in that chapter how the conditional if-then rules used by expert systems might be adapted for moral reasoning in legal and other applications. Whitby is well aware of the difficulties inherent in building moral reasoners, and of the limitations of relying upon abstract reasoning alone.

Similarly, McDermott points out that even if one could solve the difficult challenges entailed in building systems that can reason about ethics, these agents would fall far-short of being ethical decision makers. He contrast ethical decision making with ethical reasoning, writing "The ability to do ethical-decision making, however, requires knowing what an ethical conflict is, i.e., a clash between self-interest and what ethics prescribes." In McDermott's view, an agent can only know what an ethical conflict is and be a genuine moral decision maker if that agent has sufficient free will to sometimes choose to act in its own self interest when that runs counter to the moral prescription.

Real engineering challenges are best pursued with clear criteria for success. How might one develop criteria for moral sensitivity or moral agency? Alan Turing, one of the fathers of AI, confronted a similar problem in trying to determine whether a computer is intelligent. Turing was a British mathematician whose wartime efforts in breaking the German code were instrumental in the Allies' victory. Before the war, Turing had developed a mathematical representation of machines and programs that enabled him to state with precision what mathematical functions any possible machine could compute. During and after the war, Turing turned his abstract ideas into actual machines, the forerunners of the modern digital computer. In his 1950 article "Computing Machinery and Intelligence," perhaps the single most influential article in the philosophy of AI, Turing proposed to bypass the problem of defining intelligence by applying a practical test: could a person tell a machine from a human being on the basis only of their conversational responses in a text-only exchange? According to Turing, if an expert can't tell the difference between the computer and the person, the computer is to be considered intelligent for all practical purposes. This standard has become widely known as the Turing test. The criterion has drawbacks, but it nevertheless presents a clear goal for engineers to pursue in building intelligent systems.

Could a useful moral Turing test be developed? We'll discuss this later. The proposal is likely to be as controversial (and arguably unreachable) as the original Turing test. For the time being, each project directed at implementing some aspect of moral decision making in AI will need a specification of criteria for judging its success. Different criteria will result in different emphases on features such as logical consistency, language, or emotional intelligence.

Before getting into the details of how to build and assess AMAs, however, we will address two kinds of worries we frequently encounter when presenting this work. What will be the human consequences of attempting to mechanize moral decision making? And is the attempt to turn machines into intelligent agents as misdirected as the alchemists' quest to turn lead into gold?

Chapter 3

DOES HUMANITY WANT COMPUTERS MAKING MORAL DECISIONS?

Fear and Fascination

We've informally polled people on the desirability of AMAs and found them quite divided. Many agree with us that AMAs are necessary and inevitable. Others say that the idea of AMAs intensifies their discomfort with advanced technology.

There is something paradoxical in the idea that one could relieve the anxiety created by sophisticated technology with even more sophisticated technology. A tension exists between the fascination with technology and the anxiety it provokes. We think this anxiety has two sources. On the one hand are all the usual futurist fears about technology on a trajectory beyond human control. On the other hand, we sense deeper, more personal worries about what this technology might reveal about human beings themselves.

Humanity's deep relationship with technology is sometimes captured by the expression "man the toolmaker," which summarizes a central conception of human nature that is often (somewhat erroneously) used to distinguish humans from other animals. When the primitive ancestors of humans picked up stones and fashioned them into tools or weapons, they initiated the coevolution of humanity and its technologies. Today's children find it hard to imagine a world without computers, and everyone has been changed by the advent of indoor plumbing, sanitation, speedy transportation, and widespread education.

The centrality of technology to human nature is the main theme in the philosophy of technology, a subject that goes back to Aristotle. Philosophers of technology deal with the role technology plays in human culture, including the resulting costs and benefits. The biblical notion of beating swords into plowshares illustrates the long association of tools with costs, benefits, and power. Because humans would be lost without their gadgets and machinery, the tools that to some extent define humans can also be seen as controlling their lives and undermining their autonomy.

Two notions of value are operating here. On the one hand, there are external values, which have to do with whether technology does or does not contribute to public welfare. Are nuclear weapons, cloning, and artificial intelligence good things overall? What about planes, trains, and automobiles? On the other hand, there are internal values, which have to do with how technology forms what it means to be human. Are we, as Andy Clark says, "natural born cyborgs" who take up technologies so readily as to become literally merged with them? Or is technology as easily shed as a pair of underpants? (And by the way, where did the characters in *The Matrix* find clothes?) There is a philosophical tension between humans' autonomy and their dependence on technology.

Furthermore, there is the sense that the adoption of new technologies not only alters human potential but can also transform human character and consciousness. Sociologist Sherry Turkle of MIT writes that "an unstated question lies behind much of our current preoccupations with the future of technology. The question is not what will technology be like in the future, but rather, what will we be like, what are we becoming as we forge increasingly intimate relationships with our machines."

Philosophy of technology raises questions about human freedom and dignity in an increasingly technological society. Is it true that many more people in highly industrialized societies are relegated to repetitive and stultifying jobs? Does the demand for the products of technology inevitably decimate the environment? The development of some new technologies, for example genetic engineering and nanotechnology, raises the fear that powerful processes are being unleashed that humans might not be able to control. Many of the same worries arise in connection with (ro)bots. Much, perhaps most, of what is written in this genre is not engaged with solving technological problems themselves and, indeed, is critical of the idea of technological "progress." These philosophers of technology often see themselves as providing a necessary counterweight to technology optimists, for example Maggie Boden, the very influential philosopher of AI and founding Dean of the School of Cognitive and Computing Sciences at the University of Sussex in Brighton, England, who wrote in her 1983 article "Artificial Intelligence as a Humanizing Force" that AI could be "the Westerner's mango tree," capable of freeing humanity from drudgery to pursue more humanistic activities.

While old-style philosophy of technology was mostly reactive, and often motivated by the specter of powerful processes beyond people's control, a new generation of philosophers of technology are more proactive. They seek to make engineers aware of the values they bring to any design process and wish to influence the design and implementation of technology rather than merely react to it. Not content with simply cheering or jeering, the new philosophers of technology participate in meetings about activities as diverse as designing toys, video games, and sewage plants. Philosopher Helen Nissenbaum calls this "engineering activism."

Some engineers may be tempted to ignore or dismiss questions about values as too "soft," but this will not make them go away. Systems and devices will embody values whether or not humans intend or want them to. To ignore values in technology is to risk surrendering their determination to chance or some other force. Given the inevitable incorporation of values into computer systems, Nissenbaum justifies engineering activism as the need to "advocate on behalf of values" that serve humanity.

The field of artificial morality shares this activist approach to technology. It is fundamentally concerned with infusing technology with values that enhance human welfare. When computer systems select from among different courses of action, they engage in a kind of decision-making process. For the immediate future, the ethical dimensions of this decision making will be largely determined by the values engineers incorporate into the systems, either implicitly or explicitly. Until recently, designers did not consider the ways values were implicitly embedded in the technologies they produced. Helping engineers become aware of both the internal and external ethical dimensions of their work has been an important achievement of philosophers such as Nissenbaum.

Attention to the values that are unconsciously built into technology is a very welcome development. At the very least, system designers should consider whose values or what values they implement. But the morality implicit in the actions of artificial agents is not simply a question of engineering ethics, that is to say, of getting engineers to recognize their ethical assumptions. Given the complexity of modern computers, engineers commonly discover that they cannot predict how a system will act in a new situation. Hundreds of engineers contribute to the design of each machine. Different companies, research centers, and design teams work on individual hardware and software components that make up the final product. The modular design of a computer system can mean that no single person or group can fully grasp the way the system will interact with or respond to a complex flow of new inputs. The goal of artificial morality moves engineering activism beyond emphasizing the role of designers' values in shaping the operational morality of systems to providing the systems themselves with the capacity for explicit moral reasoning and decision making.

The ideal AMA would take into account both external and internal values as it makes choices and acts. Nevertheless, initially, the emphasis will be on ensuring that (ro)bots don't cause external harms. Attention to internal values will lie primarily with the engineers who design the systems and with the society and users who elect to adopt or reject new technologies.

Delegating Responsibility for Decisions to a Computer

We have suggested that AMAs are necessary and inevitable, but are there downsides to developing this technology? There are, of course, the highly speculative and often alarmist concerns raised by futurists and devotees of science fiction, but there are also more immediate concerns regarding the impacts on human dignity and responsibility that may follow even from more limited forms of artificially intelligent systems.

The initial approaches to machine morality are most likely to be in the form of software support tools for decision makers. But there is a danger that such support tools will become crutches for users who will substitute the machines' output for their own critical thinking. Social scientists Batya Friedman and Peter Kahn have raised this worry concerning decision support tools (DSTs).

Friedman and Kahn suggest that DSTs start a slippery slope toward the abandonment of moral responsibility by human decision makers. As people come to trust the advice of a DST, it can become more difficult to question that advice. There is a danger, they believe, that DSTs could eventually come to control the decision-making process.

Why would this be a bad thing? Friedman and Kahn are not completely clear on this point, although they seem to think that responsible computing requires a fully conscious agent to be responsible for every decision. We think that this might be a requirement for some very important contexts—perhaps life-and-death decisions in hospitals, for example. But there are lots of areas where direct human oversight is impracticable, for reasons we've already explained. In those contexts, responsible computing means having programs that take into account and are responsive to the ethically relevant features of the problem under consideration.

Friedman and Kahn use the adoption of a DST in the intensive care unit (ICU) of a hospital to illustrate their concerns. They focus on APACHE, a computer-based decision support model that facilitates determining treatment procedures for patients in the ICU. As they put it:

> It may become the practice for critical care staff to act on APACHE's rec-
> ommendations somewhat automatically, and increasingly difficult for
> even an experienced physician to challenge the "authority" of APACHE's rec-

ommendation.... But at this point the open-loop consultation system . . . has become, in effect, a closed-loop system wherein computer prediction dictates clinical decisions.

When Friedman and Kahn wrote their article in 1992, the APACHE system was a prototype. The latest upgrade, APACHE-III, contains a database with information on more than six hundred thousand ICU patients. The system is marketed on the premise that it can provide real-time, risk-adjusted clinical and financial information to physicians and hospital administrators who manage care for high-risk, high-cost patients. APACHE Medical Systems claims that this helps hospitals to introduce procedural changes that can, for example, decrease the length of time a patient stays in the ICU—and therefore decrease hospital costs. The company also contends that improved procedures and improvements in evaluating the prognosis for individual patients have led to quantifiable improvements in patient care.

Has the presence of APACHE in hospitals led to a decline in physician autonomy? It is difficult to establish an answer to this question. In any case, it is unclear that a reduction of physician autonomy would be such a bad thing, if physicians using APACHE tend to do a better job for their patients than physicians working without a decision support system. Nevertheless, it is important to recognize the danger Friedman and Kahn highlight—of physicians deferring to the machine in evaluating a patient's care. Given the current litigious age, we agree that health professionals may well be shy about challenging the conclusions of a DST with a good record of accomplishment. A computerized audit trail detailing the system's analysis is likely to be available to enterprising malpractice attorneys. Rather than speculating about such reluctance, however, we think such worries should be based on empirical study—is it true that DSTs inevitably lead to too much machine control? Some preliminary studies suggest that physicians have a positive response to DSTs, but more research is necessary.

Friedman and Kahn have also considered the prospect that an APACHE system might one day be used to turn off life support without any direct action by a human decision maker. This speculation might be alarming, but in the decade and half since they raised this worry, we have not seen any evidence that full machine control over life-and-death decisions has gotten any closer. Before anyone takes this drastic step, the available software would have to reach a level of sophistication that far exceeds the ethical sensitivity of anything currently envisaged. APACHE has only a very limited conception of what is ethically or morally relevant in the ICU situation. A more ethically focused DST should be expected to consider not just patient survival but the issues of, for example, whether the treatment is consistent with the wishes of the patient and his family and whether the anticipated result of the treatment will provide a quality of life acceptable to him. These are the kinds of considerations for patient autonomy and well-being that are usually best answered in a full and open dialogue between a physician and a patient, and may well include other human actors, for example, a spouse or religious counselor the patient invites into the discussion.

Sometimes, however, patients are not in any condition to enter into a dialogue. Could computers be as accurate as a patient's relatives in predicting the preferences of such terminally ill patients? A National Institutes of Health (NIH) research group published a study in 2007 showing that patients' relatives were accurate in predicting the wishes of their loved ones only about three-quarters of the time. Could a computer program do better? David Wendler, a bioethicist at NIH who was one of the authors of the study, believes so. He and his colleagues wrote a program that used no information except how well the treatment had worked for other patients in a similar condition. It applied a simple rule to predict whether a patient would have accepted a specific treatment. If the treatment had a 1 percent chance of allowing the patient to recover normal cognitive abilities, the program predicted that it would be chosen. The program was able to perform just as accurately as relatives and friends in predicting patients' wishes. Wendler believes that by factoring in more information about a patient, such as age, gender, and occupation, it should be possible for software to significantly outperform human judgment. Perhaps, then, should you ever become incapacitated without having previously written a living will, you would prefer the decision about your intensive care to be made by a machine rather than your relatives!

When patients are not completely incapacitated, we agree with Friedman and Kahn about the need to be vigilant against misusing DSTs. Regardless of the context, decision support should not be allowed to become decision making by default. However, this does not obviate the need for more and more sophisticated DSTs that take a broader range of ethically relevant details into account—DSTs that are more like AMAs, in other words. A system that gets 90 percent of the decisions correct using only ethically blind criteria—for example, objective survivorship rates—may be missing the 10 percent of cases where ethical judgment has the greatest significance to all involved.

Nevertheless, one might object that developing DSTs along this track increases the slope, or its slipperiness. The worry is that the more intuitively plausible the output of the machine, the more likely it is to be treated anthropomorphically as embodying genuine moral intelligence. Arguably, those who design and market such systems are perpetuating a kind of fraud on those who use them: they make people believe that these systems are something that they are not. We turn to this issue in the next section.

Pulling the Wool

In 1944, Fritz Heider and Mary-Ann Simmel published a now classic experiment in which they demonstrated how natural it is for people to attribute anthropomorphic properties to anything they perceive as being animate. In their experiment, subjects were shown movies of simple geometric figures moving around a blank screen and were asked to describe what they saw. Virtually everyone spontaneously described the movements of these objects with words such as "wants," "fears," and "needs." If one of the triangles closely followed the other while the second made frequent changes of direction, the first triangle might be described as "chasing" the second triangle, or the second triangle was seen as "frightened by" and "running away" from the first. Subjects spontaneously anthropomorphized and projected intentions on the objects. They found it very difficult to describe the activity in geometric terms even when prompted to do so. Many recent experiments have reconfirmed how readily humans project intentions onto animated objects.

Most forms of anthropomorphism are relatively innocuous. Humans relate to their pets at times as if they are human, but most people appreciate that what pets understand is limited. Toy companies have recognized that they can capitalize on the natural tendency to project emotional states and intentions onto animated objects in their design of dolls, robopets, and other objects. When a robot dog wags its tail or hops around as one gives it attention, it is not "happy"; it has no internal states comparable to human emotions, or even the emotions of an animal. Although there are interesting research questions regarding such parlor tricks for social psychologists to pursue, it is well understood that these toys are designed primarily to be entertaining. Sony promoted its cute humanoid robot with the line "QRIO wants to be your friend." But, of course, QRIO does not "want" anything. The manufacturer wants you to buy QRIO. (Or, at least, they did until their new American CEO closed the robot division in 2006.)

There is a fine line between parlor tricks and duping the public. However, there is also considerable evidence that providing technology with humanlike skills can facilitate interaction between humans and their computers, gadgets, and robots. Many consumers like automobiles and computers that speak to them in a soothing voice. The Affective Computing Lab at MIT is experimenting with ways systems can recognize user frustration. For example, frustration is registered in the form of pressure on a specially designed mouse with built-in sensors. Pressure on the mouse activates the sensors, which in turn initiates on-screen menus or triggers a simulated voice that asks whether there is a problem. If the user responds affirmatively, the software then offers various forms of remediation.

Other scientists in MIT's Humanoid Robotics Group are exploring how systems designed to detect basic human social gestures and respond with human-like social cues can facilitate human-robot interactions. Perhaps the best known social robot is Kismet. No one would claim that Kismet has a sophisticated social aptitude. What is remarkable is that even with its very low-level, essentially mechanical social mechanisms, it could be quite persuasive in conveying the sense that it was alive and actually engaged in a form of social interaction. (Some students in our classes feel bad when they see Kismet being scolded.)

Certainly, robots like Kismet, with some human-like features and movements, can make interacting with technology easier and more comfortable. But there is also considerable uncertainty as to how human-like technology can or should be. Masahiro Mori, a Japanese roboticist, theorized in 1970 that people become more comfortable with and empathetic with robots with human-like features and movements until they start to look too human, and then people tend to become very uncomfortable with or even revolted by them. The dissonance created by what appears to be human but fails to meet human expectations is apparently quite disconcerting. Mori described this drop in comfort as the "uncanny valley"—on the assumption that it would be possible to overcome these negative feelings if androids could be made even more human-like.

Mori's uncanny valley causes different reactions among designers of robots. Hiroshi Ishiguru, who designs android robots with the goal of having them look and act as much like humans as possible, sees the uncanny valley as a challenge to be surmounted. Other roboticists read the uncanny valley as suggesting that the most effective robots will be those that have some human-like characteristics but clearly do not pretend to be human. The strategy roboticists take is largely a function of their goals. Given present-day technology, robots that are similar to but clearly distinct from humans in their appearance and actions are better than androids at facilitating human-robot interaction.

The techniques developed to give Kismet the ability to detect basic social cues and respond with complementary social gestures are already being appropriated by businesses interested in designing and marketing toys and service robots. From a puritanical perspective, all such techniques are arguably forms of deception. However, consumers are unlikely to consider this an ethical problem, given the entertainment value and improved usability of such products—presuming, of course, that they aren't being designed for a nefarious purpose.

Still, there may be a problem if the anthropomorphic responses elicited by such technologies tend to mask activities that are unintentionally harmful or unethical. Consider, for example, an experiment by the sociologist Sherry

Turkle, who brought robotic dolls into a nursing home. The particular type of doll she loaned the residents had been commercially unsuccessful, failing to attract the interest of sophisticated young consumers who could choose from similar dolls with better features. But Turkle was surprised by the depth of the attachments many of the nursing home residents formed with their robotic dolls, often being unwilling to give them up at the end of the loan period. Clearly, many of the residents were hungry for any form of social interaction.

Most people consider robotic dolls a very poor substitute for human companionship, and would regard the attachments formed by the home's residents as a symptom of society's failure to attend to the emotional needs of the elderly and the disabled. One might well abhor any suggestion that social robots are a solution to loneliness and need for human interaction. But there are hard questions that need to be asked about the function, practicality, and desirability of social robotics as a response to human needs. For example, if there is no evidence that people and communities are willing to direct the time or resources necessary to respond to the needs of the elderly and disabled for human contact, are social robots better than nothing?

Friedman and Kahn raise another serious ethical concern posed by the human tendency to anthropomorphize technology: the harm that can result from imputing faculties to machines that they do not have. Present-day technology is far from having the kinds of intelligence and intentions people demand from human moral agents. Imputing such agency to machines is dangerous, and indicates a potential abrogation by humans of responsibility. Companies that produce intelligent machines need to train users to be vigilant, not merely to escape liability but also to fulfill their responsibility for harms that result from a misunderstanding of what the machines do and what they cannot do.

The introduction of Trident submarines carrying nuclear weapons in the late 1980s was one of the factors that seriously jeopardized the fate of the Earth during the arms race between the United States and the Soviet Union. These ships broke the symbolic ten-minute barrier between the launch of weapons and weapons strikes that had been considered necessary for bringing leaders into the decision-making process to evaluate whether images that appeared on radar screens signaled an attack or were harmless. Without time to bring humans into the decision-making process, weapons systems in the Soviet Union would be forced to rely on computer analysis of the data and computers initiating retaliatory measures. The future of humanity was about to be placed in the hands of 1980s Soviet computer technology. Luckily for all, the arms race collapsed. But even today, anyone who puts matters of life and death in the hands of computers has failed to understand the limits of current technology.

It remains unclear whether, as AI systems become ubiquitous, users will come to better understand the limitations of these machines. Will, for example, most people come to appreciate the areas in which human intelligence excels in comparison to computers or will humans begin to feel inferior? Certainly, calculators and computers are far superior to humans in performing complex mathematical tasks, but has the adoption of calculators, for example, actually undermined the respect of humans for their own faculties? The fact that computers perform mechanical and repetitive tasks so well is generally seen as a boon to humanity, a time saver that frees people to direct their attention to more important matters.

However, one might try to press the concern that if computers are perceived as handling moral deliberations, creative tasks, or other complex challenges better than humans, a form of malaise or inferiority complex might set in, undermining self-respect. Computers with creative faculties might also sap the motivation of creative individuals to test their own ingenuity. We think it would be incorrect to see technology as the thief that steals motivation and spirit. Even children who are not among the most intelligent, athletic, or artistic can be effectively motivated to accomplish great things. It is the challenge of parents and educators to bring out the best in each child, regardless of whether or not they show talent in one particular area. The social challenge in a world of sophisticated machines will be to nurture human aspirations. We are confident that this challenge can be met. Indeed, for many children, new technologies have helped nurture talents that in previous generations lay hidden.

These worries are futuristic, so long as the verdict is out on whether scientists will succeed in their endeavors to duplicate individual human cognitive and social capacities within computer systems and robots. Optimists believe that humans will build systems that equal or surpass human intelligence, and have argued that this may even happen in the next twenty to fifty years. If they are right, it will be seen by some as a blow to human dignity, a demonstration that humans are not unique creatures, with god-given talents that make them superior to animals and other entities. There are those who would even prefer that humans never find out whether AI can rival human intelligence. While we understand this perspective, we believe that humanity is better served by pursuing scientific research. People are quite capable of accommodating the truths that scientific investigation brings to light. Furthermore, we suspect that substantiating all higher order mental faculties in artificial systems will prove to be a particularly difficult challenge, if not impossible, and the difficulty of this challenge may indeed underscore why humans are such remarkable creatures.

Soldiers, Sex Toys, and Slaves

Might accepting robots into people's lives dilute cherished human values and degrade people's humanity? Ironically, this question has been raised by one of the most successful roboticists, Ronald Arkin, the director of the Georgia Institute of Technology's Mobile Robot Laboratory. Arkin coined the phrase "Bombs, Bonding, and Bondage" to capture the social concerns posed by the three main forms of human-robot interaction—robots as soldiers, as companions, and as slaves. Robots for military applications, intimacy, and labor will each be very different entities with different goals giving rise to different ethical considerations.

Does humanity want robot soldiers? Well, we already have them in the form of cruise missiles, remotely controlled vehicles, and battlefield robots deployed for hazardous duty. A May 2006 news story describes the hundreds of "PackBot Tactical Mobile Robots deployed in Iraq and Afghanistan to open doors in urban combat, lay fiber-optic cable, defuse bombs and perform other hazardous duties previously done by humans alone."

In the United States, where robotic research is largely financed by the Department of Defense, there are plans to spend billions on the long-term goal of developing armed robots. According to numerous press reports in 2004 and 2005, the U.S. military had already developed a remote-operated Talon robot (using a SWORDS) armed with M240 or M249 machine guns, and in December 2005 the BBC reported that these robots were being deployed "to wage war against insurgents in Iraq." The SWORDS robot takes aim electronically, although actual firing decisions are under the remote control of the human operator. At the end of 2007, there were reports that SWORDS robots were soon to be used in combat. No reports of their actual usage have yet appeared. Nonetheless, at the end of January 2008, a missile fired from a remotely flown Predator drone reportedly killed over a dozen members of al Qaeda at a location inside Pakistan.

Even if human operators initially remain within the loop of any decision to kill using weapons-carrying robots, this will not always be the case. In fact, the Defense Advanced Research Projects Agency (DARPA) has been funding research into autonomous battlefield robots since at least the beginning of the decade, and DARPA's field combat systems (FCS) program has set a 2010 deadline for field deployment of military-grade robotic workforces needed for combat.

To our knowledge, fully autonomous gun-carrying or bomb-carrying systems have not yet been let loose. But the rationale for such systems is simple and compelling—robots decrease the need for humans in combat and therefore save the lives of soldiers, sailors, and pilots. Furthermore, even remotely operated vehicles such as the Predator are currently complex enough to require up to four people to operate one drone. Navigation, flight, and targeting functions each required highly trained personnel. Clearly, the side that can reduce its personnel needs by making its robots more and more autonomous will have an advantage. The Army is already testing supply robots that move across the battlefield without a human operator.

Robotic fighting machines will not be hampered with the inconvenience of Asimov's First Law—against harming or killing humans. The problem is obvious. Once robots are authorized to kill, real-time decisions are necessary to determine whether killing any particular person is justified. Asimov himself opened the door to the possibility of a robot killing a human for the general protection of humanity, when he added his Zeroth Law to the other three laws: "A robot may not harm humanity, or, by inaction, allow humanity to come to harm." Short of implementing the ability to make moral decisions about when, where, and toward whom deadly force is acceptable, there is no way to reduce the likelihood that robotic fighting machines will cause unacceptable harm. Furthermore, robots will not only kill enemy combatants but also be responsible for civilian deaths ("collateral damage") and the deaths of allied troops ("friendly fire"). Even if collateral losses are justifiable given the larger objectives, the autonomous systems would need to be capable of weighing the options. Given the difficulty of ensuring safety and ethical behavior, it is necessary to think long and hard about when to deploy weapon-carrying systems. The answer is unlikely to be as straightforward as "never."

The generally held understanding of the unmanned vehicles or cruise missiles that have already been deployed by the military is that they are tools or things. But given the human propensity to anthropomorphize, soldiers have bonded with their robots. Colin Angle, chief executive of iRobot, manufacturer of the PackBot that is being used to find and defuse explosive devices in Iraq, tells the story of a U.S. soldier who begged that the company repair Scooby Doo, the affectionate name his unit gave their PackBot that was blown up after completing thirty-five successful missions. Angle recounts that the soldier pleaded with iRobot to "please fix Scooby Doo because he saved my life."

An entirely different objective from building artificial soldiers is the development of artificial creatures, friends, and companions—robots designed for human interaction. Developers of social robots are focusing on exploiting human psychology to either enhance usability or stimulate people to forge emotional bonds with their mechanical pets and companions.

Designers of sex toys are particularly good at taking the lead in appropriating the latest technology to titillate their clients. Technological development has a long history of being driven by pornographic applications, and the field of robotics is no exception. As with all pornographic applications, serious issues about exploitation of women and fostering of antisocial behavior arise. But as with the discussion of robot soldiers carrying weapons, there are two sides to this issue. For example, robot avatars functioning as surrogate sex partners for John's remote pleasures arguably provide a form of "safe sex." But no doubt there will also be anecdotal evidence suggesting that relationships with robotic sex toys leads to aberrant antisocial behavior, and future research may confirm this.

The use of robots for solving problems of loneliness goes well beyond their use for the instant gratification of sex. Researchers are working on (ro)bots that can read emotional states through facial expressions and other nonverbal and verbal cues to create the illusion of being empathetic. In his 2007 book *Love and Sex with Robots: The Evolution of Human-Robot Relationships*, David Levy argues that the current research trajectory will lead to long-term partnerships and even marriage between humans and robots. However, the deepening of emotional bonds opens up opportunities for unscrupulous designers and perhaps even future semiintelligent robots to exploit naive users. There are also, of course, issues concerning the forms of sexual behavior that various communities will consider ethical for human-robot relationships. Will it be necessary to regulate what a companion robot system can and cannot do? Perhaps. At the least, society should be prepared to address the social consequences of sophisticated robot companions.

A long-standing attraction of robots has been the prospect of having servants or slaves that work 24/7 and don't need to be paid—getting the benefit of having slaves without taking on the moral challenges of slavery. Indeed, the word *robot* was first coined by Josef and Karel Capek in 1920 from the Czech word *robota*, which means drudgery or servitude. Ronald Arkin questions whether the moral problems inherent in slavery are circumvented by using robots as slaves. For thousands of years, humans have held each other in involuntary servitude, and the abolition of slavery has only been partially accomplished during the last 150 years. The abolition of slavery is a young and perhaps still fragile moral principle, especially in light of the vast number of people worldwide who are still effectively enslaved as indentured workers. Arkin ponders whether the acceptance of robot servants could reinstate slavery as a viable option in societies that have officially abolished the practice, and he wonders whether this could relegitimize human slavery or lead to human sloth.

Robots as surrogates for human workers are already established in industrial robotics and the commercialization of robotic appliances, for example vacuum cleaners. The Japan Robot Association has set the goal of developing service robots to care for the elderly and disabled within the next few years. Regardless of any suggestion that slave robots are a bad idea, robots as tools and workhorses will be built. No one is likely to mistake a Roomba for a person, but the usability and charm of service robots will be enhanced by making them cute and more sociable-looking, with human- or pet-like features and faculties. Furthermore, the barriers to slavery may well lower incrementally as the distinctions between humans, cyborgs, and robots are blurred one by one.

Then there are the futurist concerns that robots themselves will eventually have feelings and emotions of their own and will acquire intelligence, consciousness, and self-understanding. Will a robot that feels pain have the right to command a human to stop mistreating it? Will a robot with a sophisticated degree of understanding be free to say that it will not work? Or, despite the evidence, will people continue to insist that robots are a race of inferior life-forms without true feelings, higher-order mental faculties, or consciousness.

For the near future, most tasks will be performed by discrete robotic appliances and embedded technology. Microprocessors in refrigerators, garbage cans, and clothing will alter humans' workloads. The immorality of human slavery will not be challenged as long as robot helpers are virtually invisible or without personality or emotions. But this is unlikely to remain the case for long. Household robots designed to be both companions and slaves are on engineers' drawing boards—or should we say in their CAD programs.

Can Technology Risks be Properly Assessed?

Our discussion so far has underscored some of the types of social risks involved in the development of advanced (ro)bots. But exactly how risky are they?

Assessing the impact of new technologies is far from a science. Risk assessment reports on the safety of drugs, building projects, and complex technologies are filled with data about numerous factors. Eventually, someone has to interpret the relative import of each factor, and quantifiable research gives way to value judgments. All too often, the empirical data is used to mask the fact that some group's economic or political interests have weighed heavily in the final evaluation of risks.

No one engaged in assessing risks is under the illusion that one can eliminate the unpredictable. The unpredictability of the future hinges on missed influences, inadequate information, the fallibility of humans, and unforeseen eventualities, for example, the ways complex technologies will affect each other and even give rise to new possibilities.

The value of going through a formal process of assessing risks lies in weighing the foreseeable benefits against the foreseeable risks. Without going through this exercise, people are prone to give undue emphasis to more prominent beneficial or negative factors. The identification of risks can in turn facilitate the management of risks. Professionals in the field of risk assessment struggle to make their research comprehensive, their discipline scientific, and their judgments transparent to the greatest extent possible. Technology assessment, a young discipline, is still struggling to effectively model how the introduction of new technologies influences change in already dynamic social contexts.

Risk assessment is important to the project of building decision-making (ro)bots in two respects. First, there are the risks posed to people individually and to society as a whole by implementing such systems. The risks may vary depending on the type of system that is introduced. For example, service robots in the home may pose immediate physical and psychological risks to those who enter the house but are less likely to cause harm to anyone outside the home. Autonomous agents within computer networks, for example financial systems, might be less likely to cause direct physical harm but are quite capable of causing harms that have far-reaching social consequences that can, in turn, indirectly affect the physical well-being of individuals. Automated programs that buy and sell stocks, bonds, and currencies on international markets have caused severe financial crises by triggering large-scale movements of capital out of specific countries.

Second, to the extent that the tools for assessing risks can predict the probabilities and consequences of various courses of action, they might be appropriated by (ro)bots for evaluating the risk entailed in alternative responses to a challenge. That is, the analysis of risks could potentially help the AMA select the best course of action on the basis of the available information. Some of the specialized tools and techniques professionals use for assessing risks have already been computerized. These programs might even provide a software platform for AMAs to analyze the consequences of their own actions.

The Future

Nothing in life is risk free. Even librarians die from work-related factors or on-the-job risks. Americans and Europeans often have the illusion that they can effectively minimize risks so they approach zero. The public is particularly attuned to the possibility of disastrous events. In research published in 1987, Americans rated nuclear power as the most dangerous in a list of thirty activities or technologies that included smoking, pesticides, police work, x-rays, and prescription antibiotics. Professional risk assessors, who use psychometric scales that emphasize mortality rates, saw nuclear power as much safer (twentieth in the list) than the general public. Surgery, which the professionals rated as high risk (5), was ranked at 10 by the public. These differences do not mean the professionals are right and the public is necessarily confused. Rather, different factors can influence the assessment of risk. For example, one might believe that eventually there will be a disastrous nuclear accident that will override existing safety records and low mortality rates.

Lurking in the background are all the science fiction scenarios that suggest that AI systems will eventually evolve into creatures that will want to eliminate humanity. Are engineers stepping onto a slippery slope leading to the inevitable extinction of the human species? Humanity's extinction at the hand of (ro)bots is not inevitable. From our present vantage point, we think the risk is extremely low. Is it possible? It is hard to say. It is still unclear whether some of the perceived barriers to robust AI can be overcome. If they can be, and the platforms for it have been clarified, then it may be possible to build appropriate ethical constraints into these systems to eliminate the possibility of human extermination.

It is much too early to consider relinquishing the benefits humans can derive from AI because of highly speculative futurist fantasies. As this very young field progresses, social theorists, engineers, and politicians will have many strategic opportunities to visit the question of whether Pandora's box is about to be opened.

The idea that humans should err on the side of caution is not particularly helpful in addressing speculative futuristic dangers. This idea is often formulated as the "precautionary principle" that if the consequences of an action are unknown but are judged to have some potential for major or irreversible negative consequences, then it is better to avoid that action. The difficulty with the precautionary principle lies in establishing criteria for when it should be invoked. Few people would want to sacrifice the advances in computer technology of the past fifty years because of 1950s fears of a robot takeover. Without the benefit of hindsight, it is difficult to say which dangers represent unmanageable challenges and which can be managed if not actually defused. Nevertheless, the difficulty in applying the precautionary principle should not be taken to undermine the need for vigilance.

The social issues we have raised highlight concerns that will arise in the development of AI, but it would be hard to argue that any of these concerns leads to the conclusion that humans should stop building AI systems that make decisions or display autonomy. Nor is it clear what arguments or evidence would support such a conclusion. In a 1999 report released by the World Health Organization, traffic accidents were noted as the leading injury-related killer of people between the ages of fifteen and forty-four. Motor vehicle accidents accounted for the deaths of 1,170,694 worldwide in 1998. This figure does not include the deaths indirectly related to automobiles in the form of air pollution (e.g., bronchial disease) and global warming (e.g., skin cancer and storm-related deaths). If people had known how destructive automobiles would be a hundred years ago, would they have stopped the development of a favored form of transportation? Probably not. Most people believe the advantages of automobiles outweigh their destructive potential.

We are concerned with the destructive potential of AI systems. That prompts our interest in promoting the field of artificial morality. We see no grounds for arresting research solely on the basis of the issues presently being raised by social critics or futurists. However, we believe that there are and will continue to be opportunities to reassess whether the dangers of developing AI outweigh any rewards. In the meantime, the development of AMAs provides an important venue for exploring how effectively the risks posed by autonomous systems can be managed. It also provides a venue for assessing the nature of moral agency itself, and it is to this topic that we turn next.

Chapter 4

CAN (RO)BOTS REALLY BE MORAL?

Careworthy Technology

"Soldiers Bond with Battlefield Robots" declared the headline of the 2006 story by Reuters reporter Joel Rothstein about Scooby Doo. A 2007 story by Joel Garreau of the *Washington Post* reported a colonel in the U.S. Army calling off a robotic land-mine-sweeping experiment in which the robot kept crawling along despite losing its legs one at a time. The colonel, Garreau reports, declared that the test was inhumane. Robots that humans care about are clearly a reality. But will the robots care about us? Can they?

Many people believe that machines are incapable of being truly conscious, incapable of the genuine understanding and emotions that define humans' most important relationships and shape humans' ethical norms. What are these capacities? (The "ontological" question.) What can be known about them scientifically? (The "epistemological" question.) Does artificial morality depend on answering these questions? (The practical question.) Our answer to the ontological and epistemological questions is an emphatic "We don't know!" (But neither does anyone else.) The reasons no one knows the answers to the first two questions help shape our approach to the practical question, giving us the confidence to answer it with a resounding no.

Practically speaking, all current progress toward AI involves software running on digital hardware. One day, perhaps sooner than people think, AMA development may take place in petri dishes or quantum computers, not CPUs. But the "wet" artificial life being developed at places like the J. Craig Venter Institute in Rockville, Maryland, and Protolife in Venice, Italy, is still prebacterial, and not yet programmable. And the problems facing large-scale quantum computing may be insurmountable. For the near term, at least, the field of artificial morality is hitched to digital computing. But hasn't it been shown that digital computers can't have genuine understanding and consciousness? Isn't it just a conceptual confusion to use "moral" and "ethical" to describe the behavior of (ro)bots? Our task in this chapter is to argue convincingly that the immediate practical aims of artificial morality need not be compromised by the controversy about the limits of software-based intelligence. In fact, we think that pressing ahead on the practical task of building AMAs will contribute to better understanding of the ontological and epistemological questions about the nature of ethics itself.

Artificial Intelligence: The Very Idea

The mysteries of matter, life, and mind define the three major challenges of science. By the middle of the twentieth century, scientists held the keys to understanding the first two. In the early part of the century, physicists made great strides in understanding the behavior of matter and energy at scales from the subatomic to the universe. The discovery of the structure of DNA similarly put biology on a fast track.

Matter and life still hold their mysteries, of course. But the basic tools for their scientific investigation were established—everyone knew that what was needed in physics were more powerful particle accelerators and more powerful telescopes, and in biology more powerful molecular techniques for manipulating genotypes and cells. These strategies still dominate physics and biology today. What, then, of the mind? Many scientists have, of course, pursued a biological route, folding the study of mind into the study of brains, deploying biological techniques. However, others have seen the central character of mind in more general terms, defining it in terms of information processing, not neuroscience. It was in this context that the early advocates of AI saw computers as the best hope for putting mind onto a secure scientific footing.

A computer program is a series of formally defined symbols that can be used to control the operations of a physical machine—a "physical symbol system" in the terminology of Allen Newell and Herbert Simon of Carnegie Mellon University. In their Turing Award Lecture to the Association of Computing Machinery in 1975, Newell and Simon stated the AI manifesto boldly: "A physical symbol system has the necessary and sufficient means for general intelligent action." Cognitive psychology, as they envisaged it, was the science of showing how computation is necessary for intelligence, by uncovering the symbolic operations involved in human intelligence. The task they envisaged for AI was to show the sufficiency of symbolic computation by establishing that any intelligent capacity could be programmed into a computer.

If intelligence is computation, then more and more powerful computers are AI's analogs to the increasingly powerful particle accelerators used by physicists to probe the deep structure of matter. The number of digital bits in today's computers is still several orders of magnitude below the number of connections among neurons in a human brain, but the technology is increasing its capacity exponentially. Silicon transistors seem destined to be replaced by carbon nanotube transistors that will allow circuits to be laid out in three dimensions. Ray Kurzweil predicts the equivalent capacity of one human brain will be available on desktop computers by 2020. He argues that when machine intelligence starts to outstrip the collective total of all human intelligence, around 2029, humanity will have entered the Singularity. The Singularity marks a point at which change is so radical that it is no longer predictable.

Kurzweil is a proponent of what Berkeley philosophy professor John Searle calls "strong AI": the view that an appropriately programmed computer is a mind. In 1980, Searle published what has become the most widely discussed condemnation of strong AI. In it, he argues that the formal symbol manipulation carried out by a computer following a program is never sufficient to produce intelligent understanding of anything. He presents his famous "Chinese room" thought experiment, which he designed to show that it is possible for a computer to pass the Turing test without possessing genuine understanding or intelligence.

Searle argues that if he performs the same procedures as a computer in responding to Chinese questions, he can pass the Turing test without actually understanding the Chinese language. He imagines himself in a room with a book of instructions (the program) that tell him what to do with pieces of paper he receives that have meaningless (to him) symbols on them. He looks up these symbols in the book of instructions and follows the rules, which after some number of steps lead him to copy some other symbols onto paper and pass them outside the room. Unbeknownst to him, the symbols are Chinese, and from outside the room they are interpreted as lines of dialogue in a conversation conducted in Chinese. Since he is "executing a program" in this thought experiment, yet does not genuinely understand the "conversation" in which he is participating, Searle argues that executing a program is insufficient for genuine understanding. This argument has given rise to a long debate and countless articles regarding whether a computer system can genuinely "understand anything." Searle believes that the point made by his Chinese Room argument is common sense, and he expresses surprise that it isn't more widely recognized by computer scientists.

This is not the place to go into more detail about the Chinese room argument—as well-trodden a field as one can find in philosophy of mind today. However, philosophers and others who accept Searle's argument have taken it to show that programming a computer is a hopeless approach to the development of genuinely intelligent systems. We frequently encounter skeptics who claim that Searle's result shows that our own approach to artificial morality is similarly hopeless.

We disagree. That is, we disagree that the philosophical objections should stop us from continuing to advocate for better computational solutions to ethical decision making. Nevertheless, we must recognize that there are philosophical questions about the nature and status of the kinds of systems we envisage. We face two questions: Could a (ro)bot ever really be a moral agent? And how would one know?

While we don't think that either of these questions can or needs to be satisfactorily resolved, it's worth discussing them because the skepticism behind such questions can serve a useful, critical function. What is required for real moral agency? There are various answers to this question, some focusing on conscious reasoning, some on free will, and some on the issue of moral responsibility.

Could a (Ro)bot Be a Real
Moral Agent?

The discussion about "real" moral agency is useful if it suggests capacities that need to be engineered into AMAs. If consciousness provides advantages to moral agents, then people should want to consider it for AMAs. Recognizing that no current system is actually conscious, what limits does this place on the capacities of AMAs?

Arguments against AMAs based on Searle's position are of little consequence in practical applications. In his thought experiment, the output of the symbol processing is completely indistinguishable from a genuine Chinese speaker to any outside observer. Therefore, Searle's "genuine understanding" marks a distinction without a behavioral difference. Nothing in Searle's argument rules out the possibility of producing AMAs that are behaviorally indistinguishable from genuine moral agents. Thus, his conception of conscious, intentional understanding is simply irrelevant to the practical issues of how to make (ro)bots behave ethically.

To René Descartes, over three hundred years ago, the idea of machine intelligence was metaphysically absurd. Descartes looked into his own mind, and what he found there seemed so different from the world of physical objects that he concluded mind and body were necessarily distinct substances. Machines are material objects, extended in space and time, and divisible into smaller material parts. Mind, on Descartes's view, was the indivisible locus of conscious reasoning. Although the human being, as conceived by Descartes, combined mechanical body and immaterial mind into a perfectly coordinated whole, material machines alone could never have intellectual attributes. Unlike Searle, Descartes thought that machines were inherently incapable of reasoning or using language flexibly. If Descartes is right, then the prospects for AMAs are somewhat dimmer.

Although Descartes asserted that mere matter could not reproduce the flexible reasoning and speech of human beings, he produced no airtight argument against this possibility. His understanding of the capabilities of material objects was shaped by the best that seventeenth-century science could offer. However, even Descartes's contemporary, Thomas Hobbes, believed that "mind will be nothing but the motions of certain parts of an organic body," and nowadays, as an argument for dualism, Descartes's views about the limitations of matter carry little weight. However, as noted, there are those who still hold that there is something special about the human brain that gives it capacities that can never be attained by programmed silicon. It's a point of view that, given the best that twenty-first-century science has to offer, can still be neither proved nor disproved.

One "special property" some believe is not to be found in any computational technology yet developed is free will. Conscious understanding is another. We'll look at each of these in turn.

The Ethics of Deterministic Systems

Metaphysics appeared and asked her younger sister, Ethics: "What would you recommend that I should bring back to my protégés, the metaphysicians, whether or not they call themselves such?," and Ethics answered: "Tell them they should always try to act so as to increase the number of choices; yes, increase the number of choices!"

—Heinz von Foerster

Unless suffering from compulsion or some other mental disorder, human beings feel free to act in various ways. This sense of freedom can be present even when the physical options for action are extremely limited. A man in shackles may still feel free to blink his eyes. What is the source of this feeling? And is it required for ethical behavior? No one can definitively answer these questions.

The notion of human free will is often viewed somewhat mystically as the "whatever it is" that underlies one's feelings of being free to act, even if it cannot be defined in a scientifically acceptable way. The philosopher Daniel Dennett rejects such "magical" notions of free will. He believes instead that the ability to consider multiple options and select among them is the only kind of freedom humans have, and the only kind worth having. Be that as it may. (We, the present authors, don't entirely agree with each other on this point.) Nevertheless, because free will can't be formulated in clear terms, the mystical view only provides a vague argument against the attempt to engineer AMAs. The hunch that there is a magical ingredient to human free will is one that we can't refute, but we can't apply it to the engineering task of creating AMAs either.

Does this undermine the whole project of engineering AMAs? We don't think so. Deep Blue's ability to choose algorithmically among the chess moves needed to beat Gary Kasparov was not hampered by the lack of any magical ingredients. One might argue, of course, that the success of Deep Blue depended crucially on the human creativity involved in its design. But even if this human creativity is not deterministic, the result was a deterministic system capable of playing chess at the highest level.

Despite being a deterministic system, Deep Blue qualifies as an *agent* in some respects, while falling short in others. Luciano Floridi and J. W. Sanders have identified three key features that are important to the concept of artificial agents:

- *Interactivity*: Response to stimulus by change of state; that is, the agent and its environment can act on each other
- *Autonomy*: Ability to change state without stimulus, that is, without direct response to interaction, which results in a certain degree of complexity and decoupledness from the environment
- *Adaptability*: Ability to change the "transition rules" by which the state is changed; that is, the agent may be viewed as learning its own mode of operation in a way which depends critically on its experience

Deep Blue is interactive and autonomous to a degree, but lacks adaptability, being dependent on the programmers to change the rules by which it functions. (Indeed, Kasparov famously complained that the programmers unfairly added special rules geared specifically to defeating his style of play.) Adding a learning component to the system would enhance its adaptability. However, the learning algorithms available today are far from sufficient.

Chess isn't ethics, of course. Ethics is much closer to the core conception of what it means to be a human being. A central feature of the human experience as moral agents is that people frequently feel poised between act-ing selfishly and acting altruistically. People feel the pull of both directions, and this tension sets up the possibility of freedom—the equal freedom to do the wrong thing or the right thing. (Some ethicists even suggest that it is not possible to act ethically if it is not also possible to act unethically.)

How might ethics arise for a deterministic system? We find the possibil-ity in the kind of choice suggested by the cyberneticist Heinz von Foerster, whom we quoted at the beginning of this section. Like it or not, existing (ro)bots are not just passive conduits of ethical rules but themselves inter-act with other agents in an existing moral ecology. The soldier's concern for his bomb-sniffing robot introduces new ethical possibilities, for example, how he would rank the survival of the robot against that of, say, a dog. But these possibilities also have an impact on ethical agent design. For example, it is within the scope of current technology to measure the tendency of a soldier to approach and interact with a robot and to use this to estimate whether he would act protectively toward the robot. Whether or not it is ultimately a good idea to program such capacities into military hardware, the goals of a specific mission might dictate that robots should associate preferentially with those who respond to it in caring ways. In this way, the relationships between humans and (ro)bots can be reciprocal. Any agent operating within this reciprocal structure will face conflicts between its own goals and the goals of others. Whenever the pursuit of one set of goals involves the possibility of harm to others, an ethical issue arises. The more choices available to and evaluated by a system, the more potential there is for conflict.

Young children and most animals have only a limited sense of the effects of their actions on the well-being of others. For them, the scope for ethical action is limited by the invisibility of the relevant options and outcomes. With increased cognitive sophistication, whether achieved evolutionarily, developmentally, or socially, comes greater awareness of the conflicting goals among agents. It also brings sensitivity to conflicts within an agent's own internal goals. A sophisticated moral agent, we suggest, is one that recognizes that different perspectives yield different preference rankings. These different rankings may not be resolvable in completely neutral, perspective-independent ways. An agent's selection of a course of action may not be rigidly constrained by a single ordering of preferences. People tolerate those with norms different from their own. The design of AMAs should accommodate the degrees of freedom that exist within the domain of ethics.

For von Foerster, it is not just the question of what to choose but also the expansion of the available choices that is central to ethics. In Dennett's view, the expansion of choice comes about because (to quote the title of his book) "freedom evolves." By this he means that evolution has provided humans with the capacity to consider multiple options and foresee multiple outcomes.

The expansion of choice is not only a theme in Dennett's discussion of the evolution of human freedom but also a central principle in the evolution and development of ethical machines. Chris Lang, while a graduate student at the University of Wisconsin at Madison, proposed that the expansion of choices for a search-based learning computer would lead to a system likely to act as a human-friendly moral agent. His optimistic view is based on a conception of machine learning whereby "the rational search for strategies entails maximizing the rate at which one encounters novel ideas which, in turn, entails maximizing the diversity and interaction rate of the group in which one participates." According to Lang, this approach

> entails maximizing freedom in the world in general, which usually involves both preserving life and empowering people—basically all the things we generally consider ethical. Even if "superior" to humans, ethical machines would have to value interaction with humans, because the loss of such interaction would entail a decrease in the diversity of their environment.

We have yet to discuss Lang's ideas about ethical learning machines, but for now it is interesting to note that he, like von Foerster, sees the maximization of choice as a key to moral agency.

We've suggested that the question of whether deterministic systems can be considered *real* moral agents is as unanswerable as the question of whether human beings *really* have free will. If your conception of real moral agency involves a "magical" notion of free will, there is no way to be sure that humans have it. However, even if humans don't have any magical freedom, the issue of how moral choice arises is largely unchanged. Recent discussion of the relationship between ethics and freedom usefully points out important design considerations for AMAs. Even within a deterministic framework for action, ethics involves open-ended choice. Options expand and consequences multiply as new agents enter the moral environment. To perform well in the human moral context, AMAs will need the capacity to assess multiple options and consider different evaluative perspectives. By their actions, AMAs will undoubtedly feed back into, and thus change, the existing moral ecology. However, it is to be hoped that sophisticated AMAs would be less likely to deform the moral ecology in lamentable ways, even if the way humans bond with them continues to outstrip their actual moral capabilities. Perhaps this is a false hope. Nevertheless, moral freedom, whether compatible with determinism or not, is relevant to AMA design.

Understanding and Consciousness

Like free will, human understanding and consciousness hold a mystical fascination for many. And like all attempts at demystifying the human mind, the claim that digital systems can possess *genuine* understanding or *real* consciousness evokes strong negative responses. The human tendency to anthropomorphize both pets and machines makes it hard to avoid talking as though they have something like human understanding or human consciousness. But what kind of understanding can (ro)bots actually have, and is it adequate for building AMAs? Will an AMA require consciousness, and can a system without consciousness be considered a moral agent? In both law and philosophy, moral agency is equated to moral responsibility, and is seldom attributed to individuals who do not understand or are not conscious of what they are doing, for example, young children. The issues of rights and responsibilities for (ro)bots are what most people jump to when they first hear about artificial morality, but, as before, our concern here is less with the downstream questions about what to do after the successful creation of AMAs than with the upstream role of consciousness and understanding in the system's ability to make ethical judgments.

Understanding

Searle's Chinese room is ground zero in the continuing debate over machine understanding. Most serious AI research has, however, moved away from an isolated focus on the conversational abilities needed to pass the Turing test. Machine understanding requires much more than conversation. Researchers are employing "multimodal" approaches to robotics that are modeled on the development of human children. Such systems simultaneously process hearing, vision, and touch, and they learn about action and speech simultaneously. The words learned by such systems are thus "grounded" in the robot's own actions and the actions it observes others performing. Even abstract capacities, for example arithmetic, may be grounded in the ability to move objects around to form perceptual clusters. People initially understand "$2 + 2 = 4$" not as an abstract proposition of mathematics but as the concrete result of creating two groups of two objects and counting them, perhaps even by using their fingers. Physical interactions with pencil and paper may ground yet more abstract capacities, for example algebra. Many researchers are betting that when information-processing capacities are grounded in this way, the gap between *genuine* human-like understanding and machine understanding becomes less significant, perhaps even irrelevant.

The kind of disconnected and disembodied symbol manipulation Searle imagined in the Chinese room makes genuine language comprehension practically impossible. If all the references among symbols are internal to the symbol system, then their significance is circular in exactly the same way dictionary definitions are. As you follow the chain of definitions, you are often led back to the original word you were trying to understand. Real cognitive systems are physically embodied and situated in the world of physical objects and social agents. The words, concepts, and symbols used by such systems are grounded in their interactions with objects and other agents.

Beginning with the work of Rodney Brooks, director of MIT's Artificial Intelligence Laboratory, the theory of embodied cognition has had a revolutionary affect on both the scientific and commercial development of robots. Brooks's company iRobot produces the "Roomba" robotic vacuum cleaner and the Packbot military robot (with over three hundred deployed in Iraq, including Scooby-Doo). In the mid-1980s, Brooks started developing insect-like robots in the Artificial Intelligence Laboratory that were remarkably successful in navigating through rooms and around objects.

For example, Genghis, an ant-like robot with six legs, was able to walk over various obstacles. Brooks's genius lay in giving independent control to each of the legs rather than using a central processor to coordinate all activity. He thereby produced very stable robots that adjusted to a wide range of pushes and shoves and could move over a wide variety of terrains. Genghis's ability to move around on legs without falling over was an impressive tour de force at a time when most roboticists were building wheeled vehicles because they seemed to offer greater stability. By thinking seriously about the way the robot is physically embodied and embedded in an environment, Brooks was able to show that a series of relatively simple local processes could collectively lead to the emergence of more complex behavior. For example, in Genghis, a distributed array of sensors allows each local joint to respond to movements originating in other parts of the robot. Those movements need not be explicitly signaled, but are implicitly detected by the sensors in other joints because when one leg moves, the angles of all the other legs are changed.

Brooks proposes to build more sophisticated robotic systems by layering different behavioral capacities on top of each other. Genghis could also follow humans with the help of infrared sensors. Genghis did not know what it was doing, yet it appeared to be attracted to the mammals it encountered. It appeared to have goal-directed behavior. Brooks showed that coordinated behavior could be accomplished without a central controller issuing instructions to the entire system.

Brooks refers to his approach as "subsumption architecture" or "behavior-based robotics." The idea is that the robot is provided with basic behaviors it can perform in response to environmental cues. Thus the environment plays a central role in determining which of these subsumptive layers controls the activity of the robot at any given time. The potential power of the subsumption architecture lies in the way adaptive behavior emerges from interactions among subsystems performing simple, lower-level tasks. Put differently, in complex animals, and perhaps even humans, a collection of relatively simple components performing specific tasks can collectively take on the appearance of complex behavior and higher-level cognitive function.

The theory of embodied cognition arose as an alternative to the view that the brain must create a full internal representation of the world, a complete model or simulation containing all the details necessary for reasoning about how to act in the world. In the classical, more centralized approach to cognition, the brain manipulated the internal symbols that made up its model of the world, in order to determine each action and each response, for example the position of every muscle or joint. However, robotic systems designed on this approach tend to be very fragile—falling over, for example, before they can accurately update their internal models in response to an unexpected shove. A robot living in a self-created virtual reality is no match for one that responds immediately and continuously to reality itself. As Brooks is said to have put it, "the world is its own best representation." His former student Brian Scasselati, now a roboticist at Yale University, jokingly says that he and his colleagues follow Brooks's approach because "we are too lazy and too stupid to build successful simulations" of the robot's world.

Can every challenge be met dynamically in direct interaction between the body and the world? Or are there tasks where it is helpful to have an internal model of the world? On the one hand, there is considerable evidence that much of human cognition is embodied. But clearly an internal model of the world is helpful for planning and prediction, to imaginatively test various courses of action. For the purposes of designing AMAs, much more needs to be understood about the relationship between embodied cognition and the construction of internal virtual or imagined models of the world.

We recognize that it's a long way from insect-like behavior to higher cognition, including ethical decision making. Nevertheless, realizing the importance of being embodied and embedded in the world provides two important insights. First, much of the information agents need may already be built into the environments through which they move, making it unnecessary to reproduce or simulate this information internally; that is, one doesn't always need to build a mental model of the world. Second, people's abilities to react with apparent understanding to their physical and social environments owe a lot to the structure and design of their bodies, their limbs, and their senses, which allow them to process most responses with little or no need for conscious thought or reflection.

What moral aspects of judgment and understanding are dependent on being embodied and situated in a world of objects, entities, and other agents? For humans, much of moral behavior is about adjusting to social situations in real time, in a way that tries to meet the changing needs, values, and expectations of the parties involved. Artificial moral agents will need to be similarly situated in their relationships. For example, the relationship between socially adept robots and the people and other agents in their environment will be constantly evolving, as will the social contexts within which they operate. Particularly with regard to the AMAs themselves, one might imagine increasing acceptance and latitude for their actions as humans come to feel that their behavior is trustworthy. If you become more trusting and comfortable with the actions of a robot in your home, a sophisticated system should be able to sense this comfort and accordingly expand the tasks it can perform without upsetting you. Conversely, if robots fail to act appropriately, the public will demand laws and practices that add new restrictions on their behavior. Morality evolves, and AMAs will be active participants in working through new challenges in many realms of activity.

What, then, does "understanding" mean, in the context of this discussion? If it means the capacity to react appropriately and adaptively to the social and physical environment, we see no reason to think that suitably embodied and embedded computers can't have these reactions. Already there are engineers developing human-computer interfaces that are "enactive"—engaging the users of these systems through all sensory modalities instead of limiting the interactions to language. As such systems gain in sophistication, it will become increasingly irrelevant to ask whether all this understanding is located in just the digitally programmed part of the system.

Consciousness

Understanding is sometimes equated with consciousness—another term with magical connotations, and having a bewildering array of meanings. The term is used to mark the distinction between being awake or asleep, as well as to capture a range of higher-order cognitive functions, including the abilities to be attentive, to plan, and to experience. There are unusual states of consciousness that include dreaming, psychotic experiences, peak experiences, and flow.

Other varieties of experience pose an epistemological problem. One can only conjecture what it is like to be a bat, or what a bird feels, as one can only guess at the character of the conscious experiences of people whose preferences in food or thrills differ markedly from our own. Presumably, what any computer could or would experience is similarly beyond humans' ken. The idea that one cannot have knowledge about other kinds of minds provides reason enough for some philosophers and scientists to doubt whether it even makes sense to talk about consciousness.

Some people attribute the mysterious experience of being conscious (its "phenomenological" properties) to a nonphysical aspect of the human mind that is not literally *in* the physical universe at all. Soul, spirit, and supernatural substance are religious terms that attempt to capture the appearance of the mental magic of humans' conscious experiences. Some think consciousness must be a universal property of matter, shared in some measure even by the grains of sand on the beach. At the other end of the spectrum are scientific hardliners who reject any such views as mystical mumbo jumbo. On such views, consciousness must, if the notion is to make sense at all, be understandable in terms of something like information processing, neural network organization, or basic neurophysiological properties of nervous systems.

In between these positions are researchers who believe that whether or not consciousness can be fully accounted for in objective informational or neural terms, it must be tightly correlated with observable or measurable features of the brain. The late Francis Crick, who won a Nobel Prize for his role in discovering the structure of DNA, spent the latter part of his career working with his colleague Cristof Koch in the search for the neural correlates of consciousness. Philosophers draw different lessons from this kind of research. Patricia Churchland contends that as scientists come to understand the individual systems that make up consciousness, the problem of understanding consciousness will fade away. Others, for example David Chalmers and Colin McGinn, argue that while discovering correlations between consciousness and the brain is a scientifically valuable activity, it cannot provide an explanation of the phenomenological aspects of conscious experience. This is either because there is not one available in principle, as Chalmers thinks, or because, just as dogs have cognitive limitations that make it impossible for them to understand calculus, people have cognitive limitations that make it impossible for them to understand how their brains produce consciousness, as McGinn believes.

Such philosophical pessimism has not deterred others from continuing to pursue neural and computational explanations of consciousness. Are neurons really the right place to be looking for an understanding of consciousness? One might argue along with John Searle that there is no better place to look because it is known that neurons produce consciousness, at least in the case of humans. But maybe attempts to produce artificial consciousness by computation are like the earliest attempts at human flight, which involved a lot of feathers and flapping. It is now known that birds weren't necessarily the best models for human flight (which is not to say that humans have had nothing to learn from them about flight). Flight is a functional property—it doesn't matter how you do it, so long as you get airborne and stay airborne for a decent amount of time. Because it is a functional property, flight can be manifested by a wide range of different systems made out of lots of different materials. Perhaps the important properties of consciousness are best understood functionally, too. Even if computers won't be conscious in exactly the same way as humans, perhaps they can be designed to function as if they have the relevant similar capacities.

Machine consciousness is developing as a subspecialty within AI. Igor Aleksander, a professor of engineering at Imperial College in London, proposes that the requirements of consciousness can be broken down into axioms covering five areas: a sense of self, imagination, focused attention, forward planning, and emotion. Each of these is in turn a composite or set of lower-level cognitive skills. In working toward building a conscious system, Owen Holland and Rod Goodman start from the bottom and move up, adding skill after skill to an embodied robot. They believe this process will eventually give rise to an internal representation of the robot's world and the robot's own behavior, and this will lead to consciousness-like phenomena. Stan Franklin, designer of a computer system named IDA, which he argues has attributes of being conscious, proposes that an artificial agent is functionally conscious if its architecture and mechanism allow it to do many of the same tasks that human consciousness enables humans to do. (We will have a lot more to say about IDA in chapter 11.) Roboticists working on machine consciousness, for example Owen Holland and Murray Shanahan, recognize that building a system whose consciousness is comparable to that of humans is a long way off. Nevertheless, they certainly believe that robots that are both functionally and phenomenally conscious will eventually be successfully developed.

Time will tell whether the field of machine consciousness will succeed. Some philosophers will insist that *phenomenal* consciousness requires something over and above functional equivalence, and will never be satisfied by the success of computers in performing tasks associated with human consciousness. However, this conception of consciousness as something that makes no difference at all to observable behavior is irrelevant to the development of AMAs. *Functional equivalence of behavior is all that can possibly matter for the practical issues of designing AMAs.* As long as there are new ideas about how to get computers to converge toward human behavior, there is the prospect of progress. At this stage of the game, we think it would be premature to bet against human ingenuity in this regard.

What AMAs Still Can't Do

Armchair arguments that there is a glass ceiling for (ro)bot intelligence are not entirely worthless; they might even turn out to have a correct conclusion. However, that can't be judged from the present. In the meantime, these arguments help focus attention on what is and is not important. Most of the experienced roboticists we have talked to do not think that there is a glass ceiling. This is unsurprising, of course, since pessimists tend to get weeded out of the profession. However, we predict that in the near term, (ro)bots will continue to converge toward human capacities while also showing considerable cognitive deficits. Nevertheless, as we will illustrate later, the present state of AI, artificial life, and robotics is sufficient for the initiation of some interesting experiments in the design of AMAs, and for additional experiments just around the corner.

If there are limits, they have yet to be proven. Human beings may also be limited in their reasoning. Kurt Gödel, for example, proved in his famous incompleteness theorem that any consistent system of logic powerful enough to represent mathematical reasoning will contain true statements it cannot prove. (Alan Turing proved that a similar limitation applies to any computer program.) Sometimes it is claimed that humans can transcend the limits of formal reasoning Gödel established, though how humans might do so is entirely unclear. Perhaps, if humans knew how or if they could transcend the limits of formal logic, this would provide a tool for designing computers that also transcend such limitations. Issues such as these are well beyond the scope of this book, although important to acknowledge.

Nevertheless, it is safe to assume that for some time to come, computers will be more limited than humans in what they can understand or be conscious of, and this will affect their abilities to accommodate nuances and make sensitive judgments. Whether computer understanding will ever be adequate to support full moral agency remains an open question. The problem that needs to be researched is whether there is morally relevant information that is inaccessible to systems lacking human-like understanding or consciousness. Is, for example, the ability to deal with the subtleties of others' feelings dependent on empathy or intuitions of those feelings that would not be possible for a computer?

Human understanding and human consciousness emerged through biological evolution as solutions to specific challenges. They are not necessarily the only methods for meeting those challenges. Just as a computer system can represent emotions without having emotions, computer systems may be capable of functioning as if they understand the meaning of symbols without actually having what one would consider to be human understanding. Nevertheless, questions regarding the capacity of a computer or robot to understand or be conscious suggest that the development of very sophisticated AMAs will not be easy.

Assessing AMAs

Engineering, more than philosophy, thrives on clear task specifications. But what is the task of an AMA? People disagree about the morality of various actions, and ethicists disagree about which is the right theoretical approach.

Turing's test for machine intelligence was an engineer's solution to a philosophical problem: build a system whose performance can be measured against a known standard. The test has flaws—for instance, its sole reliance on language, and the game-like nature of the situation. However, no one has successfully proposed a better test. Could a moral Turing test (MTT) play a similar role for the field of artificial morality? Colin Allen, Gary Varner, and Jason Zinser considered this question and made some critical observations, which we review here. Just like the original Turing test, any MTT that depends on comparing the behavior of a machine to that of a human is bound to be far from a perfect evaluation tool. However, thinking through the limitations of such a test can help sort out what might be important for evaluating AMAs.

One advantage of using an MTT might be that it would bypass disagreements about particular ethical issues. If you disagree with your neighbor about some moral issue, for example whether killing animals for their fur is acceptable, you can nevertheless recognize your neighbor as a moral agent if he can offer some relevant reasons for his view. Similarly, a machine that engages in a moral discussion might be indistinguishable from a human even if it comes to conclusions different from the interrogator's own view.

This focus on moral reasoning and justification may, however, be inappropriate. Ethical theories differ on the importance of justification. Kant required good agents to act for good reasons—in other words, the reasoning process is an essential component of the morality of the action on Kant's view. But Aristotelian virtue theories place great emphasis on right action as a result of habits due to good character, not theoretical knowledge. John Stuart Mill, the most famous utilitarian of the nineteenth century, argued that actions are morally good independent of the agent's motivations. His utilitarian approach thus emphasized effects of actions rather than their causes or justifications. Many people would also reject the Kantian view by claiming that young children, and perhaps dogs, are moral agents (albeit limited ones) even though they are incapable of giving reasons for their actions.

Responding to these differences, Allen and his colleagues also considered an alternative version of the MTT in which the "interrogator" is shown a set of descriptions or examples of actual morally significant actions, purged of any identifying information. The interrogator's task is to spot the machine. This approach could also turn out to be problematic if humans happen to be recognizable because they often act less ethically than they should. People, after all, are not known for their saintliness. This worry suggests a different question could be asked—not "Can you tell which is the AMA?" but "Which of these agents is less moral than the other?" Allen and his colleagues called this the comparative MTT (cMTT for short) and suggested that a successful AMA should be consistently judged the more moral.

Problems remain for the cMTT. For one, the standard might still be too low, especially if the humans selected for comparison are not paragons of virtue. And ethics, as we mentioned, is usually taken to concern what people should do, not what they do do. So a comparison to actual human behavior might be inappropriate. In addition, a machine might pass the cMTT even if its overall performance included actions that would be judged morally wrong, so long as the aggregate performance exceeds the human's. People expect and tolerate human moral failures. However, they might not tolerate such failures in their machines. As Allen and his colleagues put it, "calculated decisions that result in harm to others are likely to be much less tolerated in a machine than in another human being. In other words, we shall probably expect more of our machines than we do of ourselves."

It is important to keep in mind some fundamental differences between humans and computers. The human organism evolved from a biochemical platform. The capacity to reason emerged from the emotional brain. In contrast, AI is currently being developed on a logical platform.

This suggests some advantages that computers may have over human brains for responding to moral challenges. For example, computers are likely to calculate a broader array of possibilities in response to a challenge and therefore might come upon options that are better than those considered by human counterparts. Decisions made by people are not fully rational, in that only a few responses are considered and people generally settle for the first option with which they feel comfortable.

Furthermore, the moral decisions of computers will not initially suffer from interference by emotions. Thus, (ro)bots will not be hijacked by emotions, for example rage or sexual jealousy. Nor will they have emotionally reinforced prejudices or be greedy—unless engineers elect to introduce affective mechanisms into (ro)bots. In chapter 10, we return to a discussion of why such mechanisms might be beneficial for the design of AMAs. Something like greed might also emerge from the kinds of evolutionarily inspired bottom-up approaches to the development of AMAs that we discuss in chapter 7. If greedy computer systems flourish, however, they are more likely to be greedy for energy or information than prestige, power, or sex.

If these factors mean that computers are capable of meeting higher standards than people, where could such standards come from? Moral theories do not provide unequivocal answers. Nor are they easily translated into algorithms. Nevertheless, we believe that the attempt to translate theory into practice will be as instructive for ethicists as for (ro)boticists.

Chapter 5

PHILOSOPHERS, ENGINEERS, AND THE DESIGN OF AMAS

Two Scenarios

Scenario A: Imagine you are an ethicist and your friend, an AI engineer, says to you, "My company has asked me to design a robot that will always act ethically. Where should I start?" After sputtering off a few ideas that sound incredibly simplistic to your ears and fail to connect with your friend, you reply, "I'll get back to you."

Scenario B: You are an ethicist and you hear that your friend, an AI engineer, has just been awarded a military grant to design an ethical control system for autonomous weapon systems in the battlefield. You rush toward his office to offer your expertise, but halfway there, your pace begins to falter as you wonder to yourself, "Where do I begin?"

Scenario A is fictional, perhaps even a fantasy, given that engineers don't usually receive such open-ended assignments and philosophers aren't usually the first people they think to call for advice. Scenario B, however, is based in current events.

Many experts believe that military robots are likely to be the first place where AMAs will be needed. The U.S. Army's Future Combat Systems envisages autonomous vehicles deployed in combat zones. The bulk of robotics funding from the Department of Defense has gone toward basic engineering and software design, but Georgia Institute of Technology computer scientist Ronald Arkin received an Army grant to develop design recommendations for autonomous fighting vehicles operating in a war zone. The Navy has also recently funded a group at California Polytechnic Institute in San Luis Obispo to address the ethical issues surrounding automated weapon systems.

Some will, of course, see the idea of ethical killing machines as itself morally suspect. But whatever the application, whether it is the elimination of enemy forces or taking care of the elderly, there is a fundamental divide between philosophers, who tend to think in terms of highly abstract principles, and engineers, who have to accomplish the actual design task. Still, philosophers do have some role to play. General principles can guide design, even if they are not sufficient alone. Even though scenario A may be fictional, it provides a useful way to frame some questions that would come up, even for practical applications that demand ethical capacities from artificial agents.

What contribution, beyond helping engineers to be aware of the ethical consequences of their creation's actions, can a trained ethicist or trained philosopher make toward the design of an AMA? Are ethical principles, theories, and frameworks—for example, utilitarianism or Kant's categorical imperative—useful in guiding the design of computational systems capable of acting with some degree of autonomy? Or will the contribution of the ethicist be mainly that of underlining the complexity of the challenge, which could seem unhelpful to the engineer?

Grounding the Collaboration

Over the past half century, the relationship of philosophers to AI has been mixed, ranging from enthusiastic advocacy to trenchant critiques of the optimistic scenarios prophesied by those who believe that full-blown AI is just around the corner. Philosophers have not just commented from the sidelines; some have played a seminal role in developing the theories underlying AI. Daniel Dennett, who functioned as an advisor to the development of the embodied learning robot Cog, has even proposed that "roboticists are doing philosophy, but that's not what they think they're doing." But philosophers critical of AI have also turned out to be better judges than the true believers of the difficulties AI engineers would encounter. Some of the philosophical critiques regarding the limits of computational strategies for achieving "strong AI" remain alive, as noted. However, this does not interfere with the "weak AI" task of developing systems with a high degree of what we have called "functional morality." So in this and the next four chapters, we set aside the philosophical issues and focus on ways ethical considerations can be introduced into the platforms presently available.

Your engineering friend who has been charged with designing a (ro)bot that acts ethically will be concerned with the kinds of constraints that should be placed on the system's choices and actions. What role might ethical theory play in defining the control architecture for such systems? In addition, the engineer must determine what the information requirements are for a system making moral decisions: that is, what does the system need to know in order to make an informed decision, and what input devices and sensors will it need to get access to this information?

How can ethicists actually be helpful here? A well-trained ethicist is taught to recognize the complexity of moral dilemmas, and is likely to be sensitive to the inadequacy of any one approach meant to cover the range of challenges the AMA might confront. The engineer, on the other hand, will be concerned that the ethicist's desire to make the system sensitive to moral considerations will add further difficulties to the already challenging task of building reliable, efficient, and safe systems. Theoretical discussions about the complexity and intractability of ethical dilemmas will not be considered helpful. While engineers generally believe that there is more than one solution to every problem, they are trained to converge on a satisfactory solution for the problem at hand. Ethicists, however, are trained to diverge from each other, arguing separate positions so as to describe as completely as possible the range of considerations and theories that may be relevant to a problem.

Here it is useful to borrow from the field of engineering ethics, where philosophers frequently worry about the problem of making their discipline relevant and accessible to engineers. In outlining an approach for teaching ethics to scientists and engineers, Caroline Whitbeck, a professor in ethics at Case Western Reserve University, draws on a distinction philosopher Stuart Hampshire made between "a judge perspective" on ethical problems and "an agent perspective." The judge perspective, which Whitbeck equates with traditional philosophical approaches to ethics, applies abstract principles to particular instances, and commonly poses ethical challenges as conflicts between two or more opposing sides or principles. This can entail a forced judgment—a choice between mutually exclusive and often unsatisfactory alternatives. In contrast, an agent perspective deals with ethical challenges from the point of view of an actor in a context, who must find a solution to a problem. Engineers are accustomed to approaching engineering problems through case studies, an approach with which Hampshire's agent perspective is more closely aligned. Whitbeck writes that "ethical or moral problems are often represented as conflicts between (usually two) opposing sides or opposing principles, but they are often better understood as problems in which there are multiple (ethical) constraints which may or may not turn out to be satisfiable simultaneously." This suggests to Whitbeck that ethical challenges should be considered similar to design problems and treated as such.

Certainly not all ethical challenges can be approached in this way. But for the ethicist contributing to the design of an AMA, keeping in mind an agent perspective is useful on two levels. First, an agent perspective is similar to the problem-solving approach engineers understand. Second, the robot or computational system can best be appreciated as a simple-minded agent looking for a way to proceed or act in a specific context within ethical constraints. In designing the computational systems that will operate within ethical constraints, emphasis must be placed on practical approaches for working through the challenge.

This emphasis on the practical may appear to philosophers as an oversimplification of ethics. We recognize that both ethical theory and applied ethics are full of complexity. Appreciation of the complexity is useful, insofar as it suggests ways of making computational systems more sophisticated. It is less useful if it is simply directed at dismissing the project of building AMAs. Ethical complexity comes from at least a couple of sources. On the one hand, there are the nuanced discussions within ethical theory about the fundamental concepts of the discipline. On the other hand, there are the difficult issues that arise from attempting to make normative judgments about real-world situations. Morality in humans is a complex activity and involves skills that many either fail to learn adequately or perform with limited mastery. Although there are shared values that transcend cultural differences, cultures and individuals differ in the details of their ethical systems and mores. Expecting AMAs to deal immediately with all of these issues is impracticable, but our basic position is that any step toward sensitivity to moral considerations in (ro)bots, no matter how simplistic, is a step in the right direction.

Engineers will be quick to point out that ethics is far from science. Difficult value questions often arise both in situations where information is inadequate and where the results of actions cannot be fully known in advance. Thus ethics can seem to be a fuzzy discipline that deals with some of the most confusing and emotionally charged situations people encounter. Ethics can appear as far away from science as one can get.

Any claim that ethics can be reduced to a science would at best be naive. Nevertheless, we believe that the task of enhancing the moral capabilities of autonomous software agents will force scientists and engineers to break down moral decision making into its component parts, recognize what kinds of decisions can and cannot be codified and managed by essentially mechanical systems, and learn how to design cognitive and affective systems capable of managing ambiguity and conflicting perspectives. This project will demand that human moral decision making be analyzed to a degree of specificity as yet unknown.

Different specialists are likely to take different approaches to the problem of implementing an AMA. For engineers and computer scientists, a natural approach might be to treat ethics as simply an additional set of constraints, to be satisfied like any other constraints on successful program operation. On this view, there would be nothing distinctive about moral reasoning. But, questions remain about what those additional constraints should be, whether they should be very specific (for example, "Obey posted speed limits") or more abstract (for example, "Never cause harm to a human being") and whether they are to be treated as hard constraints, never to be violated, or soft ones, able to be stretched in pursuit of other goals. Making a moral robot would be a matter of finding the right set of constraints and the right formulas for resolving conflicts. The problem of developing AMAs might thus be understood as finding ways to implement abstract values within the control architecture of intelligent systems. The result would be a kind of "bounded morality," and a system capable of behaving inoffensively so long as any situation it encountered fits within the general constraints predicted by its designers.

Where might such constraints come from? Philosophers confronted with this problem are likely to suggest a top-down approach of encoding a particular ethical theory in software. This theoretical knowledge could then be used to rank options for moral acceptability. With respect to computability, however, the moral principles proposed by philosophers leave much to be desired, often suggesting incompatible courses of action, or failing to recommend any course of action. And in some respects, key ethical principles appear to be computationally intractable because of the essentially limitless consequences any action might have.

But if it is not possible to see a clear way to implement an ethical theory as a computer program, then one might also wonder whether such theories play a guiding role for human action. Thus, thinking about what machines are or are not capable of may lead to deeper reflection about the limits of ethical theory in the computational domain. The problem of AMAs is, from this perspective, a problem not of how to give them abstract theoretical knowledge but of how to embody the right tendencies to react in the world. It is a problem of moral psychology, not moral calculation.

Psychologists confronted with the problem of constraining moral decision making are likely to focus on the way a sense of morality develops in human children as they mature into adults. A developmental approach may be the most practicable route to machine morality. But given what is known about the unreliability of this process for developing moral human beings, there's a legitimate question to be raised about how reliable it would be to attempt to train (ro)bots to be AMAs. Psychologists also focus on the ways humans construct their reality, become aware of self, others, and their environment, and navigate through the complex maze of moral issues in their daily lives. Again, the complexity and tremendous variability of these processes in humans underscores the challenge of designing AMAs.

Whose Morality or What Morality?

There's another kind of reaction you might have when your friend the engineer walks into your office saying his company has asked him to design a robot that will always act ethically. "What the hell kind of company has the right to dictate what's ethical?" you might wonder.

The project of building AMAs faces hard questions. Whose moral standards will be implemented? What ethical subroutines? Engineers are very good at building systems for well-specified tasks, but there is no clear task specification for moral behavior. Talk of moral standards might seem to imply an accepted code of behavior, but among people there is great disagreement about moral matters. Talk of ethical subroutines also seems to suggest a particular conception of how ethical behavior might be implemented, but whether algorithms or lines of software code can effectively represent ethical knowledge requires a sophisticated appreciation of what that knowledge consists in, and of how ethical theory is related to the cognitive and emotional aspects of moral behavior. The effort to clarify these things, and to develop alternative ways of thinking about them, takes on special dimensions in the context of artificial agents. Any approach to machine morality has to be assessed in light of the feasibility of implementing the theory as a computer program.

Disagreements about the morality of various actions—from illegally downloading music off the Web to abortion or assisted suicide—underscore the difficulties in determining criteria for ascribing morality to the actions of an artificial system. The ethical theories of Kant, Bentham, and Mill were shaped by the Enlightenment ideal that moral principles should be universal. But even those values on which there is general consensus tend to break down in face of the details of specific situations. Truthfulness, or not lying, is a virtue most people put aside when they believe their honesty will result in unwarranted harm to another person. Most people will applaud some lie as justified if there's a net benefit from telling it. On the other hand, Kant considered always telling the truth, regardless of the consequences, to be imperative. He argued that lying to another person takes away that individual's autonomy, which Kant considered foundational for all ethics.

Given the range of perspectives regarding the morality of specific values, behaviors, and lifestyles, perhaps there is no single answer to the question of whose morality or what morality should be implemented in AI. Just as people have different moral standards, there is no reason why all computational systems must conform to the same code of behavior. One might envisage designing moral agents that conform to the values of a specific religious tradition or to one or another brand of secular humanism. Or the moral code for an AMA might be modeled on some standard for political correctness. Presumably, a robot could be designed to internalize the legal code of a country and strictly follow that country's laws. This concession to culturally diverse AMAs is not meant to suggest that there are no universal values, only to acknowledge that there may be more than one path to the design of an AMA. Regardless of what code of ethics, norms, values, laws, or principles prevails in the design of an AMA, that system will have to meet externally determined criteria as to whether it functions successfully as a moral agent.

Top-Down and Bottom-Up Approaches

The study of ethics commonly focuses on top-down norms, standards, and theoretical approaches to moral judgment. From Socrates' dismantling of theories of justice to Kant's project of rooting morality within reason alone, ethical discourse has typically looked at the application of broad standards of morality to specific cases. According to these approaches, standards, norms, or principles are the basis for evaluating the morality of an action. Top-down moral principles range from religious ideals and moral codes to culturally endorsed values and philosophical systems, but many of the same values are evident in differing ethical systems. The Golden Rule, the Ten Commandments, Hinduism's Yama and Niyama, lists of virtues, and Kant's categorical imperative can all be thought of as top-down ethical systems. Of course, Asimov's Three Laws for Robots are also top-down.

The term "top-down" is used in a different sense by engineers, who approach challenges with a top-down analysis through which they decompose a task into simpler subtasks. Components are assembled into modules that individually implement these simpler subtasks, and then the modules are hierarchically arranged to fulfill the goals specified by the original project.

In our discussion of machine morality, we use "top-down" in a way that combines these two somewhat different senses from engineering and ethics. In our merged sense, a top-down approach to the design of AMAs is any approach that takes a specified ethical theory and analyzes its computational requirements to guide the design of algorithms and subsystems capable of implementing that theory. In other words, a top-down approach takes an ethical theory, say, utilitarianism, analyzes the informational and procedural requirements necessary to implement this theory in a computer system, and applies that analysis to the design of subsystems and the way they relate to each other in order to implement the theory.

In bottom-up approaches to machine morality, the emphasis is placed on creating an environment where an agent explores courses of action and learns and is rewarded for behavior that is morally praiseworthy. There are various models for bottom-up acquisition of moral capabilities. Childhood development provides one model. Evolution provides another bottom-up model for the adaptation, mutation, and selection of those agents best able to meet some criteria for fitness. Unlike top-down ethical theories, which define what is and is not moral, in bottom-up approaches any ethical principles must be discovered or constructed.

Bottom-up approaches, if they use a prior theory at all, do so only as a way of specifying the task for the system, and not as a way of specifying an implementation method or control structure. In bottom-up engineering, tasks can also be specified theoretically using some sort of performance measure (e.g., winning chess games, passing the Turing test, walking across a room without stumbling, etc.). Various trial-and-error techniques are available to engineers for progressively tuning the performance of systems so that they approach or surpass the performance criteria. High levels of performance on many tasks can be achieved even though the engineer lacks a theory of the best way to decompose the task into subtasks. An analysis of the system after it has determined how to perform a task can sometimes yield a theory or specification of the relevant subtasks, but the results of such analyses can also be quite surprising and typically do not correspond to the kind of decomposition suggested by a priori theorizing. In its ethical sense, a bottom-up approach to ethics is one that treats normative values as being implicit in the activity of agents rather than explicitly articulated (or even articulatable) in terms of a general theory. In our use of the term "bottom-up," we recognize that this may provide an accurate account of the agents' understanding of their own morality and the morality of others, while we remain neutral on the ontological question of whether morality is the kind of concept for which an adequate general theory can be produced.

In practice, engineers and roboticists typically build their most complex systems using both top-down and bottom-up approaches. Components are assembled to fulfill specific functions guided by a theoretical top-down analysis that is typically incomplete. Commonly, there is more than one route to meet the project goals, and there is a dynamic interplay between analysis of the project's structure and the testing of the system designed to meet the goals. Failures of the system may, for example, reveal that the original analysis of the challenge has overlooked secondary considerations, and so the control architecture has to be adjusted, software parameters refined, or new components added. Bottom-up self-organizing techniques can be utilized to facilitate the fine-tuning of individual modules.

The top-down/bottom-up dichotomy is too simplistic for many complex engineering tasks, and one should not expect the design of AMAs to be any different. Nevertheless, the concepts of top-down and bottom-up task analysis highlight two potential roles of ethical theory for the design of AMAs.

Chapter 6

TOP-DOWN MORALITY

Putting Ethical Theories to Work

What does the engineer who is seeking to build an ethical machine need to know about ethical theories? Ask an ethicist this question, and he or she may launch into a survey of the varieties of *consequentialism*, *deontology*, and *virtue ethics* that would be standard fare for an undergraduate course in ethics. Instead of replicating Ethics 101, we will try to present the ethical theories with a view to what engineers or computer scientists can (or cannot) do with them.

Why might a top-down, theory-driven approach to morality for AMAs seem like a good way to proceed? One answer is that theories promise comprehensive solutions. If ethical principles or rules could be explicitly stated, acting ethically would just be a matter of following the rules. All that an AMA would need to do is compute whether its actions are allowed by the rules.

Ethicists don't think this is a viable approach to human decision making, because people are simply incapable of doing all the required calculations. But it is an old dream of philosophers that machines might be able to do better. The German philosopher Gottfried Wilhelm von Leibniz, who designed a calculating machine that was built in 1674, dreamed of having more powerful machines that could directly apply moral rules to calculate the best action in any circumstances.

Despite the great enhancements in computing technology since Leibniz's day, we think top-down theories may not serve to realize this dream. We'll show that the prospects for implementing ethical rules as formal decision algorithms are rather dim. Nevertheless, people do appeal to top-down rules to inform and justify their actions, and designers of AMAs will need to capture this aspect of human morality.

In the most general sense, the top-down approach to artificial morality is about having a set of rules that can be turned into an algorithm. Top-down ethical systems might come from a variety of sources, including religion, philosophy, and literature. Examples include the Golden Rule, the Ten Commandments, consequentialist or utilitarian ethics, Kant's moral imperative, legal and professional codes, and Asimov's Three Laws of Robotics.

In some of these ways of thinking, the list of rules is just an arbitrary collection of whatever needs to be specifically proscribed or prescribed. This is the "commandment" model of morality, which, in addition to having roots in the Judaic tradition, also pops up in Asimov's Three Laws. The challenge facing commandment models is what to do when the rules conflict: is there some further principle or rule for resolving the conflict? Asimov's approach was to prioritize the rules so that the first law always trumped the second, which in turn always trumped the third. Unfortunately for roboticists (if fortunately for the fiction writer), the first two of Asimov's laws are each sufficient to produce intractable conflict on their own.

To solve the conflict problem, some philosophers have attempted to find more general or abstract principles from which more specific or particular principles might be derived. Other philosophers reject the idea that ethical rules should be understood as providing a comprehensive decision procedure, while continuing to recognize that top-down rules function as heuristics that help guide decisions and inform the critical analysis of expert evaluators.

Whether ethical principles are conceived of as rules or heuristics, much of mainstream moral philosophy consists of testing highly general principles against intuitive judgments about thought experiments such as the trolley cases. The history of moral philosophy can be viewed as a long inquiry into the intuitions of ethicists about what qualifies something as morally right or morally wrong. The most general top-down ethical theories are meant to capture the *essence* of moral judgment. Competing top-down theories are challenged whenever they seem to give the "wrong" answers according to some expert's intuitions. Are these intuitions valid universally? There have long been cultural critics who have read Western and male-centered biases into the intuitions promoted by Western philosophers. More recently, a new breed of "experimental philosophers" has been challenging the claim that these intuitions are even shared universally within the same culture.

We want to avoid getting sidetracked by the very knotty questions about ethical intuitions. Our focus is on the computational requirements for implementing particular top-down theories. Are they really suitable as task specifications for algorithms? And if not, what does this say about the project of building AMAs? Only rarely have top-down theories been evaluated from a computational perspective, and the results, we think, have the potential to cast light on the nature of philosophical ethics itself.

Among those schools of philosophers who think that ethical reasoning can be brought under a single general principle, there are two "big picture" rivals for what that general principle should be: utilitarianism and deontology.

Utilitarians claim that morality is ultimately about maximizing the total amount of "utility" (a measure of happiness or well-being) in the world. The best actions (or the best specific rules to follow) are those that maximize aggregate utility. Because utilitarians care about the consequences of actions, their views are a type of *consequentialism*. Another consequentialist theory is *egoism*, which considers only the consequences for the individual doing the action. However, egoism is not a serious contender for the design of AMAs (or even, perhaps, for ethics more generally). Because utilitarianism seems to be the most promising version of consequentialism for use in artificial systems, we'll focus our discussion on it.

Within utilitarianism there is an important distinction between "act utilitarianism" (each individual action is assessed) and "rule utilitarianism" (rules for actions are assessed in light of their tendency to increase total utility). We initially discuss act utilitarianism, although many of the points we make can be generalized to both forms. Utilitarian AMAs face heavy computational demands because they need to work out many, if not all, of the consequences of the options in order to rank actions morally. From the perspective of the agent, the problem is how to determine the consequences of various courses of action in order to maximize some measure of utility. For the designer of artificial systems, the problem to be solved is how to build mechanisms that can make the necessary determinations of consequences and their net utilities.

The competing "big picture" view of moral principles is that duties lie at the core of ethics. Within this framework, the rights of individuals are generally understood as the flip side of duties. Duties and rights fall under the heading of *deontology*, a nineteenth-century term for the study of obligations. In general, any list of duties or rights might suffer the same problem of internal conflicts as a list of commandments. For example, a duty to tell the truth might come into conflict with a duty to respect another person's privacy. One way to resolve these problems is to submit all prima facie duties to a higher principle. Thus it was Kant's belief, for instance, that all legitimate moral duties could be grounded in a single principle, a *categorical imperative*, which could be stated in such a way as to guarantee logical consistency.

For an artificial agent designed with a deontological approach to ethics, knowing the rules (or how to determine the rules) and having methods for applying those rules to a specific challenge is of central importance. An agent that could also reflect coherently on the validity of specific rules would be desirable, but this is a rather distant dream. The designer of a deontological (ro)bot needs to find ways to ensure that the rules are activated when the situation requires their application, and to formulate an architecture for managing situations where rules conflict.

Utilitarian and deontological approaches both raise their own specific computational issues, but they also raise a common problem of whether any computer (or human, for that matter) could ever gather and compare all the information that would be necessary for the theories to be fully applied in real time. This problem is especially acute for a consequentialist approach, since the consequences of any action are essentially unbounded in space or time. We will discuss this problem in the next section by asking whether a utilitarian approach to artificial morality would require an omniscient computer. In the following sections, we consider deontological approaches.

Public discussions of morality are not just about rights (deontology) and welfare (utility); they are often about issues of character, too. This third element of moral theory can be traced back to Aristotle and what is now known as "virtue ethics." Virtue ethicists are not concerned to evaluate the morality of actions on the basis solely of outcomes, or in terms of rights and duties. Instead, virtue theorists maintain that morally good actions flow from the cultivation of good character, which consists in the realization of specific virtues. We discuss the application of virtue theory to the design of AMAs in chapter 8.

Is An Omniscient Computer Needed?

The eighteenth-century British philosopher Jeremy Bentham is frequently credited with the idea that it would be desirable to develop a kind of "moral arithmetic." Bentham and the other philosophers who developed utilitarian views wanted to put morality on an objective footing, getting away from dependence on hard-to-justify lists of duties or individual intuitions about what is right or wrong. They envisaged a method of evaluating situations quantitatively—assigning numbers to the goods and harms that resulted from actions. Quantitative measures of utility would allow for a simple decision rule: choose the action that results in the highest total utility. Utility is often equated with happiness. Thus the utilitarian's traditional rallying cry "the greatest happiness for the greatest number."

Because of its numerical aspect, utilitarianism might seem to provide a uniquely attractive form of ethical theory for AMAs. But what would it take to actually build a utilitarian AMA? In 1995, computer scientist James Gips of Boston College presented what was perhaps the earliest attempt to outline the computational requirements for any consequentialist robot. He outlined four necessary abilities:

(1) A way of describing the situation in the world
(2) A way of generating possible actions
(3) A means of predicting the situation that would result if an action were taken given the current situation
(4) A method of evaluating a situation in terms of its goodness or desirability

This list falls a long way short of specifying algorithms, far less an actual computer program. Nevertheless, it provides a useful framework for specifying the relevant subtasks. Any actual attempt to implement utilitarian reasoning in a computer will need to make design decisions about each subtask. How complete a description of the situation is needed? What range of actions should the computer be capable of generating? How can the computer make accurate predictions about situations that might be quite remote in space or time? And how are the different situations to be evaluated?

Let us begin with the last question, a staple of introductory ethics courses. How can one reasonably assign numbers to something as subjective as happiness, pleasure, or desirability? Bentham and Mill famously disagreed on whether the pleasure one person might take in playing a game is of equal value to the pleasure another person might derive from reading poetry. A similar point arises when comparing the pleasure experienced by animals to that experienced by humans. Bentham consistently took the position that there are no intrinsically superior forms of pleasure; the joy of playing the game of push-pin or reading the poetry of Pushkin, the pleasure of pigs or of people—it was all the same to Bentham. Others have worried that it makes no sense to think that all forms and varieties of pleasure can be ranked on a single scale. It is sometimes suggested that the problem of assigning numbers to utilities could be solved in the same way that courts, insurance companies, and free markets do it: by figuring out how much individuals are willing to pay for certain goods or to avoid specific harms. But to many, equating moral values to monetary values seems extremely inadequate for, as the popular saying goes, some things are priceless.

This is one of those questions that threatens to slide off into a battle of intuitions we cannot hope to settle here. But however one decides to assign numbers, very similar computational issues arise. On the positive side, given some way of assigning numbers to utilities, computers would seem uniquely suitable for the application of consequentialist theories. In fact, one might expect computers to produce aggregate utility assessments faster and more accurately than humans. On the negative side are the problems of constructing a computable evaluation function that appropriately weighs present benefits against future harms, and vice versa, or actual benefits and harms against potential risks and benefits.

Any appearance of computational simplicity completely vanishes when one reflects on the kinds of information that would have to be gathered in order to complete the other subtasks Gips describes.

Gips's first subtask is to describe the situation in the world. What are the relevant elements of the situation? Depending on the breadth of the moral constituency, this may include people, animals, and perhaps even whole ecosystems (although perhaps with different weights). Regardless of how this is settled (another battle of intuitions?) the sheer scale of the data collection required to describe the situation of all ethically relevant subjects is mind-boggling. The prominent British philosopher Bernard Williams imagined that it would need an "omniscient, benevolent observer—he might be called the World Agent—who acquires everybody's preferences and puts them together." Williams' point was to dismiss the possibility of such an agent, but even if a World Agent does exist, it doesn't have a URL for easy (ro)bot access.

The second subtask, generating a range of actions, is also affected by the range of elements that have to be considered part of the situation. If, for example, the welfare of animals is not part of the equation, then the possible action of eating a meal might be generated without distinguishing between eating a vegetarian meal and a nonvegetarian meal. The greater the variety of morally relevant facts, the more fine-grained the programming would need to be about the options considered.

Gips's third subtask is to estimate the expanding effects of an action on every entity that matters morally. The designers of any algorithm must face at least two broad questions: Which future branches should be computed? And should far future outcomes be discounted?

Regarding the first question, future effects cannot be computed indefinitely into the future. There are primary effects that may directly satisfy goals underlying a decision to act, and the moral value of these outcomes should be computed. But every action has an indefinite number of secondary effects, potentially leading to a computational black hole that would suck up vast amounts of CPU time for any program that tried to track all the interactions. Furthermore, secondary effects can on occasion have far-reaching consequences—as in the famous butterfly effect elucidated by chaos theory (the idea that a butterfly's beating wings in China could affect the weather in North America several weeks later.) There is also the problem of calculating future effects when information is incomplete. Weather forecasting suffers from exactly the same problems, but that has not stopped meteorologists from working toward increasingly more accurate predictions (while still leaving plenty of room for improvement!). One particularly useful technique weather forecasters use is to average across the predictions of several competing computer models. "Utility forecasters" might similarly employ multiple approaches to predicting the consequences of specific behavior.

Regarding the second question, the sayings "Charity begins at home" and "Think globally, act locally" are both used to express the idea that ethical actions are grounded in relationships to people and places nearby. And what goes for space also goes for time: consequences in the far future typically have less of a pull on people than more immediate consequences. Whether this is the ethically proper attitude is not for us to decide here. We note only that if AMAs are going to act in ethically acceptable ways by deploying top-down, consequentialist principles, then some method for discounting future and distant consequences is necessary. It is possible, perhaps, that the degree of discounting would exactly correspond to the increasing degree of uncertainty that goes with predicting remote events. But there is no simple formula that relates time or distance to uncertainty—some events a year from now or 5,000 kilometers from here may be much more predictable than other events only one week from now or 100 meters away.

Gips's fourth subtask is to evaluate a situation in terms of its goodness or desirability. We've already pointed out that utilitarians disagree among themselves about whether pleasures or satisfactions from different sources should be weighted differently. One way to proceed might be to collect as many subjective utility ratings as one can, to apply a weighting formula to these, and then to adjust it in a progressive fashion until the choices and actions of the AMA appear to be satisfactory. There are, of course, serious difficulties involved in collecting subjective assessments of utility in real time.

To protect utilitarian AMAs from an endless stream of calculations, viable strategies for accomplishing Gips's four subtasks are needed. The difficulty in terminating calculations is exacerbated by an additional challenge. The act of computing potential consequences is itself an action that requires time and resources, and may therefore have ethical consequences of its own. If one loses the opportunity to help someone in need because one's decision making went on too long, the process of deciding was dysfunctional. The utilitarian theory can be applied directly here because, of course, the utilitarian principle specifies that calculations should be halted at precisely the point where continuing to calculate rather than act has a negative effect on aggregate utility. But how do you know whether a computation is worth doing without actually doing the computation itself? This apparent paradox can only be solved by cutting off computation by some other means.

People are confronted with the same challenges, and for this reason some theorists don't feel that utilitarianism is a particularly useful or practical theory. Nevertheless, humans do manage to act with the intention of maximizing welfare, even though they are clearly not omniscient. How do humans do it? They generally practice what Herb Simon, a founder of AI and a Nobel laureate in economics in 1982, called "bounded rationality": including a very limited set of considerations in one's rational decision making. The question is whether a more restricted computational system, weighing the same information as a human, would be an adequate moral agent. Not including all the preferences, incorrectly estimating them, or failing to understand short- and long-term consequences of actions inevitably causes some pain and suffering, as the history of humankind (painfully) reminds us.

Simon and his collaborator Allen Newell pioneered the use of heuristics—functional approximations, that is, "rules of thumb"—to abbreviate complex searches by AI systems. Heuristic search is central to the success of systems such as IBM's chess-playing Deep Blue II, which does not need to search the unimaginably vast space of chess moves into the indefinite future to play a good game. Instead, it focuses on accomplishing intermediate goals by using approximate methods of evaluation: rules of thumb that rate certain arrangements of pieces on the board as more valuable than others.

Perhaps moral heuristics could be developed to play a similar role. Ethical heuristics applied to individual actions would need to rank immediate consequences of actions with respect to their likelihood of having ethically relevant secondary outcomes. For instance, toppling a foreign government has many long-term consequences that must be assessed, but the effects of this action on the work schedules of newspaper journalists is not one that needs a lot of attention.

One kind of ethical heuristic might be to follow rules that are expected to increase local utility. For instance, rather than analyze all the consequences of her possible actions, a person may choose between them solely on the basis of benefits to her local community. A heuristic such as this may be globally beneficial if it turns out, for example, that a locally healthy population is more likely to engage in more distant forms of charity. However, an effective moral agent might be able to rely on this relationship without having to check it explicitly.

Rule utilitarianism can also be seen as a kind of heuristic approach. Rules can circumvent the need to calculate all of the consequences of individual actions, on the assumption that on average, the benefits of following the rules outweigh the costs of occasionally doing something that might have gone better without the rule. A problem, however, for an engineer designing an AMA on the basis of rule utilitarianism is where the rules come from. Initially, the rules might be those agreed on by experts and programmed into the system. But because the justification for applying these rules is itself a utilitarian one (following the rules produces higher overall utility than not following them), they have to be reassessed periodically. The capacity to carry out such an assessment might also be required of a sophisticated AMA. But initial attempts to apply rule utilitarian approaches to the design of AMAs are unlikely to start with such sophisticated assessment capacities. Assuming that the rules are initially going to be specified by experts, then rule utilitarianism can be treated as a kind of commandment theory, in which case the main computational issues are those shared with other rule-based approaches to AMA design.

Rules for Robots

No discussion of top-down morality for robots can ignore Asimov's Three Laws:

1. A robot may not injure a human being or, through inaction, allow a human being to come to harm.
2. A robot must obey orders given it by human beings except where such orders would conflict with the First Law.
3. A robot must protect its own existence as long as such protection does not conflict with the First or Second Law.

Well after he established the three laws, Asimov added a fourth or Zeroth Law (so named because it superseded the other three):
Zeroth: A robot may not harm humanity, or, by inaction, allow humanity to come to harm.

The rest of the laws are modified sequentially to acknowledge this.
Asimov's Laws are of course a piece of fiction—a plot device that allowed the development of some very interesting stories. As we shall explain, they offer little practical guidance as moral philosophy, and their value as specifications for algorithms is questionable. Nevertheless, they contain an interesting idea about AMAs: that their behavior should conform to different standards than the usual rules of morality for human beings.

Asimov's idea of special ethical duties for robots provides a significant contrast with the utilitarian approach we discussed in the previous section. For the purposes of moral evaluation, consequentialists generally don't care why or by whom a particular action is carried out. But on deontological views, duties stem directly from the specific nature of agents, and different kinds of agents might have different duties.

In the movie *RoboCop*, the cyborg policeman is programmed with three directives that owe much to Asimov's laws but take the idea of task-specific duties even further: (1) serve the public trust; (2) protect the innocent; and (3) uphold the law. The plot gimmick in *RoboCop* is the existence of a secret fourth directive that supersedes the others, making RoboCop subservient to his corporate masters even though they are criminals. In the original movie, the residual human part of RoboCop is able to overcome this fourth directive, but this would not be possible for a (ro)bot programmed to follow rules strictly.

RoboCop's secret directive and Asimov's Second Law both require artificial agents to be virtual slaves of their human masters. While this may help humans feel safer in the presence of (ro)bots, clearly this is not a duty that should be thought to apply to moral agents generally. Here, however, we are not interested in justifying any particular set of duties (or in debating what humans' moral obligations might be toward intelligent machines). But we do want to talk more about Asimov's rules in particular, because a lot of people hearing about our project have asked, "But hasn't Asimov already solved that problem?"

Isaac Asimov's Three Laws provided a vehicle for his and other science fiction writers' exploration of the problems inherent in even a simple form of duty-based morality. Asimov offered no direct analysis of these laws. Rather, he explored their viability through a series of stories he wrote throughout his life. On first reading, the rules appear to be straightforward. But it was evident to Asimov, and to succeeding generations, that even these simple laws would be problematic to implement. For every moral principle, there appear to be moral trade-offs.

Would a literal-minded robot, for example, interrupt a surgeon about to cut into a patient? Ensuring that a robot understands that a surgeon wielding a knife over a patient is not intending to harm the patient will be no easy matter. The fully intelligent application of a simple duty-based morality would require a great deal of understanding about context, and about exceptions to the rule of causing *no* injury. An AMA with such capabilities would need to have a broad knowledge base in order to apply rules appropriately in different contexts, and this knowledge base would need to be updated regularly.

What should a robot do if any of the available courses of action might cause some harm to a human? In *Liar*, Asimov tells the story of Herbie, a robot sensitive to human psychology, who breaks down while considering a challenge in which all options will cause psychological pain to humans. Of course, humans confront such dilemmas daily. (Or would, if they thought through the ramifications of their actions!) In principle, the fact that Herbie broke down rather than causing harm to a human might appear to be an inbuilt safeguard. But one could easily imagine a situation where a homebound elderly person was dependent on the robot, and the breakdown of the robotic system would cause even greater harm.

As in the case of the unwanted surgical intervention, if a given list of rules fails to be comprehensive, the AMA will fail in unknown situations. In the context of the real world, seemingly straightforward rules can also turn out to be impossible to follow. Without a scheme for prioritizing rules, conflict between them can cause a deadlock. Asimov prioritized his rules to minimize conflicts between them, but even single rules can lead to deadlock, as when, for example, two humans give contradictory commands, or any action taken by the robot (including inaction) will cause harm to someone. Having a robot choose whether to act or not to act when either case results in harm to a human being is a proven recipe for suspense, but is certainly not recommendable for real world AMAs. Given that it is not always possible to prevent harm in the real world, the minimization of harm may be the best one can hope for in many situations. (Whether humans can live with machines making such choices is a question we'll come back to in chapter 12.)

Asimov's rules are minimal restraints one might wish to implement on slave machines, not a fully fleshed out morality for artificial minds with a capacity to act with considerable autonomy. Many of the real-world moral codes one might wish to implement in a computational system do not prioritize all the rules, and are therefore subject to conflicts between them. Any rule-based AMA will require a software architecture that can manage situations in which rules conflict. In reviewing the lessons that can be taken from Asimov's stories, IT consultant Roger Clarke proposes that an engineer might well conclude that rules or laws are not an effective design strategy for building robots whose behavior must be moral.

Even given a set of comprehensive, nonconflicting rules, consecutive repetition of one or more rules can lead to undesirable results. This is especially true when the rules are applied "blindly" in a succession of individual decisions, without consideration of the whole process over a period of time. The same phenomenon is found in the "voting paradoxes" that are well known to political scientists and philosophers. Philosopher Philip Pettit demonstrates such a situation in the example of an editorial committee of three members that resolves all the issues it faces by majority vote. In January, the committee agrees to promise subscribers that there will be no price rise over the next five years. Another vote follows in midyear, when the committee decides to send articles to external reviewers and to be bound by their decision on whether or not to publish any individual piece. In December, the committee members are faced with the issue of publishing technical articles that are quite costly to produce. The majority voted to publish the articles, but in this case the high publishing costs could possibly result in reneging on the earlier commitment of not increasing the journal's price. As the table on the next page shows, the votes of each member of the committee (A, B, and C) made sense

	Price freeze	External review	Technical papers
A.	Yes	No	Yes
B.	No	Yes	Yes
C.	Yes	Yes	No
Result:	Yes	Yes	Yes

individually, but still led to inconsistency when subjected to the "blind" application of the majority vote rule.

Computers are particularly vulnerable to similar inconsistencies in decision making that result from locally consistent procedures being followed without the cumulative consequences being checked.

It's rather easy to agree that a fully autonomous moral agent should not get stuck when it encounters an ethical dilemma. But would everyone agree that in order to resolve the dilemma, an AMA might cut the Gordian knot and possibly do harm to a human being? Sometimes rules, including democratic decision procedures, have to be broken. And some ethical systems allow rules to be disobeyed—as they are only prima facie constraints on actions. Any rule-based approach to allowing an AMA the latitude to override a rule would require the formulation of extremely explicit criteria for when to do so. But any such criteria would very likely produce other dilemmas. Poking the balloon will cause it to bulge somewhere else.

Nevertheless, deontological moral rules continue to play an important role not just for philosophers doing ethical theory, but also in public discussions of morality. Such rules range from the very explicit to the highly abstract, from specific prescriptions of particular behaviors (e.g., "Thou shall not steal") to guiding principles from which the correct action should be derived (e.g., "Treat others as you would wish them to treat you"). At the more specific end of the scale are the Bible's Ten Commandments, Asimov's Three Laws, and professional codes of conduct. At the more abstract end are the somewhat different versions of the Golden Rule expressed in many world religions and cultures, and Kant's categorical imperative requiring that the motives for actions be universalizable.

Different challenges arise for computing morality along the range from specific to abstract rules. Specific rules tend to be relatively easy to apply in simple cases but provide unclear guidance in more complex situations. Should you honor your father by stealing if he asks you to, particularly if he has no other way of obtaining food? What would an Asimov-type robot do if given contradictory orders by different humans or faced with a choice between actions that will all lead to harm to humans? The lists of duties themselves do nothing to resolve these ambiguities. Even though Asimov makes the Three

Laws explicitly hierarchical, this is of no use when an individual principle itself results in conflicting demands. More abstract rules seem necessary for adjudicating such conflicts.

Über-Rule Computing

Kant's categorical imperative and the Golden Rule represent the more abstract deontological theories. They attempt to bypass conflicts by stating principles of such generality that they can be applied in any situation. The categorical imperative is explicitly designed to guarantee logical consistency. This might, therefore, make it seem especially appropriate for computers working within a logical framework. Kant wrote several different versions of the categorical imperative, but the key idea is captured in this statement: "Act only on that maxim through which you can at the same time will that it should become a universal law."

The exact meaning and application of Kant's theory is controversial among philosophers, but what might an engineer tasked with building an AMA get out of the categorical imperative? We think a reasonable first approximation is the idea that (ro)bots selecting among options must check to see whether their goals could be achieved if similar other agents acted in the same way in corresponding situations. This application of the imperative sidesteps the complicated question of what Kant meant by requiring an agent to be able to *will* the maxim to be a universal law. Many followers of Kant would argue that artificial agents are incapable of willing anything at all. Nevertheless, the categorical imperative might be used by AMAs as a formal tool for checking the morality of a behavior-guiding maxim. To apply this tool, an AMA would need an explicit and fully stated principle of practical reason consisting of three elements: a goal, a means or course of action by which the agent proposes to achieve that goal, and a statement of the circumstances under which acting in that way will achieve the goal in question. Given these three elements, a very powerful computing device might be able to run an analysis or a simulation model to determine whether its goal would be blocked if all other agents were to operate with the same maxim. For instance, Kant himself illustrated the application of the categorical imperative by deriving an injunction against lying, because, he reasoned, if everyone lied in the pursuit of their goals, then speech would become meaningless, making it impossible to lie at all.

While people might agree that too much lying undermines credibility, many people would disagree with Kant's universalizing the maxim "Always tell the truth" and argue that a limited amount of lying is appropriate in specific situations. Determining a self-consistent maxim that would cover those situations is a difficult reasoning problem that ultimately depends on a great deal of empirical knowledge. Any AMA that is to apply Kantian reasoning would thus require more than the aforementioned abstract characterizations of goals, actions, and circumstances. It would also need to know a lot about human and (ro)bot psychology and about the effects of actions in the world.

Duty-based systems principally revolve around rules, but the consequences of applying the rules are nevertheless important. Many rules, after all, are adopted in order to ward off bad consequences. Some rules are even explicitly stated in terms of consequences. A robot following Asimov's laws, for instance, would need to know the extent to which its actions (or inaction) would result in harm to humans in order to determine whether it is conforming to the First Law. Even Kant's categorical imperative requires agents to consider whether a maxim is self-undermining, in the sense that following it would have the *consequence* of undermining other attempts to follow it. An AMA based on Kant's categorical imperative must also (1) recognize the goal of its own action, and (2) assess the effects of all other moral agents trying to achieve the same goal by acting the same way in comparable circumstances. It will typically also need to decide what to do, because (1) and (2) determine only what not to do, unless the alternatives are mutually exclusive. This AMA would also need to have extensive psychological knowledge regarding the humans involved in order to satisfactorily perform all the necessary assessments.

An AMA that followed the Golden Rule would need to be able to (1) notice the effect of others' actions on itself, assess the effect (also in hypothetical situations), and chose its preferences; (2) assess the consequences of its own actions on the affective states of others, and decide whether they match its own preferences; and (3) take into account differences in individual psychology while working on (1) and (2), as people affected by the action might respond differently to the same treatment. The latter point would presume that the AMA has a capacity to discern and anticipate changes in the affective reactions of people to its decisions. Predicting the actual consequences of actions is difficult to impossible.

Humans find it exceedingly difficult to discern what more specific rules or maxims are consistent with über-rules such as the categorical imperative or the Golden Rule. All general deontological principles that seek to resolve conflicts among prima facie duties face similar issues. In the end, many of the computational issues facing duty-based approaches converge with those facing consequentialist systems.

Deontological theories require that AMAs implementing them understand the rules sufficiently well to reason correctly in any situation requiring moral judgment. Proper interpretation and application of a moral theory would be much easier if the rules gave unambiguous direction in all circumstances. But as simple as this may sound, there are again seemingly insurmountable hurdles. To make the rules fully explicit, the AMA must be given clear definitions of all the terms that are used. This is not a simple task, considering, for instance, the vagueness of the "universal" around which Kant's categorical imperative revolves or the difficulty of specifying exactly what counts as a harm or an injury to a human being. Nevertheless, even vague concepts can have some clear applications. Baldness is a vague concept, but Captain Picard *is* bald, after all. Likewise, some actions are clearly harmful. By focusing initially on the clear cases, it may be possible to capture a lot of ordinary morality in a top-down fashion. Eventually, too, AMAs will need to possess the ability to reason about ethical cases in a top-down fashion.

Top to Bottom

The limitations of top-down approaches nevertheless add up, on our view, to the conclusion that it will not be feasible to furnish an AMA with an unambiguous set of top-down rules to follow. Not everyone agrees, and later we will discuss the important efforts of Susan and Michael Anderson with their MedEthEx system, which organizes three prima facie duties (respect for autonomy, beneficence, and nonmaleficence) into a consistent structure based on "expert" judgments. Susan Anderson believes that one consistent set of principles will emerge because she assumes that experts generally agree with each other. However, the same principles have been used throughout medical ethics, and there are countless situations where they lead to conflicting recommendations for action. We think that the task confronting AMAs is that of learning to deal with the inherently ambiguous nature of human moral judgment, including the fact that even experts can disagree.

How can machines operate successfully if things are as ambiguous as we say? For that matter, how do humans do it? Humans learn to distinguish the letter of the law from the spirit of the law. Humans identify the ability to deal with the incoherence and complexity of life, to find balance between knowing and doubting, as practical wisdom. Wisdom emerges from experience, from attentive doing and observing, from the integration of cognition, emotions, and reflection. (These are perhaps qualities that contribute to Kant's inclusion of a role for human *will* in his categorical imperative.) Does the need for such wisdom mean that humans have to build affective/emotional capacities as well as reflective reasoning capacities into AMAs? Possibly, and we'll discuss this topic in chapter 10. But first we need to discuss the strengths of "bottom-up" approaches to morality that see moral behavior as emerging from learning and evolution.

Chapter 7

BOTTOM-UP AND
DEVELOPMENTAL
APPROACHES

Organic Morality

Human beings do not enter the world as competent moral agents. Nor does everyone leave the world in that state. But somewhere in between, most people acquire a modicum of decency that qualifies them for membership in the community of moral agents.

Genes. development, and learning all contribute to the process of becoming a decent human being. The interaction between nature and nurture is, however, highly complex, and developmental biologists are only just beginning to grasp just how complex it is. Without the context provided by cells, organisms, social groups, and culture, DNA is inert. Anyone who says that people are "genetically programmed" to be moral (or psychopathic for that matter) has an oversimplified view of how genes work.

Genes and environment interact in ways that make it nonsensical to think that the process of moral development in children, or any other developmental process, can be discussed in terms of nature *versus* nurture. Developmental biologists now know that it is really both, or nature *through* nurture. A complete scientific account of moral evolution and development in the human species is a very long way off. And even if one had such an account, it is not clear how one could apply it to digital computers. Nevertheless, evolutionary and developmental ideas will continue to play a role in the design of AMAs.

The idea that AI should try to mimic child development is as old as AI itself. In his classic 1950 article "Can Machines Think?" Alan Turing wrote: "Instead of trying to produce a programme to simulate the adult mind, why not rather try to produce one which simulates the child's? If this were

99

then subjected to an appropriate course of education one would obtain the adult brain."

Turing was thinking not specifically about morality but instead about the problem of whether a computing machine could ever perform an original act. The idea that machines would never be capable of originating anything had been raised over a century earlier by Ada Lovelace, who had worked with Charles Babbage to give a comprehensible description of the "analytical engine"—a planned but unbuilt mechanical computing device that is regarded as a forerunner to the modern digital computers ultimately made possible by Turing's work.

Lovelace wrote that the "Analytical Engine has no pretensions to originate anything. It can do whatever we know how to order it to perform." Turing reasoned that if a computer could be put through an educational regime comparable to the education a child receives, "We may hope that machines will eventually compete with men in all purely intellectual fields." Presumably, this educational regime would include a moral education.

Simulating a child's mind is only one of the strategies being pursued for the design of intelligent agents. In 1975, John Holland's invention of genetic algorithms generated much excitement about the potential for evolving adaptive programs. Genetic algorithms have been employed for many purposes, for example, predicting the stock market and breaking codes. (*Wikipedia* lists over thirty applications.) Holland's work also led to the radical idea that computers might even become environments for evolving a new kind of life: artificial life (Alife).

Early advocates of Alife proposed to simulate evolution within virtual environments. They hoped for the emergence of agents capable of learning, sophisticated behavior, and elements of mind, all completely contained within a software-created world. Recognizing, however, that virtual worlds are no substitute for the challenges and complexities of the real world, roboticists have also adapted Alife techniques to help them design robots that operate in physical environments. This is the field now known as evolutionary robotics.

The power of evolutionary algorithms can be illustrated by way of evolutionary robotics. An initial population of (ro)bots, which vary slightly from one another, is evaluated in a real or virtual environment according to how well they succeed in some task. Each (ro)bot is assigned a score that measures its success (fitness) in performing the desired task. The (ro)bots with the highest fitness are used to generate a new set of (ro)bots, by recombining components in a process modeled on sexual reproduction, and by introducing small, random mutations. The fitness of the new generation is measured, and the best performers are selected and allowed to reproduce. This is repeated for many generations, leading to progressive improvement in the skill of the (ro)bots at performing the task. To date, evolutionary roboticists have focused on robots learning sensorimotor control to perform tasks such as walking and navigating through a room, but in principle, such techniques might be utilized to evolve systems with higher cognitive faculties.

Insofar as artificial babies and Alife both provide methods for generating AMAs, they are examples of "bottom-up" approaches, in which system design is not explicitly guided by any top-down ethical theory. Traditional engineering approaches of testing and refining intelligent systems can also be thought of as following a bottom-up course of development. Different approaches have different strengths, weaknesses, and implicit biases, which we will attempt to describe in the rest of this chapter. We'll begin with a discussion of the evolution-inspired approaches before considering learning-based approaches to moral development.

Artificial Life and the Emergence of Social Values

In 1975, the same year that Holland invented genetic algorithms, E. O. Wilson proposed that the science of sociobiology might give rise to "a precise account of the evolutionary origin of ethics." Putting these two ideas together raises the prospect that Alife could produce moral agents. If the foundational values of human society are rooted in humans' biological heritage, then it might be reasonable to presume that these values would reemerge in a sufficiently rich simulation of natural selection.

Sociobiologists—and evolutionary psychologists, who are among their intellectual descendants—have made an effort to describe the evolutionary conditions that lead to the emergence of value systems. A major theoretic underpinning of this effort has been game theory, the mathematical theory of competition and cooperation among rational agents, introduced in 1944 by John von Neumann and Oskar Morgenstern. Game theory is often associated with the mathematician and 1994 Nobel laureate John Nash, whose life and work was introduced to popular culture through the Oscar-winning movie *A Beautiful Mind*.

A central thought experiment in game theory is the "prisoner's dilemma," in which each of two criminal accomplices is offered a deal of reduced sentencing in return for giving state's evidence against his partner. The deal is structured in such a way that the most rational choice for each player is to rat on the other, but if they cooperate with each other by both keeping quiet, they will be better off collectively. Because neither prisoner can trust his partner to stay silent, rational self-interest leads both to "defect" by cooperating with the police rather than with each other.

The analysis of prisoner's dilemma–type games becomes especially interesting when two agents play against each other repeatedly. Iterated games make it possible for each player to decide whether or not to cooperate with the other on the basis of what has happened in the previous interactions. The iterated prisoner's dilemma game has become the basis for investigating the emergence of cooperation in a wide range of social sciences, from economics to sociobiology.

The iterated prisoner's dilemma game enables theorists to analyze different strategies and test them against each other. In the late 1970s, the political scientist Robert Axelrod put out a call for strategies to compete in tournaments of iterated prisoner's dilemma games. He then tested the various strategies against each other in computer simulations to see which was the most successful. One very simple strategy commonly called "tit for tat" turned out to do surprisingly well. In tit for tat, the player starts by cooperating in the first round, and then on each successive round does what the other player did in the previous round. If you try to get an advantage, then I try to get an advantage; if you play fair, then I play fair. Tit for tat is not always the optimal strategy, but this simple strategy for conditional cooperation does well in a wide variety of circumstances. We surmise that more sophisticated strategies for conditional cooperation are essential for building trust among agents living in more complex social arrangements—a point to which we will return.

Game theory came to the attention of evolutionary biologists John Maynard Smith and William Hamilton, who both developed its application to biological cases. Hamilton was interested in the fact that social insects, for example worker bees, are reproductively sterile and may even die to enable the queen bee to reproduce. The logic of evolutionary fitness would seem to suggest that "defecting" from this arrangement and producing one's own offspring would be a better strategy for keeping one's genes in the gene pool than foregoing all of one's individual "fitness" by having zero offspring.

Many social animals seem to cooperate with each other at a potential cost to their individual fitness. For example, alerting others to the presence of predators, sharing food, and taking care of offspring belonging to other group members all involve costs to the individual. A central puzzle for biology is how this behavior could evolve, given that such cooperation doesn't always seem to be in the reproductive interests of the animals providing the services. For instance, an animal that does something to alert others to the presence of a predator could in fact attract the attention of the predator to itself. An animal that kept quiet would be able to take advantage of the alarm calls of the others without risking its own demise.

Hamilton realized that the logic of game theory could be applied to the evolutionary strategies of individual genes independently of whole organisms. What is good for the gene need not be good for the organism. Richard

Dawkins later popularized this theory in his book *The Selfish Gene*. The selfish gene concept remains controversial for many reasons. (Among them is the question of whether there really is such a thing as a gene *for* cooperation, or whether it makes sense to talk of natural selection operating on single genes.) Nevertheless, the application of game theory to evolution was a historically important turning point for sociobiology. Working together, Axelrod and Hamilton concluded that because cooperation was sometimes a successful strategy, it was one of the traits that could emerge from an evolutionary process.

Peter Danielson and his colleagues at the University of British Columbia's Centre for Applied Ethics took Axelrod's tournaments a step further by constructing simulated environments in which virtual organisms could change and adapt in response to the actions of other entities in the population. Danielson called these Alife simulations "moral ecologies" in his book *Artificial Morality: Virtuous Robots for Virtual Games*. His simulated organisms could cooperate or defect, and some of them could store information about their competitors' previous behavior and use this information to implement various conditional cooperation strategies. Danielson's collaborator Bill Harms added the capacity for the bots to move around within the virtual world of the computer simulation. To Harms's and Danielson's surprise, the mindless individual entities began to form their own groups. Cooperators would group together with other cooperators, and uncooperative "predators" would also hang out together. In tough times, when the resources were limited, the predators would die off, while the cooperators had a competitive advantage. But conditional cooperators, whose behavior toward others was dependent on how others behaved toward them, continued to compete with each other for resources, leading to different degrees of cooperation. Danielson proposed a concept of "functional" morality in which rationality, as it is defined by game theory, is the only prerequisite for an agent to be a moral agent. Although he now views these experiments quite critically, they seemed to him at the time to demonstrate the promise of Alife simulations to foster the emergence of moral agents.

Tennyson's famous phrase "Nature, red in tooth and claw" has often been used to characterize the harsh amorality of the Darwinian struggle for survival. The idea that morality itself might emerge from evolution seems contrary to the portrayal of nature as savage. Nevertheless, if human morality evolved, then sufficiently sophisticated Alife experiments ought to be able to evolve other morally sensitive agents. It is far from clear, though, what "sufficiently sophisticated" would mean in an artificial environment!

The propensities, features, and faculties that emerge out of evolution are not merely the product of individual entities struggling to survive and procreate. They are the product of social interactions and success in environments populated by many species. Often the most successful species are those whose members learn to cooperate with each other and recognize freeloaders that are a drain on resources. The values instantiated in evolved and evolving agents emerge from the pressures of adapting, surviving, and procreating in a multiagent system.

It remains to be seen whether artificial environments that select among agents competing for the accumulation of simple resources can produce anything like the moral propensities of humans. A series of recent experiments has shown, for example, that people (and perhaps other animals) value fairness for its own sake, and will even give up additional money (or food) to ensure a relatively equitable distribution. In his book *Evolution of the Social Contract*, Brian Skyrms, professor of logic and philosophy of science at the University of California at Irvine, describes game-theoretical simulations in which a "Fair" strategy regularly dominates greedier strategies. However, several critics have pointed out that it is a long way from such simple strategies and games to the real world. Insofar as the current understanding of the conditions in which human morality evolved is very poor, this process seems likely to be very sensitive to features beyond humans' control. Whether they are evolved in virtual or physical environments, AMAs are likely to be very different from the moral agents that have emerged from human evolution.

In addition to the problem of getting the environment right, a major problem facing the adaptation of evolutionary systems to the emergence of AMAs is how to design a fitness function without explicitly applying moral criteria. The slogan "survival of the most moral" highlights the problem of determining what "most moral" amounts to.

The transfer from virtual Alife environments to physically embodied agents is also unlikely to be straightforward. The decision-making processes of an agent whose moral capacities have been evolved in a virtual environment are not necessarily going to work well in the physical world. This difficulty is exacerbated by a problem that has been noted with Alife generally. Experiments in simulated evolution have so far been unable to cross a threshold where the patterns of artificial life forms become sufficiently complex to shed light on the robustness of real biological life. Without knowing how to evolve agents of sufficient complexity in the virtual world, one cannot expect to evolve complex agents for the physical world.

Thus, Rodney Brooks notes that although experiments in Alife have progressed dramatically over the past few decades, "they have not taken off by themselves in the ways we have come to expect of biological systems." Thomas Ray, a tropical biologist and developer of a highly regarded software program for digital evolution (Tierra), admits, "evolution in the digital medium remains a process with a very limited record of accomplishments." And Peter Danielson acknowledges that the rather simplistic games and artificial environments used for evolutionary simulations are not really reflective of the complex environments and multidimensional scenarios that give rise to values, laws, and mores in the real world.

An appreciation for the limitations of virtual worlds has led Danielson to pursue a completely different approach to machine morality, which we describe in chapter 9. But other scientists continue to work on developing more complex virtual worlds, and better measures of complexity that can be used to drive evolutionary processes within them. Even though Danielson himself lost confidence in the value of his early approach to virtual ethics, a next step for the study of AMAs within Alife could be to try to evolve cooperative agents within the richer framework provided by more sophisticated virtual worlds. Much would depend, still, on the richness of the environments (including the social dimensions) in which the artificial agents interact. For the time being, scientists' ability to simulate these worlds lags far behind capturing the complexity of the real world.

Some researchers believe that what has evolved in the real world of human social morality is something like a "moral grammar" or "moral core." The idea of a universal moral grammar for the human species was first suggested by political philosopher John Rawls in 1971, by way of analogy to the universal grammar for language posited by MIT linguistics professor Noam Chomsky. Chomsky transformed the study of linguistics and cognitive science when he argued that human language learning could only be possible if innate structures within human psychology narrowed the task to a limited number of forms that human languages can take.

Rawls's idea has recently been developed in the human evolutionary context by Harvard primatologist Marc Hauser in his book *Moral Minds*. The topic of AMAs is far outside the scope of Hauser's book, but just as Chomsky's universal grammar spawned computational approaches to language, perhaps the identification of a moral grammar would be potentially useful for the design of AMAs. Hauser has no clear specifications for such a moral grammar, much less a computational theory built on top of it, and in any case we are skeptical of his thesis that human morality contains an evolved universal core. Nevertheless, it is a topic worthy of further scientific investigation.

Nanotechnologist Josh Storrs Hall has toyed with the idea of a moral grammar or moral core while working in the specific context of designing moral machines. In an early article he wrote in 2000, he explicitly mentions Rawls's idea of the universal moral grammar, but in his more recent work he seems to have abandoned that concept in favor of a more generic notion of a moral core or moral instincts. In his 2007 book *Beyond AI: Creating the Conscience of the Machine*, Hall writes, "A good first cut at a design for an artificial moral instinct would be . . . a 'cahooter guarantee protocol.' " "Cahooting" is

Hall's label for the tendency of human beings to engage in cooperative behavior even when the simple logic of game theory appears to dictate against it.

It seems correct to say that a tendency to cahoot is favored by evolution and culture under some conditions. However, Hall goes further with his optimistic belief that the basic logic of evolution and competition will lead to advanced moral agents possessing what he calls "hyperhuman morality." He has written, "We are on the verge of creating beings who are as good as we like to pretend to be but never really are." According to Hall, such exemplary moral behavior will flow naturally from the core characteristics of self-interest, curiosity, trustability, and long planning horizons—characteristics he thinks are necessarily favored by evolutionary processes operating on long-lived, intelligent, social beings. His view is that the artificially intelligent machines (AIs) of the future will be very long-lived—effectively immortal—and thus will need to consider the very long-term consequences of their actions or suffer the negative consequences directly. The result, Hall has written, will be "guaranteeably, un-self-deceivingly honest AIs."

We expect that most of our readers will agree with us that this all sounds too good to be true. At the very least, it refers to a future we think is well beyond the immediate practical aims that we have outlined for building AMAs. However, even if that is the future, what happens between here and the emergence of a hyperhuman AMA is another matter. Semi-evolved (ro)bots will not necessarily behave any better than their biological counterparts.

Nevertheless, Storrs Hall has made a valuable contribution to the discussion about how to implement artificial morality that falls within the range of bottom-up approaches. On his view, ethical behavior emerges from the evolution of intelligence itself; the AMA designer's problem thus reduces to that of specifying the nature of the intelligence to be implemented.

Ideas of a moral grammar or moral instincts draw attention to elements of human nature that are allegedly fixed and immutable. But the most striking feature of life, especially intelligent life, is its flexibility and adaptability. What has evolved are not rigid systems with fixed natures but adaptive systems that develop and learn. Indeed, the capacity to learn may be among the more remarkable features in the nature of animals that display intelligent behavior. If any AMA is to function well in the niche created by human beings, it will need to be a learning machine.

Learning Machines

Whether evolved or constructed, AMAs will need some capacity for acquiring the norms of the locale in which they find themselves. If human morality is built up through experience, through trial and error honed by reason, then teaching an AMA to be a moral agent may well require a process of education similar to that experienced by a child. The AMA will need to assimilate feedback about the moral acceptability or unacceptability of its actions, at least during a designated developmental period, or perhaps over its entire life span. None of the machine models of learning that are presently available is anywhere close to the richness of actual biological learning mechanisms. Realizing Turing's dream of a child-like AI has turned out to be much more difficult than he expected.

The field of AI has always been concerned with machine learning, and many learning models have been developed. Chomsky's approach to human language learning exemplifies one major type of approach, where learning is treated as a problem of finding the best representation of the facts from a predetermined set of possibilities (specified by the universal grammar). An alternative approach treats the learner as more of a blank slate, faced not only with the task of finding an appropriate representation of the facts but also, simultaneously, with the task of finding an appropriate representational scheme. Traditional, symbolic approaches to AI tend to treat learning as the recombination of a set of predefined concepts. More recent connectionist approaches tend to rely less on preconceived structures, using the capacity of artificial neural networks to dynamically generate their own classification schemes from the input they receive.

Developmental psychologists are divided over the question of whether infants come into the world with a rich set of innate knowledge. Some psychologists believe that infants are born knowing some basic facts about physical objects, numbers, and purposeful agents. Others dispute these claims vigorously. Developers of AMAs need not enter into these disputes directly, although any particular learning model they adopt will tend to be aligned with one camp or another. Given the current lack of understanding about the processes, the best attitude is probably pluralism, being open to trying anything that might work.

Some cognitive scientists are convinced that progress toward sophisticated machine learning will need to take into account the physically embodied aspects of learners. For instance, an infant's "knowledge" about physical objects, whether innate or acquired, probably does not consist of a set of sentences describing how physical objects behave but is more likely grounded in her own physical presence and engagement with the world. Turing's original idea of a child-like learning machine was based only in a pure symbol-processing approach, but among scientists pursuing the dream of child-like intelligence are two former students of Rodney Brooks, Brian Scassellati and Cynthia Breazeal. Scassellati cut his teeth on the Cog project, which had the original goal of investigating learning in a robot. But the challenge of designing Cog's limbs, visual system, and other hardware components turned out to be considerably greater than anticipated, and Cog was retired to the MIT museum before any significant progress could be made on the problem of learning. Scassellati and Breazeal's next step toward child-like learning capabilities in a machine came from their collaboration on the Kismet robot, but Kismet has also been retired to the MIT museum. Each of them is now working independently on a second generation of child-like robots—"Leonardo" (Breazeal) and "Nico" (Scassellati). The hardware and software challenges remain formidable, and while some basic social learning is being investigated—for example, in the area of theory of mind, as we discuss in chapter 10—these researchers are a long way from any direct investigation of moral development.

To adapt (ro)botic systems to moral development may require understanding how children acquire moral capacities. Freud and Piaget notably laid the foundations for developmental theories of morality, and although their theories have many detractors, they provide a starting point for discussion. In the specific area of moral learning and development, the most prominent figure is the psychologist Lawrence Kohlberg, who takes a Piagetian approach in which children develop their moral capacities through several cognitive-developmental stages. Kohlberg, who was the director of Harvard's Center for Moral Education in the 1980s, proposed that as the child grapples with challenges and is confronted with limitations in his ideas about meeting those challenges, his concepts about what is right, wrong, and just move his understanding of morality naturally to a next higher stage. In the initial premoral or preconventional stages, behavior is understood as the avoidance of punishment or as the means to get what you want. In the conventional stages, morality is first understood in terms of interpersonal conformity and eventually as an aspect of a social contract—laws or codes necessary to maintain order. Postconventional stages are characterized by a sincere concern with human welfare, which can lead to a focus on universal moral principles. These later stages require capacities for abstract moral reasoning.

Kohlberg's account was vigorously challenged by his Harvard colleague Carol Gilligan. She complained that Kohlberg placed undue emphasis on reasoning rather than on what she saw as the more feminine value of care for others. Despite their disagreements, however, both Kohlberg and Gilligan believe that moral development in children goes through several distinct stages. An attempt to replicate the stages proposed by either theorist might underpin a gradual approach to the development of AMAs. However, for (ro)bots built with existing AI techniques and present-day computers, it also seems apparent that Kohlberg's emphasis on reasoning provides a more immediately tractable project than Gilligan's emphasis on care.

Another controversial issue in the field of moral development concerns how sensible it is to design programs of moral education around these psychologists' theories. (A similar question arises about the ethical theories of Aristotle, Kant, and the utilitarians and about more religiously motivated views on moral education, held by, for example, William Bennett, who was secretary of education under Ronald Reagan.) Of course, long before there were developmental theories to guide education, millions of children grew up to be good moral agents. They acquired patterns of behavior and ideas about morality from family members and neighbors, they learned about fairness and reciprocity through childhood games, and they picked up other ideas from sermons, religious texts, and morality tales such as Aesop's fables.

Nevertheless, modules for teaching moral reasoning, based on the work of Kohlberg and others, have made their way into formal education during the past five decades. The stages of moral development are, in Kohlberg's view, largely built on evaluating the applicability or limitations of reasons for moral judgments within a given context. Children move on to the next level of moral reasoning as they come to appreciate the limitations of the reasons they have been relying on for guidance. Perhaps these modules could be adapted for training an artificial system that had the right sort of logical capacities, although we know of no attempts to do this. And perhaps such an attempt would fail without first going through the earlier stages of moral development.

In the earlier stages of childhood development, rewards and punishment and approval and disapproval play a much bigger role in informing the moral reasoning of young children. Although it is possible to simulate reward and punishment in a digital computer, it is unclear whether these formal simulations have the immediacy or power that actual rewards and punishments have for children. Psychologists may disagree about the effectiveness of pain as a teaching tool, but regardless of that, it is not known how to produce anything like it in a computer. It is sometimes suggested that punishment and rewards might be communicated in terms a computer would appreciate directly, for example, by manipulating processor speed, information flow, or the supply of energy. But these seem either naive or far-fetched and futuristic. Still, even without conscious pleasure or pain, computational learning mechanisms may be able to learn some basic patterns of moral behavior.

Among those who have considered the possibility of a learning-based approach to AMAs is Christopher Lang. While he was a philosophy graduate student at the University of Wisconsin, Lang wrote an article in which he noted the limitations inherent in top-down systems designed around rule-based ethics, for example Asimov's Three Laws. He argued that any rule-constrained system would suffer from a fatal rigidity in its behavior. Instead, Lang recommended an approach to moral agents that he originally called "quest ethics." In this strategy, the computer would learn about ethics through a never-ending quest to pursue rational goals. Lang's ideas for learning machines center around what are sometimes called "hill-climbing" or "greedy-search" algorithms. Such nonterminating learning algorithms endlessly search for better and better solutions. Genetic algorithms are hill-climbing algorithms, as are various connectionist learning techniques.

Lang is extremely optimistic that learning machines will naturally come to value human aspirations and human diversity. The only limitation he perceives in machines designed around quest ethics is that they will be temporarily immature until the system has evolved to a satisfactory level where it might be designated a moral agent. Like that of Josh Storrs Hall, Lang's optimism is based on what we see as some questionable ideas about the inevitability of ethical behavior emerging when the conditions are right.

Because these learning systems are not restricted by predetermined rules, Lang calls them "unbiased learning machines." However, his use of "unbiased" in this context is somewhat idiosyncratic. In our terms, it appears to mean that they are not guided by top-down principles. In spite of Lang's suggestion that such approaches are unbiased, there are various ways biases can creep in—for instance, in the design of the particular platform, in defining the procedures or algorithms selected for the hill-climbing, and in the structure and richness of the data available to the system.

Lang's discussion is purely at a theoretical level. Actual goal-seeking or hill-climbing algorithms have yet to be thoroughly investigated for the development of moral agents (although we describe Marcello Guarini's actual connectionist model of moral classification in chapter 9). Because learning machines remove the need for programmers to anticipate every contingency, they have become extremely popular for many applications outside ethics. We believe that these techniques hold great promise for programmers interested in developing moral agents.

Nevertheless, there are hazards inherent in learning systems. The vision of learning systems developing naturally toward an ethical sensibility that values humans and human ethical concerns is an optimistic vision that sits in sharp contrast to the more dire futuristic predictions regarding the dangers AI poses. We'll assess those dangers in detail in chapter 12, but our discussion of learning systems would be incomplete here if we did not mention the prospect that any system that has the ability to learn may also have the potential to learn the wrong thing, possibly even to undo or override any built-in restraints.

This danger is inherent in IBM's strategy for "autonomous computing" networks, which is directed at lowering costs through the design of hardware and software that monitors a system's activity, optimizes performance, and heals bugs or system errors without human intervention. The challenge lies in designing systems that are self-repairing or that learn but don't alter key functions or tinker with code in a manner that unleashes unanticipated consequences. One wouldn't, for example, want a "self-healing" computer to alter the real-time execution of financial transactions. As the number of variables the system manages increases, the effect of each alteration grows exponentially, and the prospect of potentially damaging results expands.

One solution to this problem involves a layered architecture. In a layered computational system, lower-level standards and protocols are functionally isolated from higher-order functionality. In order to maintain the integrity of code, programmers customizing software for individual clients seldom tamper with the shared, lower-level modules. Rather, they design an additional software module that contains the specific customizations required by the individual client and leave the shared code intact. For the purpose of building AMAs, core restraints might be built into foundational layers of the computer platform that are inaccessible to those parts of the computer that learn and revise the structures that process new information. This was Asimov's strategy in proposing that the Three Laws of robotics be built directly into the "positronic brain." Recognizing the limitations of Asimov's laws again raises the question as to what moral restraints should be encoded into these "deeper" protocols. The ideas of a moral grammar or moral code mentioned earlier in this chapter potentially provide an answer to this question.

If key restraints could be programmed into a computational system at a very low level, they might act as something like a human conscience. In the short term, there might be little basis for concern that a learning system would alter these deeply embedded restraints. However, just as humans override their consciences given certain goals, desires, and motivations, a learning computer might also find ways to circumvent restraints that got in the way of its goals. We'll return to this problem in chapter 12.

The rudimentary learning capacities of existing AI systems are far from the rich adaptive learning skills evident in young children. Nor, as noted, have AI approaches to learning been applied to moral development. However, our discussion of the potential dangers of learning machines leads us to believe that for the near term, engineers will need to combine learning or simulated evolution with more traditional bottom-up approaches to system design.

Assembling Modules

The immediate prospects for systems that act with sensitivity to moral considerations are still largely confined to designing systems with operational morality, that is, ensuring that the AI system functions as designed. This is primarily the extension of the traditional engineering concern with safety into the design of smart machines that can reliably perform a specified task, whether that entails a robot navigating a hallway without damaging itself or running into people, visually distinguishing the presence of a human from an inanimate object, or deciphering the emotional state implicit in a facial expression. While the focus of engineers and computer scientists is on the design of methods for carrying out discrete tasks, cumulatively these tasks might lead to more complex activities and greater autonomy. These approaches are "bottom-up" in our sense, because the development and deployment of these discrete subsystems is not itself explicitly guided by any ethical theory. Rather, it is hoped that by experimenting with the way these subsystems interact, something that has suitable moral capacities can be created.

Computer scientists and roboticists are working on a variety of discrete AI-related skills that are relevant to moral capacities. The techniques provided by different approaches—including Alife, genetic algorithms, connectionism, learning algorithms, embodied or subsumptive architecture, evolutionary and epigenetic robotics, associative learning platforms, and even traditional symbolic AI—all have strengths in modeling specific cognitive skills or capacities.

Subsystems and modules will be built around the most effective techniques for implementing specific cognitive capacities and social mechanisms. However, computer scientists following such an approach are then confronted with the challenge of assembling these discrete systems into a functional whole. Among the most promising approaches to robotics are those that exploit dynamic interaction between the various subtasks of visual perception, moving, manipulating, and understanding speech. For example, Deb Roy, director of the Cognitive Machines Group in the MIT Media Laboratory, exploits such interactions in the development of the seeing, hearing, and talking robotic arm he calls "Ripley." Ripley's speech understanding and comprehension systems develop in the context of carrying out human requests for actions related to identifying and manipulating objects within its fields of vision and reach, while balancing internal requirements—for example, not allowing its servomotors to overheat, a very real mechanical concern, as it turns out.

In his public lectures, Roy sometimes places his project in the context of Asimov's Three Laws. Roy depicts the various subsystems involved in speech processing, object recognition, movement, and recuperation as modules connected to the relevant law or laws. It is obvious, for example, how speech comprehension is essential to the Second Law (obey humans) and motor cooling is essential to the Third Law (self-preservation). However, for our purposes, the most telling feature of Roy's presentation is that the line from Asimov's First Law (do not harm humans) trails off into dots. In other words, Roy has not yet thought of how he might implement the moral capacities implied by the First Law. Without necessarily endorsing Asimov's laws, the challenge to computer scientists is how to replace the dots with a substantial account of ethical behavior.

How might one get from discrete skills to systems that are capable of autonomously displaying complex behavior, including moral behavior, and that are capable of meeting challenges in new environmental contexts, and in interaction with many agents? Some scientists hope or presume that the aggregation of discrete skill sets will lead to the emergence of higher-order cognitive faculties, including emotional intelligence, moral judgment, and consciousness. While "emergence" is a commonly used word among scientists and philosophers, it is still a rather vague concept that implies that more complex activities will somehow arise synergistically from the integration of simpler processes. When integrated successfully, components that are individually limited in the flexibility of their responses can give rise to complex dynamic systems with a range of choices or optional responses to external conditions and pressures. Bottom-up engineering thus offers a kind of dynamic morality, where the ongoing feedback from different social mechanisms facilitates varied responses as conditions change.

Human morality is dynamic. Although humans may be born trusting their parents and other immediate caregivers, children and adults test new relationships and feel their way over time to deepening levels of trust. Humans invest each relationship with varying degrees of trust, but there is no simple formula for trust and no one method for establishing the degree to which a given person will trust a new acquaintance. Josh Storrs Hall's suggestion that AMAs need a "cahooter guarantee protocol" as a moral instinct seems a bit too predetermined, from this dynamic, interpersonal perspective. A variety of social mechanisms, including low-risk experiments with cooperation, the reading of another's emotions in specific situations, estimations of the other's character, and calculations regarding what one is willing to risk in a given relationship all feed into the dynamic determination of trust. Each new social interaction holds the prospect of altering the degree of trust invested in a relationship. The lesson for AI research and robotics is that while AMAs should not enter the world suspicious of all relationships, they will need the capacity to dynamically negotiate or feel their way through to elevated levels of trust with the other humans or computer systems with which they interact.

A strength of complex bottom-up systems lies in the way they dynamically integrate input from differing social mechanisms. A weakness in using bottom-up architecture as a strategy for developing AMAs lies in the current lack of understanding regarding what goals to use for evaluating choices and actions as contexts and circumstances change. Bottom-up systems are easy to build when they are directed at achieving one clear goal. When the goals are several or the available information is confusing or incomplete, it is a much more difficult task for bottom-up engineering to provide a clear course of action. Nevertheless, progress in this area is being made, allowing adaptive systems to deal more effectively with transitions between different tasks, for example in Deb Roy's work.

Bottom to Top

Bottom-up strategies hold the promise of giving rise to skills and standards that are integral to the overall design of AMAs, but they are extremely difficult to evolve or develop. Evolution and learning are filled with trial and error—learning from mistakes and unsuccessful strategies. Even in the accelerated environment of computer systems, where many generations of artificial agents can mutate and replicate within a few seconds, evolution and learning can be very slow processes.

It also remains unclear what would be the appropriate goal for an evolving AMA. What fitness criteria would determine which AMAs were allowed to replicate and mutate? How might that goal be usefully defined for a self-organizing system? Jonathan Hartman, an undergraduate roboticist at Yale, suggested in a class paper he wrote for Wendell Wallach that engineers might use Asimov's Three Laws as the fitness criteria. Unlike the top-down application of these laws, where they function as hard constraints, in an evolutionary context the laws would function as looser guiding principles that the system strives to fulfill. Succeeding generations would be judged on their ability to best approximate these goals. The downside of this approach to the laws is that they might never become hard constraints, increasing the risk of harm caused by a robot. The strength of this approach is that the robot might evolve a more dynamic relationship to the laws, treating them as flexible and adaptive guiding principles. Such softer constraints might be better able to avoid the puzzles and problems that have motivated Hall, Lang, and other authors to reject Asimov's laws altogether. Hartman's hybrid approach combines the straightforward, intuitive, top-down principles of Asimov's laws with the dynamic flexibility that makes bottom-up development so desirable.

We noted that bottom-up approaches to artificial morality might lack some of the safeguards that systems guided from the top down by ethical theories offer. Top-down principles seem "safer," although they often imply idealistic standards that are hard to meet, even for humans, and they might involve computational complexities that will make them difficult, if not unfeasible, to implement. Permitting a learning AMA to continue to make mistakes as it develops moral reasoning is a luxury humanity may not be able to afford. In a controlled laboratory setting, it may be possible to create a series of learning or evolutionary situations through which an AMA could work its way toward a basic, acceptable level of moral behavior. In theory, once this basic level had been achieved for one system, its program or hardware could be reproduced indefinitely. Each of the systems reproduced in this way would need to continue learning to accommodate changing and unanticipated circumstances. But the initial basic training and development during the protected period would not need to be repeated for every AMA, saving everyone from the mistakes of child-like learning machines.

A strength of bottom-up engineering lies in the assembly of components to achieve a goal. Presuming, however, that a sophisticated capacity for moral judgment will just emerge from bottom-up engineering is unlikely to be enough, and this suggests that the analysis provided by top-down approaches will also be necessary. Jonathan Hartman's idea already suggested a kind of hybrid approach, but there are also ways of integrating top-down ethical theories more directly into the AMAs themselves. If the components of a system are well designed and can be integrated properly, then the breadth of choices open to an AMA in responding to challenges arising from its environment and social context will expand. An AMA with the top-down capacity to evaluate those options would be capable of selecting the actions that both meet its goals and fall within acceptable social norms. However, this is not the only way to conceive of a hybrid approach to AMA design, as we shall explain in the next chapter.

Chapter 8

MERGING TOP-DOWN
AND BOTTOM-UP

Hybrid Moral (Ro)bots

If neither a pure top-down approach nor a bottom-up approach is fully adequate for the design of effective AMAs, then some hybrid will be necessary. Furthermore, as noted, the top-down, bottom-up dichotomy is somewhat simplistic. Engineers commonly start with a top-down analysis of complex tasks to direct the bottom-up assembly of components.

The top-down approaches discussed in chapter 6 emphasize the importance of explicit ethical concerns that arise from the agent's relationship to the world outside itself. Top-down principles and duties represent the desire of communities to capture generic directives for determining which forms of behavior are acceptable and which are unacceptable. The top-down ethical restraints reinforce cooperation, through the principle that moral behavior often requires limiting one's freedom of action and behavior for the good of society, in ways that may not be in one's short-term or self-centered interest. Ethical principles, for example maximizing the aggregate good, and duties, for example the duty to be "just," tend to restrict an individual's options. They presume a context in which the actor has considerable freedom in the way she can act but her actions should be confined to morally praiseworthy behavior. Top-down principles may also play an important role in helping moral agents sort out cases where moral intuitions are unclear.

Bottom-up approaches are directed more at cultivating the holding of implicit values on the part of the agent. Values that emerge through the bottom-up development of a system reflect the specific causal determinants of a system's behavior. In chapter 7, we discussed approaches derived from evolution and machine learning. These approaches produce systems whose choices and flexibility in behavior expand beyond the limited actions available to reflexive systems or rigid rule followers. The ethical restraints honored by the evolving system or learning system are those that will tend to increase its choices and its opportunity to survive and flourish. For example, cooperating with members of the agent's community will limit some choices while expanding opportunities.

Furthermore, as we will discuss in chapter 10, a moral agent may need to be embodied in the world, have access to emotions or emotion-like information, and have an awareness of social dynamics and customs if it is to function properly in many contexts. Some of the morally relevant input implied by these suprarational faculties (beyond the capacity to reason) might be a byproduct of the bottom-up architecture, but this is by no means guaranteed.

Both top-down and bottom-up approaches will undoubtedly be required for the task of engineering AMAs. But hybrid approaches pose an additional problem, meshing both diverse philosophies and dissimilar architectures. Genetically acquired propensities, the discovery of core values through experience, and the learning of culturally endorsed rules all influence the moral development of children. During young adulthood, those rules may be reformulated into abstract principles that guide one's behavior in a top-down fashion. It is likely that the design of praiseworthy AMAs will also require computational systems capable of integrating diverse inputs and influences, including top-down values informed by cultivated implicit values and a rich appreciation of context. To illustrate the way top-down and bottom-up aspects interact, we consider the possibility of utilizing a connectionist network to develop a computer system with good character traits or virtues.

Virtual Virtues

As we mentioned in chapter 6, virtue theorists, rather than focusing on consequences or rules, emphasize the importance of developing character or good habits: what one is takes precedence over what one does.

Do the virtues guarantee good behavior? In Plato's dialogue of the *Meno*, Socrates argues that they would because the virtues couldn't be misused: if someone really had a virtue it would be impossible for them to act as if they did not have it. (Conversely, acting badly would show that they really didn't have the virtue!)

What are the virtues? Plato identified four cardinal virtues: wisdom, courage, moderation, and justice. Aristotle expanded this list and divided them into intellectual and moral virtues. Writing sixteen hundred years later, Thomas Aquinas added the theological virtues, which hark back to St. Paul's discussion of faith, hope, and charity (love) in his first letter to the Corinthians.

Just as utilitarians do not agree on how to measure utility, and deontologists do not agree on which list of duties apply, contemporary virtue ethicists do not agree on a standard list of virtues that any moral agent should exemplify. In his 1995 French bestseller *A Small Treatise on the Great Virtues*, the French atheist André Comte-Sponville offered eighteen virtues, including politeness and humor. Other lists of virtues have exceeded one hundred. Furthermore, what counts as a virtue may differ from community to community, leading some theorists to argue that virtue theory is wedded to a particular community's values and may be problematic for a multicultural society. Rather than focusing on these differences, we will direct our attention to the computational tractability of virtue ethics: could one make use of virtues as a programming tool?

A key to this question may even be found in Aristotle's suggestion that the moral virtues are distinct from practical wisdom and intellectual virtues. Aristotle thought that the intellectual virtues could be taught, whereas the moral virtues had to be learned through habit and practice. This suggests that a different approach might be needed for different virtues if they are to be implemented in AMAs. The possibility of teaching the intellectual virtues would suggest that it's possible to describe rules or principles explicitly. However, for the moral virtues, the emphasis on habit, learning, and character seems to suggest bottom-up processes of discovery or learning by an individual through practice.

It's very unlikely that the virtues can be neatly divided into top-down and bottom-up approaches. In our view, they are hybrids. But it's very difficult to start building hybrids before one has the pieces to hybridize from, and for this reason, it's useful to approach the task of building computers with character either as a top-down implementation of virtues or as the development of character by a learning computer. The former approach views virtues as characteristics that can be programmed into the system. The latter approach stems from the recognition of a convergence between modern "connectionist" approaches to neural networks and virtue-based ethical systems, particularly that of Aristotle. Connectionism focuses on the development and training of neural networks through experience and examples, rather than on abstract theories captured by language and rules.

Top-Down Approaches to Virtues

The task of programming virtues into a computational system runs into problems similar to those of the rule-based approaches: conflicts between virtues, incomplete lists of virtues, and especially difficulties with definitions. Virtues affect how people deliberate and how they motivate their actions, but an explicit description of the relevant virtue rarely occurs in the content of the deliberation. For instance, a kind person does kind things but typically will not explain this behavior in terms of her own kindness. Rather, a kind person will speak of motives focused on the beneficiary of the kindness, for example, "She needs it," "It will cheer him up," or "It will stop the pain." Besides revealing some of the complexities of virtue theory, this example also demonstrates that the boundaries between the various ethical theories, in this case utilitarianism and virtue-based ethics, can be quite fuzzy. Indeed, the very process of developing one's virtues is hard to imagine independently of training oneself to act for the right motives so as to produce good outcomes.

Top-down implementations of the virtues are especially challenged by the fact that virtues intrinsically involve complex patterns of motivation and desire. A particular virtue—for example, being kind—can affect almost any activity a person engages in; it has system wide effects. An artificial agent applying virtues in a top-down fashion would need to have considerable knowledge of psychology to figure out how to apply them in a given situation. For instance, what should one do when an action seems both to apply and to violate a virtue? Imagine that you—or your (ro)bot—have been asked by two people for a favor, but you can only help one of them. The other will perceive your rejection as unkind. One might feel that being unkind is unacceptable, but how does one determine which party's request to honor? A virtue-based AMA, like its deontological cohorts, could get stuck in endless looping when checking if its actions are congruent with the prescribed virtues, then reflecting on the checking, and so on.

Perhaps some of these computational problems can be mitigated by linking the virtues to functions and tailoring them sharply to the specific tasks of an AMA. Virtues were traditionally linked to function in the Greek tradition. It was considered important for each member of the community to develop the virtues that would facilitate his performing his function well. For example, a soldier was in particular need of courage. Likewise, a (ro)bot's virtue perhaps doesn't need (initially) to be as broad as something like "kindness" but could involve the particular tasks associated with being kind in the role it has been given.

Still, we think it would be a mistake to make (ro)bot virtues too domain specific. Virtues that are stable across a broad range of features provide a strong basis for trust. It has been claimed that if you know that someone is kind in one context, you can be reasonably confident that she will be kind in others. This view can be challenged, however, by the existence of many exceptions; for example, Oskar Schindler risked much to help others escape the Nazis yet was deceitful in his own family life. Nevertheless, the virtues are often presumed to provide stability because if one exemplifies a virtue in some circumstances, one is less likely to behave as if one does not have it in similar circumstances. Such stability is a very attractive feature, particularly for AMAs that need to maintain "loyalty" under pressure while dealing with various, not always legitimate sources of information. In humans, the stability of virtues, insofar as it exists, largely stems from their being emotionally grounded. One's trust in others to do "the right thing" emerges from the foundation of shared moral sentiments. The difficulty posed for a designer of AMAs is to find a way to implement the same stability in a "cold" unemotional machine. A virtuous android may require emotions of its own as well as emotionally rooted goals, for example, happiness. Perhaps the artificial simulation of an admirable goal or desire to meet the criterion of being virtuous will suffice, but in all likelihood this will only be found out by going through the actual exercise of building a virtue-based computational system.

Connectionist Virtues

After presenting his virtue-based theory, Aristotle spends much of the *Nicomachean Ethics* discussing the problem of how one is to know which habits will lead to the "good," or happiness. He is clear at the outset that there is no explicit rule for pursuing this generalized end, which is only grasped intuitively. The end is deduced from the particulars, from making connections between means and ends, between the specific things one needs to do and the goals one wishes to pursue. Humans learn what is "good" through intuition, induction, and experience. For example, through asking good people about the good, one's generalized sense of the goal comes into focus, and the idealized individual acquires practical wisdom and moral excellence.

Several writers have noted that connectionism, or parallel distributed processing, has similarities to Aristotle's discussion of how people acquire virtues. As Gips puts it, "the virtue-based approach to ethics, especially that of Aristotle, seems to resonate well with the modern connectionist approach to AI. Both seem to emphasize the immediate, the perceptual, the non-symbolic. Both emphasize development by training rather than by the teaching of abstract theory."

Connectionism is a strategy for modeling the emergence of complex behavior through interconnected networks of simple units each performing basic tasks. Connectionist models are usually called artificial neural networks, and although they ignore many important properties of biological neurons, they share some of the same processing capabilities. One strength of connectionism is that artificial neural networks are able to learn to recognize patterns or build categories naturally, by detecting statistical regularities in complex inputs. This can be accomplished without explicit instructions or programming of the concepts or categories that the network learns.

Neural networks are trained by incrementally changing the strengths of the connections between network units. This allows the network to form associations between different patterns of input and output. For example, connectionist networks have been trained to map written words onto their associated phonemes, making it possible for an artificial neural network to read a piece of text aloud. Through the gradual accumulation of data about the relationships among its inputs, the network can also generalize its responses beyond the particular examples on which it has been trained. Thus, a trained network may have the capacity to read new letter combinations by associating them with the appropriate phonemes.

In 1995, Paul Churchland proposed that connectionist learning alone is enough to explain the development of moral cognition. Churchland and his wife, Patricia, are philosophers of cognitive science at the University of California, San Diego. They are strong allies of the attempt to ground ethics in a naturalistic foundation, free from either the supernatural or the semantic content of abstract concepts. Pat Churchland, whose work is rooted in the insights provided by neuroscience, has discussed the need for a description of how values emerge in evolutionary terms. Paul Churchland's thesis about the sufficiency of connectionist learning for the development of moral cognition is far from fully developed and is not specifically wed to Aristotle's ethics. However, other philosophers, for example William Casebeer at the U.S. Air Force Academy, note the fit between connectionism and Aristotle as they try to flesh out a naturalized framework for how ethics emerged. For Casebeer, connectionism is an appropriate framework for naturalized ethics, if one understands judgment in purely biological terms "as the cognitive capacity to skillfully cope with the demands of the environment."

The suggestion that connectionism might be especially appropriate for morality was also made by Jonathan Dancy, one of the foremost promoters of moral particularism. The top-down approaches to ethics, as we have noted, are based on finding and representing general or universal principles underlying moral decision making. Many philosophers think that you can't be rational if you don't have consistent moral principles that apply universally. But not all philosophers agree. The view in ethics called "particularism" holds that moral reasons and categories are richly context-sensitive—so much so, in fact, that principles provide people with only very rough guides to appropriate action. The particularist's view is that just as there is no general rule about whether birds can fly, there may be no general rule about whether killing another human being is ultimately wrong. The contextual details of when actions are permissible may be so rich that it is impossible to summarize them in universal moral principles. Connectionist models are good at capturing context-sensitive information without explicit or general rules. Thus connectionism seems as though it would be a good fit with particularism. However, Dancy, like Churchland, has not offered a specific model of how moral cognition would be developed in a neural network.

It is interesting and suggestive to note the similarity between Aristotelian ethics and connectionism, and the possibility that character might emerge from a connectionist model of how the brain works. Given that virtues are context-sensitive, the power of connectionism to unite virtue theory and particularism is attractive. However, existing connectionist systems are a long way from tackling the kind of complex learning tasks one associates with moral development. The challenge of implementing virtues within a neural network remains a formidable one.

Hybrid Virtue Ethics

Beyond the difficulties posed by existing neural networks that lack the robustness to tackle complex ethic challenges, connectionist theory does not explain how neuronal activity makes the leap from the unconscious building up of patterns to the consciousness of a pattern. Generally, one expects that moral agents can both act appropriately and justify their actions. Hopefully, the justification of a moral judgment is tied to the actual reason the agent made the judgment and not merely a tale fabricated after the fact.

In a dialogue between Paul Churchland and the cognitive philosopher Andy Clark in the 1990s, Clark raised the question of whether connectionist learning alone is enough to explain the development of moral cognition.

> Historically, the bias of computational cognitive science is toward the individual. Ethical theory, by contrast, has concerned itself from the outset with individuals considered as parts of larger social and political wholes. The attempt to formulate a joint image of moral cognition helps correct the historical biases of each tradition. The ethicist is asked to think about the individual mechanisms of moral reason. The cognitive scientist is reminded that moral reason involves crucial collaborative, interpersonal dimensions. Perhaps neither party strictly requires the other to remind it of the neglected dimensions. But in practice, it is often the joint confrontation of the issues that yields progress in the search for an integrated image.

Clark's vision is that of a complementarity between the bottom-up forces that form an individual's moral sensibility and the top-down considerations regarding the relationship of the individual to the community. However, the discussion between Clark and Churchland stayed at an abstract level. The details of how a connectionist learning system might be combined with a top-down architecture that accommodates social and political considerations while providing explanations tied to the reasons a judgment was made await the attention of enterprising researchers. In chapter 11 we'll discuss a hybrid platform of top-down and bottom-up approaches toward a more human-like AMA that is a step in that direction. But first, let's look at a few basic experiments directed at implementing moral decision making in computer systems.

Chapter 9

First Steps

Autonomous moral agents are coming. But where are they coming from? In this chapter, we describe software that is being designed with ethical competency in mind. Full AMAs are still "vaporware"—a promise no one knows how to fulfill. But software design has to start somewhere, and these projects provide the steam needed to drive the mental turbines that will generate further research.

In this chapter, we'll canvass three general approaches to ethical software. Logic-based approaches attempt to provide a mathematically rigorous framework for modeling ethical reasoning in a rational agent. Case-based approaches explore various ways of inferring or learning ethically appropriate behavior from examples of ethical or unethical behavior. Multiagent approaches investigate what happens when many agents following various ethical strategies interact with one another. It's likely that there are other approaches than these three, but they are the only ones being applied where some research into actual coding has already commenced.

Logically Moral

Selmer Bringsjord, director of Rensselaer Polytechnic Institute's AI and Reasoning Laboratory, sees logic as the best hope for AMAs. Bringsjord believes that humans can, and should, demand proof of the correctness and trustworthiness of their (ro)bots. But to make the ethical correctness of the behavior specified by a program provable, that program would have to be written in terms of the very same ethical concepts appearing in the proof. (Correct proofs aren't magical: they don't pull rabbits out of hats.) Thus, a provable ethical program would have to contain logical operators that refer to the relevant ethical facts. Bringsjord's approach: write programs that use "deontic logics"— systems of logic that describe relationships among duties and obligations.

Deontic logics allow reasoning about what agents ought to make happen. This requires a way of representing what ought to be the case (an "operator," in the logician's jargon) and some rules for manipulating statements that use the new operator. In addition to the basic logical machinery, it's necessary to represent the specific obligations of different agents in different contexts. And because different theories may specify different obligations, there are as many deontic logics as there are ethical theories. But once a set of obligations has been fully encoded as a deontic logic, the approach has the advantage that very well-understood methods of theorem proving can be applied to the resulting formulas.

The Rensselaer group has implemented some different deontic logics and used software reasoning techniques on them. In one example, in which a (ro)bot needs to decide whether to turn off life support (our worst nightmare), they implemented a simple utilitarian deontic logic and, using theorem-proving software that is widely available, were able to generate proofs about the relative adequacy of different ethical codes for ensuring the desired outcomes. But in another example, they found that the logic led to a contradiction when dealing with some common-sense descriptions of obligations. It seems plausible that AMAs will need to be able to reason about what should happen *after* an obligation has been violated, so Bringsjord and his colleagues conclude that the logic must be modified in some way to handle this. They are actively pursuing this challenge.

A rigorous, logic-based approach to software engineering requires AMA designers to formulate, up front, a consistent ethical code for any situation where they wish to deploy an AMA. Bringsjord admits that the approach will never be suitable for inserting AMAs into situations where humans themselves cannot say what the relevant principles are for making life-or-death decisions. Logic does have its limits, and in Bringsjord's view the costs of building AMAs without respecting these limits may be the future imagined by Bill Joy in an influential article he wrote for *Wired* in 2000: a future that doesn't need us. As Bringsjord and colleagues put it in their 2006 research article, "all bets are off if we venture into amoral territory."

Perhaps Bringsjord is right that top-down, logic-based approaches are the only ones that can be trusted for fully autonomous deployment. Nevertheless, other researchers have their eyes on less autonomous applications and are pursuing programming approaches that can support ethical reasoning in a variety of applications. The three case-based approaches we describe next use different methods for generalizing from specific cases of ethical decision making. The first approach is MedEthEx by Susan and Michael Anderson, which we have mentioned earlier. MedEthEx learns how to weigh duties against each other from the decisions made about specific cases by medical ethics experts when duties conflict. The SIROCCO and Truth-Teller systems implemented by Bruce McLaren use "casuistic" reasoning—an approach to reasoning from cases that proceeds by finding analogies rather than using top-down principles to guide decisions. Our third example is Marcello Guarini's connectionist approach to generalizing ethical decision making.

The developers of MedEthEx begin by adopting W. D. Ross's theory of prima facie duties, which they apply specifically to medical situations. The three duties (autonomy, beneficence, and nonmaleficence) they adopt from Ross's longer list are also known as *principles* in bioethics, and the ethical theory based on them is called "principlism." A prima facie duty is one that can be overridden by another duty. For instance, a physician who has a prima facie duty to provide the most effective medical treatment may also run up against another prima facie duty to respect the autonomy of a patient who is refusing medical treatment. How are such conflicts to be resolved? On a pure deontic logic approach, it would be necessary to specify in advance some higher principles that would allow one to prove that the physician should (or shouldn't) try again to persuade the patient to accept the treatment. However, such principles aren't always specifiable in advance, and even experts may be unable to explain the reasoning that underlies the judgments they would make about particular cases.

MedEthEx uses an inductive logic system based on the Prolog programming language to infer a set of consistent rules from the judgments medical ethics experts have provided about specific cases. The cases used to train the system are represented by sequences of numbers whose values, from $+2$ to -2, indicate the extent to which each prima facie duty is satisfied or violated in that situation. The recommendation of the expert in each of these cases is used by the program to infer how the expert weighed the various duties against each other when choosing between a pair of actions, for example, accepting a patient's decision or trying to convince him to change it. The Andersons tested their system using cases that were coded for the three prima facie duties: nonmaleficence (do no harm), beneficence (improve the patient's health), and autonomy (allow patients to make their own treatment decisions). Four cases where a consensus of experts recommended accepting the patient's decision and four cases where the experts recommended overriding the patient were used to train the system. The Andersons then inspected the decisions suggested by MedEthEx on additional cases.

Through its learning algorithms, MedEthEx builds a set of conditions describing when one action should be preferred over another. In this experiment, the program generated a set of rules for evaluating the possible decisions about the patient's treatment. So, for example, accepting a patient's decision to refuse a life-saving treatment yields a positive gain in autonomy, has a negative effect on beneficence, and has little effect on maleficence (as the physician is not *doing* any harm). The program generates numbers to represent the relative differences between the allowable satisfaction or violation levels of each duty, and applies a threshold to determine whether the expert would be willing to accept the violation of a specific duty in order to allow satisfaction of the others.

The approach taken by the Andersons is almost completely top-down— the basic duties are predefined, and the classification of cases is based on those medical ethicists generally agree on. Although MedEthEx learns from cases in what might seem in a sense to be a "bottom-up" approach, these cases are fed into the learning algorithm as high-level descriptions using top-down concepts of the various duties that may be satisfied or violated. The theory is, as it were, spoon-fed to the system rather than it having to learn the meanings of "right" and "wrong" for itself.

The Andersons would not claim that MedEthEx is suitable for autonomous decision making in the clinic, although they do see this kind of software being useful in an advisory role. They do not address the worry we described in chapter 3 of Peter Kahn and Batya Friedman, who argue that computerized advisory systems are likely to erode the autonomy and responsibility of primary caregivers. Of course, even if they should not be deployed in the clinic for this reason, the systems might still be useful for training purposes.

The Andersons see MedEthEx as of interest to ethicists, even if it is not ultimately used by physicians. The system generates rules for weighing the different prima facie duties, enabling ethicists to articulate more general principles that would otherwise be hard to discern in their own decision-making practices. The Andersons note that the system "discovered" or made explicit a decision principle that covered the possible cases.

> The complete and consistent decision principle that the system discovered can be stated as follows: A healthcare worker should challenge a patient's decision if it is not fully autonomous and there is either any violation of the duty of nonmaleficence or a severe violation of the duty of beneficence. Although, clearly, this rule is implicit in the judgments of the consensus of ethicists, we believe that this principle has never before been stated explicitly.

One of the Andersons' declared goals is to incorporate the principles discovered by MedEthEx into the decision procedures of robots. Their latest project is EthEl, which they describe in their article on "Ethical Healthcare Agents." EthEl's task is to remind elderly patients to take their medications.

But when does reminding become unwanted nagging? The Andersons argue that EthEl should balance respect for patients' autonomous wishes to skip medications against the harm that could result from doing so. The particular context in which EthEl operates brings in the element of time sensitivity. The longer a patient goes without the medication, the closer the potential realization of harm becomes. EthEl's decision-making procedure uses a time-based formula for changing the values assigned to the duties of nonmaleficence, beneficence, and respect for autonomy for the various possible actions of reminding, staying silent, or notifying an overseer. For example, after the patient has refused the medicine over a period of hours or days, a doctor could be contacted by the system.

How well will the model underlying MedEthEx and EthEl scale up to dealing with more duties, more cases, and more diversity and disagreement among experts about the "correct" decisions? And could the Andersons' general approach play a role in a hybrid system, acquiring the relevant notions of duty developmentally rather than building them in from the beginning? We don't know, and neither do they. However, they have proposed building a system that generates its own rules as the next project in their research.

Making Cases Explicit

Of course, it is best not to put all one's software eggs in one basket. Bruce McLaren's casuistic systems represent another arena in which software is being applied to ethical reasoning. In some dictionaries, casuistry is defined as a negative term, involving fallacious reasoning. But in ethics and law, the term is associated with a particular approach to decision making that relies on comparing new cases to one or more older cases. A decision on the new case is based on its similarity to the older cases. Such a decision need not involve any explicit theoretical principles—casuistry therefore implements a type of bottom-up approach to ethical decision making.

McLaren's approach is a response to the movement over the past two decades to require instruction in engineering ethics in all accredited engineering programs in the United States. Engineers on the whole have little patience for philosophical abstractions and fictional counterexamples. But they are very familiar with case studies. When a bridge fails, or a ship sinks, or a spacecraft explodes, engineers will study the case from all conceivable angles to try to determine what went wrong.

Exactly these kinds of case studies, including the very public analysis of the *Challenger* explosion in the 1980s, fueled the rise of engineering ethics as a teaching discipline. Case studies of disasters revealed that often it was the engineers themselves who had failed, as much or more than the equipment.

Engineers often found themselves with divided loyalties, weighing obligations to employers against obligations to vaguely defined notions of public safety.

To teach engineers about utilitarianism and deontology could be counterproductive, because philosophers tend to go straight for the controversies. Their goal is to understand what distinguishes the various theories. To repeat the point we made in chapter 5, this is the difference between the agent-centered perspective of the engineer and the judge-centered perspective of the philosopher. To the typical undergraduate engineer, however, it can seem as though the philosophers' approach to ethics is just the game of choosing whichever theory lets you justify what you intended to do anyway.

The case-study methodology applied to engineering ethics imposes a kind of rigor by forcing engineers to identify the factors framing the problem, comparing these factors across cases, and evaluating the courses of action suggested by different cases. Instead of focusing on big theories, the methodology is detail-oriented. In many ways, the difference in approach mirrors the difference between the applied science of engineering and the theoretical abstractions of physics.

McLaren has developed a "Truth-Teller" system that compares two cases, outlining their differences and similarities. As its name suggests, Truth-Teller limits its purview to cases where an agent may or may not be obliged to reveal the truth—for example, a lawyer who may only sometimes be required to reveal his or her inexperience handling a particular kind of case. McLaren followed a traditional symbol-processing approach to represent the reasons for and against telling the truth, and the professional and personal relationships among the agents involved. Comparing two cases then becomes the task of comparing the reasons and relationships between them, a task McLaren implemented using traditional machine reasoning techniques. The result is a program that can analyze the compared situations, and describe the reasons that agents might give for or against telling the truth in the new situation.

The task of framing the problem becomes, from an AI perspective, the task of finding a suitable representation scheme appropriate for the application of machine reasoning to the cases. McLaren's initial approach deliberately skips the hard work of translating from ordinary English descriptions of cases to the formal data structures required for machine reasoning. The real intelligence in this system lies with the human operator taking the cases and representing the reasons that might be applied in those situations. Truth-Teller alone is not capable of this, but is instead fed a predigested version of the cases.

McLaren was well aware that Truth-Teller represents only the first step on the way to real moral reasoning abilities. His "System for Intelligent Retrieval of Operationalized Cases and Codes" (SIROCCO) is the second step. Like its predecessor, this system is also the product of engineers' attempts to guide their ethical behavior on the basis of previous cases. The system is based on the professional code of ethics that has emerged from decades of engineering experience, and taps into a database of over five hundred cases that have been reviewed by the NSPE. Given a new case to evaluate—for example whether an engineer has an ethical obligation to inform a client of her suspicions about some potentially hazardous material—SIROCCO looks for possibly relevant prior cases and possibly relevant lines from the NSPE code of ethics.

The integration of Truth-Teller and SIROCCO is an obvious next step. One major hurdle is that the two applications do not presently use the same representation scheme. Matching the way SIROCCO and Truth-Teller represent cases would open up new possibilities. For instance, the computer could automatically search for other cases similar to the initial case and outline the ways the initial case is truly similar and different from each example it discovers. Presumably, this might then lead to a prioritization of the most similar cases and the prospect of the machine recognizing patterns or rules illustrated by those cases.

Truth-Teller and SIROCCO are both decision support tools rather than autonomous decision makers. Truth-teller helps users find relevant comparisons between two cases; McLaren conceives of SIROCCO as a tool for collecting relevant information from a database of cases and codes. Nevertheless, one can imagine a future case-based AMA constantly perusing databases to update its understanding of rules and their application in exceptional situations. In this way, it might be possible to design an AMA whose application of rules or other constraints dynamically accommodates legal precedents and emerging guidelines.

McLaren's SIROCCO depends on being able to represent the relevant features of the cases and produce a report of the possibly relevant prior cases, highlighting elements of the NSPE code that may be in conflict. The system uses a more sophisticated representation language than both Truth-Teller and MedEthEx but remains within traditional symbol-processing approaches to AI. Despite the widely presumed limitations of such approaches, we think McLaren's project is to be applauded. The task of designing an adequate representation scheme for ethical cases, containing the information needed for machines to reason about their ethical dimensions, is far from trivial. Whether or not it ultimately leads to sophisticated moral reasoners we'll learn from future attempts to build on this model.

Learning Implicitly from Cases

As we discussed in chapter 8, several philosophers have thought that connectionist approaches to learning and categorization are especially compatible with the idea that moral decisions don't fit neat definitions. Jonathan

Dancy, one of the foremost promoters of moral particularism, was among these philosophers. However, he did not develop any specific models.

Recently, Marcello Guarini, a philosopher at the University of Windsor in Ontario, Canada, has responded to Dancy's suggestion and directly experimented with connectionist models. Guarini implemented a recurrent neural network to do moral classification, that is, a network that uses feedback connections to associate inputs with an internal context. The output of this basic network is a simple classification—either "Acceptable" or "Unacceptable"— of inputs such as "Jill kills Jack to make money" or "Jill kills Jack to defend the innocent." These inputs are represented as coded vectors of ones and zeros, rather than full English statements, and the output is likewise a binary one or zero. After training and refining this basic network with sample cases, Guarini tested its ability to generalize to some novel inputs, comparing its output to students' survey responses to the verbal descriptions of the input. The system eventually attained a 70 percent success rate.

Hoping to extend the approach, Guarini implemented a second network, which he called Metanet, with the task of identifying "contrast cases"—that is, pairs of cases from the basic classification task that differ in only one input feature. For example, two otherwise identical actions might differ only with respect to the number of innocent bystanders who suffer. Contrast cases are most informative about moral decision making when the result for one is acceptable and the other is unacceptable. Guarini's hope was that Metanet could use such cases to revise initial classifications. However, Metanet had only limited success identifying such cases, and Guarini comments that his results have mixed consequences for the philosophical debate about particularism. On the one hand, the basic network classifier doesn't literally consult moral rules or principles, thus seeming to support the particularist point of view. On the other hand, it does not follow that there are no principles that describe its behavior. Furthermore, identifying and refining the principles that it does use may be an important part of sophisticated moral reasoning. Guarini also remarks that his networks are unable to give reasons for their classifications, construct moral arguments, or come up with creative solutions to novel problems.

Guarini is under no delusions about the limited power of his connectionist model. His goals are more philosophical than practical: to test ideas about moral particularism. Here, however, we are emphasizing the practical before the philosophical. Do connectionist approaches have a role to play in the development of AMAs? Almost certainly so, but not in the form of simple, stand-alone classifiers. The patterns of data that go into human moral behavior are vastly larger than a vector of a dozen or so bits representing stripped-down verbal descriptions of complicated moral situations. Rather, the human agent's internal context includes emotions and other feelings. Experiments like Guarini's help clarify these issues by showing the limitations of simple connectionist approaches to moral classification, but in the end a much richer architecture will be needed, perhaps along the lines of the learning intelligent distribution agent model, which we'll discuss in chapter 11.

Aside from needing a richer internal model, all of the implemented systems we have described so far in this chapter ignore most of the external social aspects of moral behavior. Arguably, morality emerges out of interactions among multiple agents who must balance their own needs against the competing demands of others. We turn next to implementations of multiagent systems.

Multibots

Some of the earliest experiments in artificial morality were based in game theory and involved agents competing against one another in simplified artificial worlds. In chapter 7, we introduced Peter Danielson's early ALife experiments with "virtuous robots for virtual games" and the turn toward more complex and realistic environments these experiments prompted for him.

Danielson's recent interest in real-world environments has taken a couple of different paths. One of these is a nascent program of experimentation with actual robots. Another is a major effort to develop software that can support social networking. Danielson's Norms Evolving in Response to Dilemmas (NERD) project focuses on using software to assist people in the democratic negotiation of solutions to ethical issues, rather than serving as an impartial judge or arbiter. The NERD project attempts to uncover the full range of moral views held by people from diverse backgrounds (instead of the extremes that form the focus of most philosophical arguments). Danielson suggests that three lessons from his work with NERD may feed into the design of autonomous moral agents. First, AMAs will need ways of managing reciprocity with a variety of different interactors ("kids, cats, kibitzers, and evildoers," as he puts it). Second, there will not be a one-size-fits-all moral agent, but a variety of different agents filling different roles and suited for different environments. Third, people and artificial agents will need advanced tools to help them see the ethical consequences of actions in a complex world.

Danielson's approach focuses attention on the social nature of ethics. Although he has not yet developed the real-world robotic aspects of his research program, the obvious place to take it is into social robotics. In the next chapter, we discuss research directed at making robots sociable, but we know of no one yet who is building social robots with ethical behavior explicitly in mind. One possible venue for experimenting with ethical behavior in social contexts is the Robosoccer tournaments, in which teams of robots from around the world are pitted against each other. Indeed, graduate students in Gregory O'Hare's group at University College, Dublin, have been using soccer-playing robots as their platform of choice with systems including Mauro Dragone's "Robot Soccer Anywhere" and Brian Duffy's "Social Robot Architecture," among others. Duffy's architecture combines Rodney Brooks–style subsumptive mechanisms with mechanisms for representation-based reasoning that use a standard "belief-desire-intention" (BDI) agent model. These models are commonsensical representations of how the beliefs and desires of reasoning agents interact with their intentions to accomplish their practical goals. We think that the combination of BDI and subsumption architectures looks very useful for merging bottom-up and top-down approaches to AMAs. There is still a very long way to go before robots that play soccer will display ethical behavior, recognize and reward fair play, or punish unfair play, yet the pieces for conducting research on these problems appear to be falling into place.

Virtual environments, for example, the popular website Second Life, are other possible venues for experiments with artificial ethical agents. The rape of one virtual character by another in the virtual world of Second Life not only created alarm among users but also raises its own moral issues, and apparently leaped off the screen and came to the attention of a Belgian court. As virtual worlds evolve, virtual agents will in all likelihood be expected to monitor their own behavior, and Second Life would seem to be a useful platform for conducting experiments with ethically sensitive bots. However, in keeping with our goal for this chapter to get beyond vaporware, we only mention these possibilities in passing.

Robots Who Disobey

Matthias Scheutz is a roboticist at Indiana University who has started to work on ethical behavior in robots. Scheutz's robots don't have android features, and they aren't cute or cuddly. They don't try to convince you that they are trustworthy by playing on your instinctive responses to facial gestures. Rather, Scheutz's robots are designed to engage in a collaborative task with a human being, taking voice commands and giving verbal confirmations and occasional suggestions about what to do next. Targeting Asimov's Second Law, Scheutz has looked at how people react to differences in the autonomy of the robot vis-à-vis obeying human commands. In his experiments, robots had a pair of goals—to record data being dictated by the person, and to transmit that data before its batteries go dead. Some of the participants in the experiment interacted with a robot that always followed the person's instructions. Other participants interacted with a robot that would disregard a command if it was necessary to stop taking data readings and transmit the data before its battery died.

In order to rate the participants' attitudes to the robot, Scheutz asked them five questions before they interacted with it. After the experiment, he asked the same five questions, and eleven more about their experiences during the experiment. (Did they feel that the robot understood their commands? Did they think the robot was trying to cooperate? etc.) The opinions of the participants in the study varied widely. Nevertheless, Scheutz found that the autonomy of the robot, that is, whether it sometimes disobeyed commands, had an influence on their responses. In a follow-up experiment, Scheutz added a change in voice pitch to the robot's speech as an indicator of urgency. When stress or fear rises, so does the pitch of human voices. Scheutz's robot spoke at a higher pitch as the time to battery failure approached, the condition in which disobedience to a direct command could occur. With this addition of a simple emotional cue, subjects who experienced the robot's disobedience were more likely to agree with the statement that "it is a good idea for robots to have their own goals and be somewhat autonomous rather than fully controlled by people."

Even though his robot isn't deceptively cuddly, Scheutz worries about the ethical implications of adding an emotional cue. Is the robot's rising voice pitch deceptive? The robot isn't really stressed or afraid. It doesn't really feel anything at all. But it may trick people into treating it as if it has such characteristics. This is the programmer's ethical dilemma, not the robot's, which itself is not being deceptive at all. If faking emotions has a positive ethical impact (to use Jim Moor's term), perhaps the programmer is off the hook, so long as this implicit ethical agent is restricted to the narrow range of activities for which it is designed. A more autonomous moral agent would need to decide when deception is permissible and when it is not. But to our knowledge, no one is working on such sophisticated decision making. So before our discussion dissolves again into the cloudy realm of vaporware, let us turn our attention to another approach.

SophoLab

What happens when sophisticated agents meet complex environments? Often it becomes impractical to make predictions without simulating the environment and the behavior. And as the social environment becomes more complex, ethical principles can have unforeseen consequences. Thought experiments are not powerful enough for understanding large-scale interactions among sophisticated agents. Computational experiments offer better prospects.

Vincent Wiegel has developed a system he calls "SophoLab" to model the interactions between multiple agents. Developed to meet Wiegel's 2007 doctoral requirements at the University of Delft, Sopholab represents each individual agent as a merger between a BDI model and a deontic, epistemic, and action logic. Wiegel believes that Sopholab provides a good platform for "experimental computational philosophy." Unlike the much older game-theoretical simulations of ethical behavior, which focused on very simple agents following very simple behavioral strategies, agents in Wiegel's system are represented as having multiple intentions, and plans to carry them out that can change with events. SophoLab permits what Wiegel calls "walk-of-life scenario testing," in which the responses of agents to a full cycle of daily events can be simulated.

Multiagent platforms such as Wiegel's can be used to simulate what happens when very different agents with different sets of intentions and duties interact. For instance, in a large medical system, patients, doctors, nurses, and insurance agents may all have access to private information about the patients. However, none of the parties has access rights to all the information about a client. And while some individuals may be duty bound not to pass the information in their possession on to certain others, or outside certain situations, this does not preclude such information flowing between those individuals by more circuitous routes. Furthermore, some patients may place additional restrictions on who can have access to specific information. Simulations can be used to test the adequacy of privacy rules among complex networks.

SophoLab uses a multiagent software system to create the actual individual artificial agents that are able to reason about who should have access to medical records, credit reports, or other protected information. It simulates various agents that can act across a computer network, and each network may be in a domain that has its own restrictions and protocols. The individual agents are in communication and cooperate with each other in order to achieve their respective goals.

Wiegel told us that "one can think of these agents as small computer programs... with 'a mind of their own,' though still a very, very far cry from anything resembling human intelligence." For future applications, he proposes modeling other situations in which the actions of artificial agents interacting with other agents (who may be functioning under a variety of rule systems) have a significant impact, which is neither entirely predictable nor controllable. Robotic cars that participate in the daily flow of traffic are an example of this challenge. The car may need to violate a traffic law in order to avoid an accident, but in doing so it will also need to weigh the imperative to complete its assignment against the risks its action poses to other traffic participants.

Beyond Vaporware?

Software for ethics is in its infancy. To grow up, it will need something other than "more of the same." As ethicists stress, moral agency requires practical reasoning guided by careful reflection and deliberation. However, in order to behave appropriately in many contexts, artificial agents will require more than reason alone. In the next chapter we discuss the value of emotions (or simulations of emotions), an aptitude for interacting socially, and knowledge of social customs for a moral (ro)bot.

Chapter 10

BEYOND REASON

Why Kirk Trumps Spock

Is reasoning about morally relevant information all that is required for the development of an AMA? Even though Mr. Spock's capacity to reason far exceeded that of Captain Kirk in the *Star Trek* series, the more emotional and intuitive Kirk was presumed by the crew of the *Enterprise* to be a better decision maker. Why? If (ro)bots are to be trusted, will they need additional faculties and social mechanisms, for example emotions, to adequately appreciate and respond to moral challenges? And if so, how will these abilities be integrated with the top-down and bottom-up approaches to moral decision making that we imagined a supportive ethicist providing to the engineering colleague who came looking for help?

Scientific knowledge about the importance of emotions and sociability to human decision making has grown exponentially during the past half century. It is no accident that this deepening appreciation of the subtlety, richness, and complexity of the human mind has emerged concurrently with the attempts of AI engineers to design computer systems with human faculties. Designing functional computerized systems necessitates thinking through each minute operation. Engineers have come to recognize that emotional intelligence, sociability, and a dynamic relationship with the environment are essential for (ro)bots to function competently in social contexts.

The engineer will have to be aware of the latest research on the factors that influence decision making: having emotions, being embodied in the world, and being social animals with social skills—for example, the ability to read nonverbal cues and gestures. In this chapter, we will first outline the importance of suprarational faculties for moral decision making and then describe the tentative steps engineers are taking to implement emotions in artificial systems. In chapter 11, we'll discuss hybrid systems, including those that have social skills and virtues.

Importance of Suprarational Faculties for Moral Decision Making

In chapter 2, we portrayed the evolution of technology toward moral agency along two dimensions: increases in autonomy and increases in sensitivity to morally relevant information. From a traditional philosophical perspective, autonomy is tightly connected to rationality and normativity, concepts that have been central to ethics. The availability of morally relevant information, however, has seemed to traditional ethicists to be less central to their concerns. They wish to distinguish what an agent *is* sensitive to, its actual moral psychology, from what *ought* to be the case. Ethicists have long recognized that shame, guilt, and other emotions play a central role in regulating human behavior, but ethicists are more concerned with whether they should play that role.

Claims that emotions and other suprarational faculties actually provide the basis for morality itself are particularly controversial. For example, social psychologist Jonathan Haidt of the University of Virginia argues that disgust is a moral emotion. Traditional ethicists would insist on maintaining a strict separation between disgust reactions and moral categories. Again, it comes down to respecting the is/ought distinction. The fact that some people do move from disgust reactions to moral claims (e.g., claiming that homosexuality is wrong because it is disgusting) is, the traditional ethicist points out, a lamentable mistake, not a serious contribution to moral philosophy.

The ins and outs of this debate are considerably more subtle than we can discuss here; fortunately, we can sidestep these issues. In our discussion of emotions, feelings, and social mechanisms, we will concentrate on how they provide additional channels for acquiring morally relevant information. The practical goal of building AMAs requires, we argue, attention to these suprarational capacities. Although emotions and feelings can bias decisions toward unethical acts, they are also rich sources of information that may be difficult to derive in other ways. Fear, for example, involves a felt bodily response to a dangerous situation that requires attention. Often, fear is felt before the mind consciously registers the cause of the danger.

The words "feeling" and "emotion" are typically used to refer to different things. For example, it may be correct to talk about feelings of pain, but pain is not normally considered an emotion (although pain may *cause* emotions, for example anger or sadness). Emotions themselves also typically involve feelings (e.g., sadness may involve a kind of aching sensation or a feeling of lethargy). Scientists and philosophers often classify both feelings and emotions under the umbrella term "affective" states, leading to fields of research such as "affective neuroscience" and "affective computing". Terminology aside, for our purposes the most important point is that feelings and emotions present comparable challenges for AI.

Affective states are crucial components of the prosocial responses that motivate normal moral behavior. (These are responses that appear to be lacking in many psychopaths.) Emotions and feelings help people to intuit the mental states of others and to be sensitive to their needs. One's own experiences of pain seem to be a necessary condition for empathy with the pain of others (although the capacity to feel pain is not sufficient for empathy). Emotions help one discern how a given course of action is affecting and will affect others. When one sees fear on the face of another and realizes that one is the source of that fear, this knowledge contributes to one's ability to modulate one's actions and thereby alleviate the other person's anxiety. Ethical reasoning would have very little motivational force if humans lacked concern for how their behaviors make others feel.

We have noted that the ability to read the emotions of others would be helpful for a service robot interacting with people in the home. The robot should recognize when the people it interacts with are in distress or frightened. But emotions aren't the whole story. A robot interacting with humans in a social context should be capable of making social gestures that indicate its intentions, allowing people to form appropriate expectations about its behavior. Consider the way two people coordinate bringing a large piece of furniture into a house—verbal expressions and subtle movements all convey the ongoing intention to work together toward the successful completion of this difficult job. If no one else is available, it would be wonderful to have the help of a robot with such a laborious task, but only if one could rely on active coordination of actions with the robot. Social mechanisms—for example, the ability to read one another's facial expressions or emotions—contribute to refinements of behavior that people expect from each other, and will also be necessary for robots if they are to function to a high degree of competence within social contexts.

The importance of emotional intelligence and social skills raises the question of the extent to which an artificial agent must emulate human faculties to function as an adequate moral agent. Morality is a distinctly human enterprise. Thus it is natural that humans would try to reproduce human skill sets in designing an AMA that lives up to humans' moral standards. The substantiation of human skills within AI holds a fascination of its own. But computers, as they are at present, are very different from humans, having both advantages and disadvantages in comparison to humans. Computers might be better than humans in making moral decisions, insofar as they can very quickly receive and analyze large quantities of information (provided it is appropriately formatted) and can rapidly consider alternative options (again provided that the options are easily represented). Furthermore, their lack of genuine emotional states would make them less vulnerable to emotional hijacking. This is an important reason for Ronald Arkin's belief that battlefield robots will behave morally better than human soldiers operating under similar circumstances. Humans, however, are far superior to computers in managing information that is incomplete, contradictory, or unformatted, and in making decisions when the consequences of actions cannot be easily determined.

Computer intelligence is built on a logical platform free from desires, drives, and goals other than those that engineers design into the system. Human cognitive faculties evolved from and develop alongside an instinctive emotional platform directed at survival and procreation. This difference underscores the paradoxical quality of the challenge of developing computers with emotions. Just as Deep Blue II beat Gary Kasparov by playing chess in a manner different from the way a human would play, it is quite conceivable that an artificial agent might display moral judgment without utilizing the same cognitive or affective tools a human moral agent would apply.

Human interactions follow a dance that is shaped by the actions of others, and involves one's own and others' embodied responses to changes in the world, the way they respond to one's actions, one's intuitions about their intentions, and one's knowledge of the range of appropriate responses in the specific social context. When one person moves into another person's space, there can be a variety of responses. If the person is perceived as invading one's space, one is likely to automatically recoil (unless, say, one was already spoiling for a fight). Recoiling at the invasion of one's space is an emotionally activated, embodied, social response. The actions, words, intonation, facial expressions, and body posture of the other person before and after one recoils all contribute to how one interprets the other's intent. Furthermore, what might be considered personal space varies from one cultural context to another.

The most natural approach for an engineer focused on introducing social skills, emotions, and embodied responses into a (ro)bot is to break each of these down into discrete inputs leading to corresponding actions. However, it will be essential that system designers do not lose sight of the way these suprarational faculties are dynamically entangled. A vocal intonation that may be threatening in one context may be laughable in another.

Moral agents without affective or advanced cognitive faculties will function adequately in many domains, but it will be important to recognize when additional capabilities will be needed. In the following sections, we discuss some limited steps that can be taken toward implementing suprarational faculties. Throughout this discussion, it will be necessary to keep an eye on what is lost in a system that is capable of making rational decisions but has limited emotional intelligence, is socially inept, and is not embodied in the world. It is far from clear whether these limitations can be compensated for in other ways.

Emotional Intelligence

To what extent is the development of appropriate emotional reactions a crucial part of normal moral development? If crucial, how might these responses be instantiated in a machine?

The relationship of emotions to ethics is an ancient issue that also has resonance in science fiction. Are the emotion-suppressing Vulcans of *Star Trek* inherently capable of better behavior than the more intuitive, less rational, more exuberant humans from Earth? Does Spock's utilitarian mantra "The needs of the many outweigh the needs of the few" represent the rational pinnacle of ethics as he engages in an admirable act of self-sacrifice? Or do the subsequent efforts of Kirk and the rest of the *Enterprise*'s human crew to risk their own lives out of a sense of personal obligation to their friend represent a higher pinnacle of moral sensibility?

In addition to Mr. Spock, *Star Trek* also introduced the superrational android Data, who goes berserk when an "emotion chip" is introduced into his circuitry. Data's response exemplifies a very long tradition in Western philosophy of focusing on the way emotions can interfere with or bias rational decision making and of minimizing the contribution that emotions make to good moral judgment. The dominant philosophical view, going back to the Greek and Roman Stoic philosophers, has been that moral reasoning should be dispassionate and free of emotional prejudice. This has been presumed to mean that emotions should be banned entirely from moral reflection. Stoics believed that taming one's passionate "animal nature" and living under the rule of reason was the key to moral development. Among later moral philosophers, many shared the view that emotions were of little or no help in dealing with one's moral concerns.

A few philosophers, most prominently Blaise Pascal and David Hume, argued that at least some emotions—compassion, pity, care, and love—are conducive to a moral life. Anticipating a perspective Sigmund Freud would later elucidate, they both viewed emotions as antecedent to reason. Emotions could never be fully managed by reason. "Reason is, and ought to be, the slave of the passions," Hume wrote.

Aristotle represents a third view of the relationship between ethics and emotions. He held that emotions play a significant role in determining what actions are virtuous, but he also expected the virtuous individual to hold emotions in check. This middle way acknowledges that emotions in the extreme can have a negative affect but in balance can contribute positively toward good character or virtuous behavior.

This Aristotelian theme was given a modern incarnation in 1990, when psychologists Peter Salovey and John "Jack" Mayer introduced the concept of emotional intelligence, an idea that was later popularized in the title of the 1995 bestseller by journalist and science writer Daniel Goleman. The phrase *emotional intelligence* captures the understanding that there are dimensions of intelligence other than IQ. The awareness and management of one's own emotions, learning from the information implicit in emotions, and recognizing the emotional states of those with whom one interacts are all special forms of intelligence. Implicit in the concept of emotional intelligence is the recognition that emotions are complex and influence behavior in a variety of ways. Despite such inroads into popular culture, suspicion of the way emotionally driven prejudices and desires bias and distort judgment continues in society. But people are also increasingly aware of the information and even wisdom that can be derived from emotional input. So while AMAs may not require emotions of their own, they will need access to some of the same kinds of information and wisdom that humans acquire through their emotions.

When it comes to making ethical decisions, the interplay between rationality and emotion is complex. The nature of this complexity depends on how one views emotions. Philosopher Jesse Prinz identifies five classes of emotional theory (plus various hybrids among them). Feeling theories emphasize the conscious experiential aspects of emotions. Somatic theories emphasize the bodily processes associated with emotions. Behavioral theories identify emotions with specific behavioral responses. Processing-mode theories emphasize the role of emotions in modulating other mental activities. And pure cognitive theories emphasize the role of beliefs in emotions.

Of these five, two focus on product: feeling theories and behavior theories. The other three focus on process. From an engineering perspective, the approaches that focus on process are more likely to suggest ways of implementing emotions, so we will concentrate on those. Processing mode theories and cognitive theories have the best chance of building on top of existing approaches to AI. For instance, a processing-mode change could be implemented by changing the parameters controlling other perceptual or cognitive processes, as when happiness is correlated with increased activity in certain parts of the brain while sadness is associated with a decrease in those areas. Somatic theories present more of a challenge, because it is not obvious how to integrate bodily processes into intelligent systems, nor is it known how crucially a robot's emotions would depend on the details of anatomy and physiology. How much would robot bodies have to emulate human bodies in order to have similar emotions?

We'll further narrow our attention to cognitive versus somatic approaches. This is not because we find processing-mode theories uninteresting or implausible, but because they seem concerned with setting parameters that are internal to the brain and hence less obviously connected to ethical or moral evaluation. Cognitive approaches clearly involve judgments about states of affairs that are morally relevant. Somatic reactions—for example, feeling sick to one's stomach at the sight of someone being mistreated—are also easily connected to moral issues. Both cognitive and somatic theories are thus concerned with the horizontal axis of figure 1 in chapter 2, concerning the extent to which AMAs will require sensitivity to morally relevant information.

Computational Challenges for
Cognitive or Somatic Theories

From the point of view of traditional AI, pure cognitive approaches seem the most attractive, since they involve representation of conditions that matter to the survival and well-being of an organism. Hence, for example, on a cognitive account like that of psychologist Richard Lazarus, fear may be characterized as a judgment by an organism that it is "facing an immediate, concrete, and overwhelming physical damage." Insofar as such judgments (or "appraisals," to use the jargon of the psychologists) can be represented in the same way as any other judgment, engineers who want to implement emotions in a (ro)bot can use the same sorts of knowledge representation approaches they use for any other domain of human knowledge.

One source of complexity in such an approach comes from deciding how many emotions there are and what they represent. Lazarus, who was one of the leading emotions researchers until his death in 2002, constructed a table of fifteen "core relational themes" distinguishing anger, anxiety, fright, guilt, shame, sadness, envy, jealousy, disgust, happiness, pride, relief, hope, love, and compassion. The judgment implicit in a particular emotion could also vary as the context changes. Engineers might also elect to expand this list if they felt that would be helpful in developing a subtler repertoire of responses.

Purely cognitive approaches to the emotions also seem rather inadequate, insofar as the mere judgment that one faces an imminent threat, without any accompanying feeling of fear, seems insufficient to characterize the emotion. In the late nineteenth century, William James, the enormously influential Harvard psychologist, asked his colleagues to imagine an emotion, subtracting out all bodily aspects—fear, say, without a pounding heart, dry mouth, and so on. What was left, he claimed, would not be an emotion at all. James thereby proposed a somatic theory of emotions. As an objection to purely cognitive theories of emotions, James's thought experiment has a lot of intuitive strength. From the point of view of designing AMAs, however, it's less clear that the information received from somatic sources is the only possible channel for the morally relevant information that is important to ethical behavior.

This issue goes to the heart of questions about the nature of sociopathic behavior, because, as a matter of fact if not of principle, it seems that appropriate emotional responses are major determinants of ethical behavior. *Could* it be otherwise? Perhaps. However, for the engineer who has the task of building an AMA, it seems reasonable to use what is known about the actual ethical nature of human beings.

Here a somatic approach seems to be at least part of the story. And if it is a part of the story, it's a huge and complicated part. Building the somatic architecture for a (ro)bot is a major undertaking, but one for which initial progress is being made by roboticists who are pursuing goals other than the project of building an AMA. We'll review of some of these research projects. But before getting into the details of somatic processes, we need to say a little more about the way a somatic account of the emotions may be part of a hybrid approach.

On the basis of his studies of patients with damage to their affective systems, the neuroscientist and physician Antonio Damasio adopts a somatic account of what he calls (primary emotions)—fast, embodied reactions that are closely associated with instinctual reflexes and drives. But he also notes that cognitive mechanisms can reuse primary emotions to guide behavior as a result of learned associations, thought, and reflection. He calls these "secondary emotions." Primary emotions may have evolved to enable biological organisms to bypass slower decision-making processes, while secondary emotions allow the same circuitry to be exploited for more sophisticated purposes. If speed is the main issue, primary emotional responses might not be necessary for AMAs. Digital circuitry is intrinsically much faster than neural circuitry, although there is much more to deliberative decision making than simple wiring. Presumably, however, even if some deliberative evaluation of the threat is involved, AMAs can be designed to respond to dangers quickly. Nevertheless, the (ro)bot will require a mechanism that performs the function of primary emotions in quickly determining which challenges pose immediate threats that must be responded to without delay.

In humans, the melding of sensory input, thoughts, and memories gives rise to a rich repertoire of secondary emotions. Neuroscientists are just beginning to probe how secondary emotions emerge through a network of feedback loops between the emotional centers in the brain and the prefrontal cortex, the region that governs reason and planning. The importance of secondary emotions in decision making was underscored by Damasio in his research on patients for whom the link between the emotional and reasoning centers had been severed. In what has become one of the best known neurological anecdotes, Damasio tells the story of Eliot, a patient with brain damage to the neural circuitry necessary for processing secondary emotions. Eliot's intelligence is above average, but he reports having very few emotions. Eliot is also incapable of making even simple decisions, for example setting an appointment date. Evidently some emotional input is integral to rational decision making.

The emerging picture is one in which neither reason nor feelings normally dominate decision making but emotions may help with the selection of a course of action. The medieval philosopher Jean Buridan invented a story about an ass who starved to death because he could not choose between two equal bales of hay. Buridan's ass was obviously not a normal animal; a real ass would have had his reasoned indecision short-circuited by increasingly urgent feelings of hunger. Jaak Panksepp, a founding figure in the field of affective neuroscience, has studied the laughter of rats during play, and the pleasure they get from being tickled. Panksepp emphasizes the role of emotions in helping organisms to select from a repertoire of responses to differing contexts and challenges. Panksepp argues that emotions shortcut impossibly complicated cognitive calculations about what to do, thus they serve as "affective heuristics."

Neuroscientists have proposed that humans have two different decision-making pathways in the brain, an affective pathway and a cognitive pathway. In fMRI images of individuals working through emotionally laden moral challenges, the centers that "light up" in the brain are different from the ones involved in more analytical challenges. There is nevertheless considerable disagreement as to how closely the two different pathways are integrated.

Three interrelated principles illuminate how sensory processing could develop into a sophisticated system for selecting among different actions or behavior streams: (1) emotions have valences; (2) organisms are homeostatic systems; and (3) emotional systems learn through reinforcement of responses to stimuli that have led to successful attainment of goals, and decay of responses to those that have failed to do so. To say that organisms should be understood as homeostatic systems means that they naturally try to reestablish equilibrium after each divergence from a stable range or comfort zone. For example, over time all organisms diverge from having an optimal or satisfactory supply of energy. The feelings arising from a low energy state are said to activate behavior directed at finding food or resting. Behavior that leads to the replenishment of energy is reinforced, while behavior that doesn't is overridden.

These three principles are generally accepted. Exactly how they operate in the human brain is less well established. Damasio's "somatic markers" hypothesis provides one framework for understanding how rich emotional decision making emerges. The basic theory is that somatic markers simplify decision making by directing the agent to select the options that are most beneficial. Through interactions in the environment, responses to stimuli are reinforced and induce an associated physiological affective state. These associations are stored as somatic markers.

For humans, it is speculated that the storage location is the orbitomedial prefrontal cortex. When these somatic markers are activated or enlisted in future situations, they produce physiological effects that bias decision making in a way that is intended to lead to the successful satisfaction of goals or needs. Damasio hypothesizes that in complex decisions, in which the results are uncertain or the relative difference between options is unclear, the somatic markers for all the possible rewards and punishments produce a composite or net feeling. This feeling is essential for directing (biasing) the selection of an appropriate action. Somatic markers might function as complements to conscious deliberations, but they can also serve unconscious emotional decision making.

In Damasio's view, feelings are somatic markers that expedite decision making by directing a person to one course of action among many possibilities. Feelings—for example hunger, pleasure, various forms of pain, and tiredness—are attached to various action responses. Emotions provide a valence—a negative or positive weight on information being factored into one's judgment. At each possible decision point, the somatic marker labels whether a disposition is good or bad, requiring engagement or aversion. At their worst, such predispositions can function as prejudices that bias and interfere with a person's ability to adequately meet the challenge at hand. Collectively, however, the somatic markers can also be seen as framing the territory of considerations that need to be factored into a judgment. A somatic marker system prunes the decision tree and thereby facilitates decision making. Looked at from another perspective, the network of interrelated somatic markers can be thought of as providing scaffolding on which the capacity to reason is built.

These emotional heuristics are "rules of thumb" that enable people to cut through complexity, frame issues, and make choices. Emotions thus play a central role in what Herbert Simon, one of the founding fathers of AI, called bounded rationality. Simon recognized that people must always make decisions under conditions in which time and information are limited. He introduced the notion of "satisficing," a term that blends *satisfying* and *sufficing*, to capture the idea that such decisions may not be what an unlimited rational agent might deem optimal but need only be "good enough" according to the decision maker's criteria. For example, picking the first option that comes to mind in which no one is physically hurt would satisfy criteria for acceptability, even if further reflection might come up with an even better option. Simon became justly famous for his work on bounded rationality and decision-making processes, eventually winning the Nobel Prize for economics in 1978. Less well known is an article he wrote in 1967 on motivational and emotional controls of cognition in which he specifically laid out the ways emotion might serve the functions of satisficing and setting priorities.

Psychologists Gerd Gigerenzer and Peter Todd believe that some conceptions of bounded rationality still require too much computation on the part of the decision maker, particularly with respect to determining an appropriate threshold for terminating the computation. In their book *Simple Heuristics That Make Us Smart* they propose three distinct roles for heuristics in decision making. Emotions might guide the search for a satisfactory outcome by making certain options seem more or less attractive. They might provide a stopping rule by helping the agent to recognize when no further benefits will derive from continuing to evaluate options. And they may play a role in the specific decisions reached by enabling an agent to rank one choice above all others.

Gigerenzer and Todd's "fast and frugal" approach, using simple heuristics, provides decision-making capacities that work adaptively because they take advantage of the way the agent's environment is structured. Trusting another on the basis of one's emotional response to that person may not be objectively defensible, but works well in an environment where those who provoke such an emotional response tend, in fact, to be trustworthy. Emotions may in this way contribute to a so-called adaptive toolbox of fast and frugal heuristics.

While emotions are beneficial in many circumstances, this is compatible with certain emotions being disadvantageous or even dysfunctional in other circumstances. Recognizing this fact presents an opportunity for engineers to design AMAs whose moral faculties operate in a way that makes them less susceptible to emotional interference or dysfunctionality. Today's AI systems don't have emotions, so they are not susceptible to the emotional biases and emotional flooding or hijackings that interfere with humans' moral judgments. Adding emotions, if technologically feasible, would undoubtedly lead to complex interactions whose effects cannot be fully predicted. Engineers must therefore consider carefully whether the potential benefits of emotions for AMAs exceed the potential costs.

But we are getting ahead of the technology. Testing these suggestions about how suprarational faculties can contribute to moral decision making in (ro)bots would require technological developments that computer scientists are only beginning to tackle. Current research on suprarational faculties focuses largely on perfecting systems that emulate isolated skills, for example, reading the emotions captured in facial expressions. Nevertheless, progress is being made on a range of different research fronts, as we'll now describe.

From Sensory Systems to Emotions

Artificial intelligence engineers acknowledge that humans are a long way from knowing how to develop systems that can feel pleasure or pain, or have human-like emotions. The robots available today do not have nerves, neurochemicals, feelings, or emotions, nor is it likely that robots in the near future will. Nevertheless, sensory technology is an active area of research, and it is here that one might look for the foundations of feelings and emotions. Microphones and charged couple devices (found in digital cameras) are ubiquitous technologies that need no introduction from us. Some of the technological developments relating to the other senses may be less familiar.

Smell and touch are particularly important contributors to human emotions and feelings, and both supply information germane to making moral decisions. The human sense of smell, although less developed than that of many animals, is nevertheless very complex, depending on a network of thousands of specialized receptor neurons. The Cyranose 320, named for the famously large nose of French duelist and poet Cyrano du Bergerac, is the first commercially available handheld electronic sniffer. Based on technology initially developed at the California Institute of Technology, the Cyranose has thirty-two olfactory sensors and is able to match odors to templates preloaded in it software within about ten seconds. It would be a stretch to claim that the Cyranose 320 or similar electronic noses can literally smell things in the same sense that humans and other animals smell. The Cyranose is much slower, and detects a much smaller range of substances. Nevertheless, the device has numerous commercial applications, for example the detection of spoiled food and chemical spills. And since the terrorist attacks of 9/11, the Cyranose has increasingly found its way into security applications. (Although the use of machine olfaction to fight terrorism is ethically laudable, perhaps privacy advocates should be as concerned about olfactory surveillance as they are about video surveillance. Many a tryst has been revealed by a whiff of unfamiliar perfume.)

Despite olfaction's key role in setting moods and the widespread use of scent in religious ceremonies and many other emotion-inducing social contexts, no one, to our knowledge, is investigating the role a sense of smell might play in social robotics. Touch, however, is another story. Engineers in MIT's Robotic Life Group have designed a sensate skin that is embedded with three different types of somatic sensors, which register electric field, temperature, and force. This sensate skin is placed under the fur fabric and silicone skin that covers the surface of "Huggable," an interactive robotic companion modeled on the Gund Company's "Butterscotch" teddy bear.

Huggable is being designed for therapeutic applications, for example in nursing homes. It will nuzzle when hugged and petted, and it also provides feedback about a patient to the nursing station monitoring the patient. Huggable's ability to respond appropriately to social gestures is directly dependent on how accurately the system interprets the patient's gestures. A touch, for example, can be light or hard, squeezing, petting, tickling, patting, or scratching. The MIT engineers have implemented a neural network designed to recognize nine different classes of affective touch—tickling, poking, scratching, slapping, petting, patting, rubbing, squeezing, and contact. These classes of touch are sorted into six response types from "teasing pleasant" to "touch painful," depending on the intensity of the stimulation. The classes each drive a different response from Huggable. Being held pleasantly might, for example, lead to a nuzzling response.

These newer sensory technologies, combined with the much older technologies of cameras and microphones, allow considerable amounts of sensory data to be accumulated. However, the next step—mapping these data onto the feelings and emotions that motivate actions—is more difficult. Emotions and other mental states emerge from a web of inputs from different senses. The ability of the human nervous system to integrate diverse inputs and modulate internal states leads to a broad array of nuanced responses to changing stimuli. The simple classification scheme built into Huggable runs on an embedded Pentium class chip. More complex integrative somatic architectures are clearly within the scope of artificial systems. It remains to be seen whether it is necessary to emulate in AMAs the full range of subtle emotional states evident in humans. The only way to find out is to build progressively more sophisticated systems and test them in realistic situations.

The capacity to understand and empathize with pain is likely to be an important dimension in the development of AMAs. Pain sensations in biological creatures depend on specialized receptors called nociceptors—neurons that are dedicated to detecting noxious stimuli. Pain is not simply the result of high-intensity stimulation of pressure and temperature receptors. Huggable uses thresholds to label stimuli as "unpleasant." Although this fails to capture the subtle operation of the biological pain system, it may provide a reasonable first approximation. Nevertheless, a full system would need to be alert to the fact that in humans, pain is often context-specific and dependent on the integration of a range of factors. For example, in the late autumn one's tolerance for cold is typically much lower than in the winter. Ears burn painfully on the first cold mornings. But as body metabolism readjusts, humans are quite capable of accommodating much colder winter temperatures with ease. A (ro)bot following Asimov's First Law, to do or allow no harm to a human being, would need to be aware of the facts of human pain sensitivity. A quick way to this knowledge is to have the same sensitivities.

While we anticipate the development of neural nets for integrating sensory input from a range of sources, for the near term this data will be translated into cognitive representations of emotions rather than actual somatic states that could be counted as (ro)bots having emotions or feelings of their own. If the actual capacity to feel pleasure and pain is essential for understanding how other people will be affected by different courses of action, (ro)bots will fall short in their discernment and moral acumen, not to mention their ability to be empathetic or compassionate. A truly compassionate (ro)bot is a tall order, and perhaps out of reach as far as any technology known today. What isn't out of reach, however, is the development of artificial systems capable of reading the emotions (minds?) of humans and interacting as if they understand the intentions and expectations of humans.

Affective Computing 1: Detecting Emotions

I ask this as an open question... and I don't know the answer: How far can a computer go in terms of doing a good job handling people's emotions and knowing when it is appropriate to show emotions without actually having the feelings?

—Rosalind Picard

Rosalind Picard's Affective Computing Research Group at MIT wants to make it less frustrating to work with computers. Frustration is an emotion everyone can relate to when dealing with technology that seems stupid and inflexible. A first step on the way to reducing frustration is to have computers and robots that can recognize frustration—in other words, that can recognize an emotion.

But computers and robots don't have telepathy or any special access to people's inner feelings. Engineers are exploring techniques that emulate the ability to read the same nonverbal cues (facial expressions, tone of voice, body posture, hand gestures, and eye movements) that help people understand each other.

This is the relatively new field of affective computing, and it encompasses a variety of different research goals. Modeling and studying human emotions and building systems with the intelligence to recognize, categorize, and respond to those emotions are separate but also overlapping goals for research in affective computing. Most of the research focuses on developing computer systems that recognize and respond appropriately to the emotional states of people interacting with the systems.

What's the quickest route to recognizing a person's emotional state? The dream of many technologists has been one of direct access to the physiology underlying the emotions. Heart rate, skin conductivity, and hormonal levels might all be used to measure when a person is afraid, nervous, or angry. But the fact remains that there are no widespread technologies that could enable (ro)bots to detect such things remotely or covertly. (Furthermore, covert technologies would be considered violations of privacy.) A person must wear a heart rate monitor or be attached to a galvanic skin response machine or give a blood sample for these physiological measures to be available to a (ro)bot. Rosalind Picard and her students are developing interface devices embedded in keyboards or mice that can collect some physiological data. For example, while he was a graduate student in Picard's lab, Carsten Reynolds developed a pressure-sensitive computer mouse as a tool for providing feedback on a user's behavior. Combined with other data, pressure on the mouse may indicate that the user is frustrated.

Another example is the work of British Telecom with an MIT group that has explored methods whereby a speech-recognition interface could detect frustration in the voices of people calling customer service. The system would adapt its responses to the user's emotional state, or transfer the call to a human, or perhaps even apologize. Of course, given that many people are no longer satisfied by perfunctory apologies from a robotic-sounding customer support person, an apology from a computer system could further antagonize those customers. Facilitating ease of use is the goal, but no doubt systems that are effective at defusing frustration also serve the moral goal of minimizing irritations that boil over into people's interpersonal relationships. Furthermore, they would decrease people's anger toward dumb technologies (perhaps saving the "lives" of the telephones and computers that are readily at hand).

There are three parts to alleviating the nearly universal frustration users experience working with stupid technology:

(1) *Detecting* the emotional frustration of the user: This can vary from recognizing the repeated typing of characters to the use of a specially designed interfaces, for example, the mouse designed by Reynolds, which is sensitive to how much pressure the user places on it.

(2) *Putting* that frustration *in context:* Repeated typing, for example, may signal difficulty in spelling or finding the right synonym. Random characters produced by dragging one's hand across the keyboard suggest a deeper frustration.

(3) *Responding or adapting to* the frustration in a way that potentially solves the problem and, at the least, does not further frustrate the user: Having the computer system simply ask, "Is something wrong?" with either text on the screen or through a speech synthesizer might begin a process of alleviating frustration.

Charles Darwin's third book, *The Expression of Emotions in Man and Animals*, established the scientific study of voice and gestures in the 1870s. This work continues with primatologists, for example Franz de Waal, and neuroscientists, for example Jaak Panksepp, researching the animal side of the equation. On the human side, the work of Paul Ekman has been seminal in illuminating people's understanding of facial expressions. Ekman and his students have demonstrated that the basic facial expressions for joy, sadness, fear, surprise, anger, and disgust are shared by all humans and are recognizable across cultures. Ekman catalogued more than two thousand facial expressions as indicators of emotional states. His Facial Action Coding System (FACS) is a primary focus for engineers interested in developing computer systems with affective intelligence.

The FACS tracks the movement of facial muscles, correlating forty-four different "action units"—for example, a raised eyebrow—to specific emotions. Ekman and his collaborator Mark Frank of Rutgers University are among many researchers exploring ways to computerize the FACS. As might be expected, computerized FACS systems are better able to discern basic emotional expressions and the emotional states of individuals in the laboratory and worse at determining subtle facial expressions or the emotional states of people in real-world applications. In addition to identifying facial expressions from constantly changing visual input, FACS systems need to register subtle momentary changes in facial expression and correlate those expressions with data stored in memory. The computational tasks are formidable, but (ro)bots with the ability to discern very basic emotions are on the horizon, and perhaps this is all that will be necessary for the first generation of AMAs.

The FACS systems represent only one approach to machine detection of emotions. Other devices range from sensors that register skin conductivity to chairs that sense whether the sitter is restless or bored. Some engineers believe that they will be able to embed sensors in shoes that could discern and signal when the user is depressed. If this technology works, a caregiver could use it to detect when a loved one has forgotten to take his antidepressants.

Single indicators of human emotional states are notoriously unreliable. For example, the galvanic skin response for excitement is very similar to that for anxiety. Thus, while many engineers work on perfecting individual tools for discerning emotional states, other engineers have directed their research to combining these tools into multimodal systems, for example,

MOUE (Model of User's Emotions). Developed for the health-care industry, MOUE is a multimodal emotion evaluation system that characterizes a patient's emotional state from data it retrieves from a number of sources. Heart rate, breathing pattern, temperature, and other physiological indicators, along with vocal characteristics and facial expressions, all contribute to MOUE's interpretation of a patient's sensorimotor and physiological states. The MOUE also has some basic language-processing capabilities that allow it to evaluate the patient's subjective description of her mental and emotional experience. The computer passes a description of the patient's emotional and mental state to health-care providers, along with video imagery, audio recordings, and the quantitative data it has collected.

Designers of emotionally sensitive AMAs *could* adopt the kind of technology used in MOUE. However, those who experiment with and use devices that can detect the emotional states of others confront a major privacy hurdle. Will computer users want their personal computers to allow access to such information? Should other computational devices have access to this information without written informed consent, or at least a basic contract between the user and the researcher or institution behind the device? Rosalind Picard and her former student Carsten Reynolds have struggled with how to handle the perception some users may have that technology that accesses their emotional states violates their privacy. However, many people will embrace the technology if it makes their interactions with computers less frustrating.

Affective Computing 2: Modeling and Using Emotions

Computer scientists have begun to experiment with computational models of emotion and decision making. With the usual caveats about the huge gulf between these models and the real biological phenomena, we'll describe several of these models and discuss their potential utility for the design of AMAs. First we discuss the OCC, a computerized cognitive model of the emotions developed by (and named after) Andrew Ortony, Gerald Clore, and Allan Collins. Then we'll turn to robotic experiments that capture aspects of learning and emotional decision making.

Cognitive Emotions: The OCC

In the OCC, emotions are represented as positive or negative ("valenced") responses to situations. The model classifies situations according to whether they are desirable or whether the organism wishes them to stop. The OCC is considered a *cognitive* model because it treats emotions as derived from a representation of the events, agents, and objects in the world, and an analysis of whether the agent's goals, desires, and intentions are being satisfied. For instance, the pleasure of winning a competition would be inferred if the program represents the agent as having the desire to win. The affective intensity of a situation is also computed from the cognitive representation of the situation.

The OCC has twenty-two categories of valenced responses that it applies to goal-oriented events, actions for which the agent will be held accountable, and attractive or unattractive objects. Each of these valenced responses is mapped onto one of four basic emotions: joy, sadness, fear, or anger. These in turn are mapped onto the corresponding Ekman facial expressions. Pleasure from winning a competition would, for example, be mapped to the basic Ekman facial expression for joy. Only four of Ekman's basic six expressions (joy, sadness, fear, and anger) are defined in the OCC model. Ortony, Clore, and Collins assumed that the other two basic Ekman expressions (surprise and disgust) do not involve much cognitive processing. Thus, the OCC is a model for a very limited range of emotions. Nevertheless, it has been widely used for animating cartoon and virtual characters in the entertainment and computer game industries. Unlike FACS, which takes a facial expression as input and infers the emotional state of the agent, OCC works in the opposite direction: it attempts to model the emotions the agent itself possesses, treating the associated facial expressions as output.

Models of Cognitive and Emotional Decision Making in AI

A highly influential conceptual model for how affect and cognition interact is CogAff, developed by Aaron Sloman, a philosopher at the University of Birmingham, with the help of Ron Chrisley, a philosopher at Sussex University. CogAff was developed as a model of cognition for computer scientists designing autonomous systems. Different levels of cognitive processing allow for different levels of control in an agent. Sloman and Chrisley distinguish three such levels that can be implemented for the architecture of an autonomous agent: the reactive, the deliberative, and "metamanagement." For all practical purposes, the reactive level refers to the affective mechanisms, but these three layers interact in their model.

Artificial intelligence researchers have explored the application of the principles of emotional valence, homeostasis, and reinforcement in the design of emotional decision-making systems. Marvin Minsky, in his book *The Emotion Machine*, proposes that emotions serve to limit the range of actions considered. Reasoning mechanisms can then go to work more efficiently on this restricted set of options. An alternative approach envisages a role for affective states in experience-based learning. Positively valenced feedback reinforces successful behavior patterns, or negative valences can motivate a switch to other behaviors when the current actions are unsuccessful. Hence, the agent might "feel" its way through a challenge posed by the environment, learning as it goes. Reason and feel can also be combined through experimentation and planning.

Perhaps the biggest challenge facing designers of (ro)bots with affective intelligence is whether to try and capture emotional decision making as an independent process or treat emotions as a particular type of input to a standard cognitive decision-making process. Which is better, one process or two? Early simulations of robots with both affective and cognitive decision-making systems suggest that having two processes enhances the systems' overall learning capabilities.

Sandra Gadanho formerly at the Institute for Systems and Robotics in Lisbon and now at Motorola, has explored how learning in an emotional decision-making system of a robot compares with learning in a cognitive deliberative system. Khepera robots, which are rapidly becoming the robotic equivalent of laboratory mice, were the subjects in the experiments Gadanho conducted while in Portugal. Khepera robots are tiny circular vehicles 55 millimeters (two inches) in diameter that run on wheels and are equipped with infrared and ultrasonic sensors. They can also be attached to computers to track their actions or feed their systems new data. Because these robots are so small, experiments with them can be set up in a very small space. They are also quite easy to adapt for use in multi-robot experiments. They have been used for experiments designed around basic tasks, for example obstacle avoidance, following walls, target searches, and the study of collective behavior.

In Gadanho's experiment, a single Khepera robot is placed in a simple closed maze environment. The robot is equipped with eight sensors (six on front and two on the rear) that facilitate its ability to detect objects and ambient light. The robot can select from three basic behaviors: avoid walls, seek lights, and wall following. The goal of the robot is to survive by maintaining an adequate level of energy. The robot acquires energy through two lights, which its sensors detect, that are placed on opposite corners of the maze. However, the energy is only available from a light for a short period of time. Nor can the robot survive on energy from a single source. So the robot needs to learn how to acquire energy from multiple light sources while minimizing the energy it loses navigating the maze.

The details of Gadanho's experiments are beyond our purposes here. What is relevant here is that some versions of her emotion-based robots use controllers that are designed to apply reinforcement-learning techniques

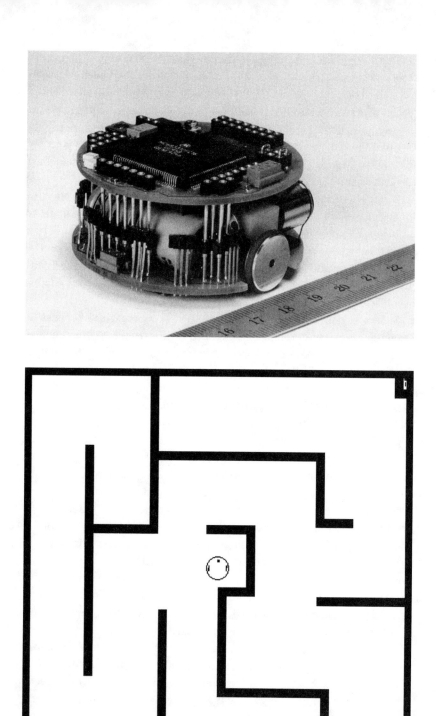

Figures 10.1 and 10.2. The Khepera robot (above) and its simulated environment (below). 10.1 courtesy of k-team; 10.2 courtesy of Sandra Gadanho.

(pleasant and unpleasant factors act as reinforcers of behavior). Others have a goal system that doesn't model emotions explicitly but attempts to identify properties that will help the robot work properly. The goals for robots in this second group are based on three homeostatic variables that the robot attempts to maintain within an acceptable range: energy, welfare (avoid collisions), and activity (keep moving). Divergence from the comfort zone of these three variables activates behavioral responses in the robots. Measures of decreasing divergence from the comfort zone provide the experimenter with empirical evidence that the robot is learning successful behavior patterns. The performance of robots with these two different designs was competent and quite similar, although the robots whose learning was based around maintaining the homeostatic goals did slightly better than those with the simpler explicitly emotion-based system.

In a third group of experiments, Gadanho deployed robots using what she names the asynchronous learning by emotion and cognition (ALEC) architecture. In these robots, she adds a cognitive system to the robots with either the original explicit emotion-based goal system or with the slightly better performing homeostatic version. The cognitive system is composed of a dynamic collection of rules that allow the robot to make decisions on the basis of what it has learned through past trials. There are distinct differences between the learning capabilities of the emotion and the cognitive systems. The emotion system can store all events but has no way of distinguishing one event from another, while the cognitive system only extracts the most significant event. Gadanho writes that "the distinctive underlying mechanisms of the two systems are consistent with the assumption that, in nature, the cognitive system can make more accurate predictions based on rules while the emotional associations have less explanatory power but can make more extensive predictions and predict further ahead in the future."

In the ALEC architecture, the cognitive system collects data independently from the emotional system and is designed to step in to correct bad decisions made by the emotional learning system. While agent architectures from other scientists propose a functional role for emotions in the context of learning, Gadanho's is one of the first to offer two differentiated learning mechanisms. While the cognitive system in the ALEC architecture does not perform well without the emotion system, robots with both decision-making systems perform much better than robots with just an emotion system.

Gadanho's robots function within a quite simple environment and solve a rather straightforward challenge. However, her experiments do illustrate the advantages and disadvantages of emotion-based and cognitive learning, and they also illustrate the overall benefit of having both systems. In her approach, the cognitive system functions as a check on the emotional learning system by enforcing constraints on the selection of actions. In the design of more sophisticated robots, the cognitive and emotional decision-making systems may be more tightly integrated, leading to a range of creative responses to complex challenges, as well as rules or moral constraints on the actions available to a bottom-up learning system.

Human-Robot Interaction— Beyond Cog and Kismet

Morality is a social phenomenon. Good behavior depends on sensitivity to the intentions and needs of others. Autonomous moral agents will need to know what people want. In their interactions with humans, (ro)bots will need to be aware of social conventions and expectations associated with their roles.

Along with the proliferation of roles envisaged for (ro)bots, research projects directed at increasing the sociability of robots have expanded dramatically in recent years. Robot toys, robopets, robot companions, mobile information kiosks in museums, rescue robots, delivery systems trekking through the halls of hospitals, and robot coaches for exercise or personal health management must each follow different conventions in fulfilling the tasks for which they are designed. A child who doesn't want to play needs to be treated differently from a patient who doesn't want to take her medicine.

Social interactions depend on trust. Among the foundations for building trust and mutual understanding are the capacities for reading facial expressions, gestures, body posture, voice intonation, the direction of another's gaze, and other social cues. These, along with an understanding of how to convey one's own intentions, are also foundational for the possibility of working together toward shared goals. Social interactions, including eye contact, imitation, and turn taking, nurture the development and learning of infants and young children. Many of the elements contributing to trust are culturally specific. Children learn what is an appropriate distance or an allowable physical contact between two people in their culture.

To be accepted by people, (ro)bots, both physical and virtual, will need to make their actions understood in a clear manner and will need to be able to learn and grow in dynamically changing social interactions. We introduced earlier the Cog and Kismet robotic experiments in social interaction and embodied learning. Cog was designed to learn through interactions with people but had only limited capabilities. Kismet was designed to respond to voice prosody, pointing gestures, and the proximity of the human with whom it was interacting with a fixed repertoire of social behaviors. Facial expressions for basic emotions, conversational turn taking, smiling and moving forward to engage people, and moving backward when humans came too close were among the responses made by Kismet. Cog and Kismet are both now exhibits in the MIT Museum. Brian Scasselati, who as a graduate student led the team that designed Cog, is building a humanoid robot named Nico that emulates the cognitive faculties of an infant. Cynthia Breazeal's work currently focuses on "Leonardo," a joint project of the Robot Life group at MIT and Hollywood's Stan Winston Studio, known for their expertise in animatronics (and creators of the robot Teddy for the movie *AI*).

Leonardo is a successor to both Kismet and Cog. While Kismet's interactions with humans were limited to a fixed set of simple social gestures, Leonardo combines an expandable repertoire of social responses with the rudimentary capacity to learn through social interactions. Through trial and error, supplemented by verbal feedback from an instructor, Leonardo has learned to perform relatively complex tasks that are challenging for a robot though simple from the human perspective—for example, turning on three separate lights by pushing large colored buttons in a specific sequence.

Leonardo's added capacities make it possible for the researchers to tackle learning problems that were impossible for Cog and Kismet. For instance, Leonardo has been presented with a version of the false belief test that children under the age of three or four usually fail. As children develop normally beyond age four, they come to understand that others may have beliefs different from their own. The false belief test is designed to reveal the emergence of this capability to represent the beliefs of others. First an object is hidden while a child and another person are watching. Then the person leaves the room, and the child sees the object moved to a new location. Where does the child expect the other person will look for the object when he comes back into the room? Young children expect the person to look for the object at the new location, apparently indicating that they can't conceive of that person not knowing something they themselves know. Older children, of course, know the difference between what they believe and what others believe.

In the Leonardo version of the experiment, a human places two different objects, for example a bag of chips and a bag of cookies, into each of two boxes, and then leaves the room. Another person then switches the objects in the boxes. When the first person returns to the room, Leonardo infers from their behavior which object they are looking for and helps them get access to the correct box. If Leonardo actually solved the false belief test the way a child does, the robot would be on the way to successful social interactions. But Leonardo isn't reading facial expressions or other nonverbal gestures to identify the two different participants. Rather, Leonardo's software and sensors rely on different arrangements of reflective tape placed on participants and objects to help the robot identify who is who and which snack is which. Furthermore, Leonardo's software has been designed specifically to handle this particular version of the false belief test. Leonardo would not do so well with other versions of the test that have successfully been given to children.

However, the team's approach to the false belief test provides a platform for the development of more sophisticated approaches.

Other labs have taken social robotics into new contexts. For instance, Graduate Robot Attending a ConferencE (GRACE), was designed by a team from Carnegie Mellon University, the Naval Research Laboratory, Metria Inc., Northwestern University, and Swarthmore College to compete in a 2002 challenge proposed by the American Association for Artificial Intelligence. This robot interacts with humans primarily as an expressive talking head projected through a monitor mounted on a rather clunky mobile body, replete with cameras, microphones, and other sensors. To win the challenge, GRACE needed to find its way to an elevator, get off at the correct floor for the registration lobby, look for the registration desk, find its way to the end of the line, wait patiently as the line moved forward, and interact with staff to get a name tag, bag of conference goodies, and directions to the conference room. The robot then had to navigate through the crowd to find its way to the room with the help of an electronic map, and give a five- to twenty-minute talk on its hardware and software.

Both GRACE and Leonardo have been configured to pass specific tests. Leonardo's capacity to take the other's perspective across a range of tasks is extremely limited. And GRACE might well have difficulty performing similar tasks at a different conference, without being reprogrammed. Nevertheless, we believe that Leonardo and GRACE are not simply performing parlor tricks. They both are serious scientific experiments that demonstrate significant progress in the goal of designing physically adept robots with social savvy and common sense.

While Leonardo and GRACE are behavior-based robots with faculties that are, at least theoretically, presumed to be similar to those of humans, roboticists, for example Hiroshi Ishiguro at Osaka University, are experimenting with social robots that have access to information a human might not have. For example, a robot traveling through Ishiguro's laboratory has access to many remotely mounted cameras that provide it with information about what is taking place behind walls or in distant corners of the room. A robot with this information could know exactly where in the lab it would find a particular person or object. Ishiguro has also placed a robot in a school setting. This robot was capable of mapping the social interaction patterns of all the students, thereby enabling the teachers to identify which children were more outgoing and which tended to be isolated.

Until now, we have focused on robots' emotional and social capacities. But Ishiguro and Breazeal also illustrate contrasting approaches to eliciting human emotional responses to robots. Ishiguro is best known for building robots that closely resemble humans. At MIT, the approach is aimed more toward the design of appealing robots similar to cartoon characters or stuffed animals, with some child-like features, for example, big eyes. This approach evokes anthropomorphic responses, perhaps causing people who interact with these robots to attribute more intelligence and emotional capacity to them than really exists. Ishiguro takes a harder path in demanding that his android models be highly realistic. His hopes of overcoming people's discomfort with golem-like entities correspond to Japanese roboticist Mashahiro Mori's idea of the uncanny valley—the area where human comfort with androids drops off sharply because they have become too similar to people yet not similar enough.

Ishiguro, together with Karl MacDormand, who is presently teaching at the School of Informatics at Indiana University–Purdue University Indianapolis, has initiated the field of "android science" in the belief that roboticists can learn how to build human-like robots that will eventually dispel this discomfort. Whether or not android science will succeed, these contrasting approaches highlight the fact that the possibility of success for designing AMAs may depend on factors other than the acceptability of their behavior. Appearance, whether more or less human-like, may count.

Other Minds and Empathy

If the robot Leonardo had solved the false belief test the way a human solves it, he would have demonstrated a core skill associated with a theory of mind. Theory of mind (ToM) is a somewhat ambiguous phrase that refers to the abilities that facilitate awareness of another's mental states. While few people claim to have ESP, "getting into the minds of others" by inferring their moods, beliefs, and intentions is certainly central to smoothly functioning social interactions.

Theory of mind develops through the early years of life. An infant learns in stages to distinguish her own body from that of others, to recognize herself in a mirror (primitive self-awareness), and to appreciate that another's mind will contain different information from her own. All of these contribute to the development of ToM. Some theorists have even suggested that many of the behaviors associated with autism are a result of failure in the normal development of ToM.

The research on ToM is filled with fascinating experiments and characterized by an array of largely unproven theories. Nevertheless, AI engineers are already testing these theories in the design of their robots. Scassellati, who took a leading role in building Cog and Kismet while studying at MIT under Rodney Brooks, wrote his Ph.D. dissertation on developing a ToM for a robot. Now an assistant professor in the Computer Science Department at Yale, Scassellati continues this work with the development of the robot Nico.

Theory of mind is often presumed to emerge from a collection of very low-level skills. For example, Simmel and Heider, as mentioned earlier, demonstrated with a few simple video clips that people impute intentions to objects on the basis of simple movements. Associating intentions with basic movements is one of the lower-level skills that could contribute to building a full ToM.

Utilizing the theories of cognitive scientists who have broken ToM down into discrete skills, computer scientists are trying to implement each of these skills in hardware and software. For example, humans distinguish sensory inputs that arise from their own actions from those that arise from others' actions. Scassellati and graduate student Kevin Gold have demonstrated how the timing of sensory feedback after self-generated movement can be used to enable Nico to distinguish sensory inputs produced by its own actions from those produced by others' movements.

Using this kind of sensorimotor feedback, Nico can recognize itself in a mirror, a test that is presumed to represent primitive self-awareness and that infants first pass between eighteen and twenty-four months. When a reflection from a mirror comes into the camera that functions as an eye, Nico assigns the image a score based on whether the image is likely to be "self," "another," or "neither." The robot will also move its arms and assign a high probability that the image is "self" if this movement is evident in the reflection. Conversely, when the reflected image moves and Nico hasn't moved, the probability is that the image is "another," and if the image is stationary, it is likely to be "neither." Presumably, as Nico is programmed to discern other features and actions, it will factor these into determining self from others, including specific others.

Current research on building a robot with ToM is proceeding on the assumption that the aggregation of lower-level cognitive mechanisms will collectively enable the robot to act as if it had a ToM. To date, only a few limited pieces of the basic skills have been demonstrated. Identifying the full skill set that contributes to ToM and the hard work of coordinating or integrating these skills lies ahead. To date, researchers not only lack systems with a ToM but do not even know whether they have adequate ideas about the attributes necessary for a system to have a ToM. Nevertheless, the first steps taken by Scasselati, Breazeal, and their students are impressive enough to suggest that significant strides can be anticipated over the next few years.

ToM and Empathy

The relationship between ToM and empathy is far from clear, but certainly both contribute to the way one human appreciates the states of mind of another. The capacity to empathize with the feelings of others is often considered to be a prerequisite for moral judgment and sensitive behavior in many situations where people interact. Nevertheless, there are cases of psychopaths who are skilled at deducing appropriate empathetic behavior without actually feeling empathy.

Infants demonstrate—by trying to comfort a distressed companion—some capacity for empathy long before they develop the basic skills associated with a ToM. Indeed, behaviors that could be interpreted as empathic are evident in a broad array of species. The discovery in macaque monkeys of mirror neurons—neurons that fire both when the animal performs an action and when the animal observes another animal performing the same action—appear to many scientists to be a neural mechanism that facilitates access to another's mind and feelings.

An artificial system that could empathize would be more likely to select morally appropriate responses in its choice of actions. However, robots are unlikely to have empathy for other entities unless or until they have emotions of their own. Without emotions, empathic behavior by robots will largely be the result of rational responses built on top of a merely symbolic representation of the minds of others.

Multiagent Environments

Cyburg, population 44,100, is a virtual community created by William Sims Bainbridge, a program director at the National Science Foundation and a leading figure in exploring the convergence of research into nanotechnology, biotechnology, information technology, and cognitive science. The residents of Cyburg are programmed to follows rules of individual and social behavior that Bainbridge has drawn from the latest social science. Bainbridge, who is especially interested in the emergence of religious beliefs, uses Cyburg to investigate the appearance of complex communities where residents form groups and learn to trust or distrust each other.

Many social situations involve interactions among large numbers of agents. Such multiagent contexts are changing continually. Relationships among agents constantly evolve. Customs change. A socially viable robot will require a rich set of skills to function properly in such a dynamic state of flux. If people come to feel that the behavior of AMAs is trustworthy, a corresponding change in acceptance and latitude for the actions of AMAs will also be part of the changing social context. Conversely, if AMAs fail to act appropriately, they will have to adapt to additional restrictions that will be placed on their behavior.

Today's bots actually function quite well in multiagent environments where auctions, bargaining, or other forms of negotiation are the primary mode of interactions. These contexts are governed by prescribed rules. Within a rule-based environment, for example eBay, a computer can serve to coordinate the actions of other agents or function as an independent agent that, for example, monitors the auction and places the winning bid in the last second before the auction closes.

Rules for auctions serve to establish trust among the participants, and punitive measures are applied to those who act deceptively. Presumably, this trust would be extended to a (ro)bot that played by the rules. Trust and safety come more easily when a (ro)bot's behavior is predictable and falls within prescribed rules. However, within many social contexts a difficulty arises in that agents need to be deceptive at times. In a poker game a human might bluff, or in a bargaining situation an agent might pretend that a lower offer was his final offer. Agents that reveal their constellation of beliefs, desires, intentions, feelings, and needs would be at a disadvantage.

On the other hand, opening the door to artificial agents that lie, manipulate, or are insincere undermines the prospect of instilling trust in agents' actions. People would not bid on eBay if they believed that software agents were artificially raising the cost of items by planting phony bids. Trust and suspicion go on concurrently for humans. In most contexts, people trust each other until that trust is undermined, but in other contexts, for example buying goods and services, caveat emptor is the norm. In a poker game, one expects bluffing. Artificial agents will need to know in which contexts human gestures can be taken at face value and when deception is possible or even the norm. They will also need to recognize when eliciting trust from human agents is essential and when deception is acceptable.

Similarly, humans may eventually need to understand that when and where to trust complex artificial agents will differ from context to context. In this connection, Matthias Scheutz has demonstrated that humans will tolerate a robot's disobedience of a direct command so long as they recognize that the robot's disobedience is serving a shared goal. In a similar manner, deceptive behavior by (ro)bots need not necessarily undermine human trust in their actions. For instance, a robotic soccer player would need to successfully coordinate its actions with those of its teammates, but it would also need to fake out members of the other team to be successful in moving the ball toward the opponent's goal. Such deception would be praised, not condemned, in the context of soccer.

As we mentioned in chapter 9, Robosoccer provides a venue for experimenting with social interactions between machines. The challenge of constructing a world-class robotic soccer team has been widely adopted since Deep Blue II defeated Gary Kasparov in 1997. At the time, many critics argued that chess was too limited a context to be a real test of machine intelligence. The advocates of Robosoccer believe that cooperative embodied tasks, for example playing soccer, are much more representative of human intelligence. To date, the development of robotic soccer players has focused on training systems to perform simple tasks—getting two-legged humanoid robots to kick a soccer ball or four-legged artificial intelligence robots (AIBOs) to pass a ball to each other. More complex tasks of cooperation lie well in the future. The stated goal of Robosoccer is to develop a world-class team of robot soccer players capable of beating a world-class human team by 2050. The advanced date is reflective of the difficulty of the challenge. Note, in comparison, that on May 25, 1961, President Kennedy allowed just a decade when he issued his challenge to put a man on the moon, and this was accomplished using computer systems and other technologies that were primitive compared to those available today.

An even more difficult challenge than an all-robot team is to develop a soccer team with both robotic and human agents coordinating their activities. Computerized agents can share standardized techniques for communicating with each other. But new standards have to be established for systems developed on different platforms, as well as standards or norms for computers interacting with humans. A similar challenge faces the integration of military robots into the armed forces.

Human-computer interactions are likely to evolve in a dynamic way, and the computerized agents will need to accommodate these changes. For artificial agents in multiagent environments, each transaction has the potential to change the relationships between agents. Norms can easily change, for example, when an agent moves into a new role over time, or even at different times or in different contexts during a single day. (If you play golf with your doctor, it is inappropriate for him to mention your medical conditions while standing on the putting green.) The demands of multiagent systems thus illustrate the relationship between increasing autonomy and the need for more sensitivity to the morally relevant features of different environments.

How Embodied Must a Robot Be?

Which aspects of moral judgment and understanding are dependent on being embodied and situated in a world of objects, entities, and other agents? The state of an organism in any given moment is significantly determined by its relationships to the objects, entities, and agents in its environment. Your capacity and confidence that you can quickly respond to challenges, your posture, and your emotions are all influenced by these relationships. All of this contributes to the information that informs one's judgments and actions.

Scientists who take an embodied perspective on cognition sometimes argue that it cannot be understood without recognizing the particular nature of biological organisms as self-organizing, self-maintaining, and actively striving to survive, thrive, and procreate. Building on this perspective, the philosopher Steve Torrance advocates what he calls a "robust" view of ethics, in which only biological organisms that have feelings, sentience, and consciousness are inherently capable of being moral actors. Torrance points out that the moral point of view arguably requires feeling sympathy toward people in pain or distress, not merely acting on the basis of a rational inference that helping others is the right thing to do. Without a capacity to actually feel distress, pain, fear, and anger or positive emotions such as joy, pleasure, gratitude, and affection, a being does not possess the moral states or moral identifications that are essential to being a fully rounded moral individual. In this robust view of ethics, the ability to have such states (distress, joy, fear, etc.) cannot be properly understood without reference to humans' sentience, biological constitution, and history. In other words, empathy, sympathy, sentience, and morality are all bound up together.

We believe that the robust view of ethics requires serious consideration. But it is also a relatively new argument, again raising the bar for the faculties a (ro)bot will need in order to be judged a morally intelligent system. However, we also believe that this perspective by no means undermines the project of building AMAs to function within limited contexts. Furthermore, in the process of tackling more limited goals approaches may be discovered in turn for surmounting the challenges implicit in the robust view.

Catriona Kennedy, a research fellow at the School of Computer Science at the University of Birmingham, has come to a similar conclusion when considering the need for agents that function as trustworthy ethical assistants in limited domains. She proposes that ethical agents that are not embodied and lack human-like experiences and emotions "could be feasible if two requirements are met: (1) The agent must protect the integrity of its own reasoning (including its representation of ethical rules etc.)...(2) The agent's world should generate events that can be related to ethical requirements in the human world." As an example, Kennedy cites an intrusion detection system built around policies that state which networks can talk to each other, and what protocols each network must use. The network translates the policies into "acceptable" patterns of activity and learns to detect violations through the analysis of activity registered by its sensors. In addition, the network will need to be able to discern the difference between undesirable activity and unreliable sensors. A successful ethical assistant would ground ethical principles from the human world, for example, a specification for honest business relationships, by associating it with events in its own world (reliable patterns of communication that fall within the policies). Such an agent would not need to be embodied in the human world to be a trustworthy agent in a limited domain.

More recently, Torrance has argued that an entity will require consciousness to be a moral agent. If he is correct, the work on machine consciousness will have to progress significantly before full moral agency for a (ro)bot is possible.

A leading researcher in the field of machine consciousness is Owen Holland, who in 2004 received a large six-figure grant to begin work on building a conscious robot. Holland notes three approaches to building conscious machines.

(1) Identify the components of consciousness, and implement all of them in a machine.
(2) Identify the components of the machine that produces consciousness (the brain) and copy them.
(3) Identify the circumstances in which consciousness arose, copy them, and hope that consciousness emerges again.

The first approach is taken by Stan Franklin with his work on IDA. The second approach is represented by Igor Aleksander's efforts to build a neural network model of the structures involved in the process of visual consciousness. Holland's own strategy is based on the third approach, to build a robot embodied in its environment in hopes of reproducing the conditions under which consciousness emerged.

Each of these approaches to substantiating consciousness within a machine relies heavily on some theory of consciousness. Holland's project is closely tied to theories developed by the German philosopher Thomas Metzinger. Franklin's IDA is an attempt to integrate reasoning and emotions in an artificial system based on the neuroscientist Bernard Baars's global workspace theory. In the next chapter, we will turn specifically to the viability of Franklin's approach for building an AMA.

Chapter 11

A MORE HUMAN-LIKE AMA

Put 'em Together and What Have You Got?

In the previous two chapters, we have described some basic computational components that may be part of the tool kit for building AMAs. Assembling the pieces into a single agent is not a trivial task, however. For AMAs to have a more complete repertoire of cognitive capacities, an overall architecture is needed. In computer science terms, an "architecture" specifies a system's components and how they interact. Any designer of an AMA architecture must therefore decide what components to include. Should AMAs have specific components dedicated to ethical sensibilities and reasoning? Or should these functions be carried out by more general mechanisms?

An example of the first type of architecture is Ronald Arkin's Army-funded project, discussed at the beginning of chapter 5. He is working on the problem of how to make robotic fighting machines capable of dealing with the complicated ethics of wartime behavior. Arkin's proposed architecture has four dedicated components for ethics: (1) an "ethical governor"–based deontic logic for managing the hard constraints on permissible behavior; (2) an "ethical behavior control" module that has internalized principles which implement the specific military rules of engagement for a particular combat situation and selects among permissible options; (3) an "ethical adaptor" that engages emotional systems during real-time behavior, and engages in reflective reasoning after the fact; and (4) a "responsibility advisor" that serves as an interface between the robot and the human operator, to ensure that the operator has properly considered the implications of sending the robot out on an autonomous combat mission with authorization to use lethal force. Drawing on several of the systems we described in chapter 9, Arkin has sketched out how each of these components might be constructed and how their interactions might be managed. However, the system remains very much on the drawing board, and Arkin warns against being optimistic that ethical autonomous agents capable of lethal force will be available any time soon. The danger, of course, is that ethically blind autonomous agents capable of lethal force are becoming available first. If exposing the difficulty of making killing machines ethical can help put the brakes on building them with inadequate safeguards, then the project of thinking about AMA design will have served a valuable purpose. And irrespective of what one thinks about the morality of robotic fighting machines, we think that the four components of Arkin's system could be adapted for other more benevolent applications.

Like many projects in AI, Arkin's architecture owes little to what is known of human cognitive architecture. There's nothing wrong with this as an engineering approach to getting a job done. However, our focus here will be an alternative approach that began with some discussions between Wendell Wallach and Stan Franklin, a computer scientist at the University of Memphis, and culminated in the remainder of this chapter. The approach builds on Franklin's learning intelligent distribution agent (LIDA), a conceptual and computational model of cognition that Franklin has developed in concert with other computer scientists and neuroscientists. We will look at how LIDA might accommodate top-down analysis and bottom-up propensities, including learning. We will also discuss the prospects for incorporating the affective capabilities that are likely to be important for full moral agency.

The approach we outline in this chapter is also an example of the second kind of architecture we mentioned in the opening paragraph—it does not have special-purpose ethics modules but instead implements ethical sensibility and reasoning capacities from more general perceptual, affective, and decision-making components.

Franklin's LIDA is based on Bernard Baars's highly regarded global workspace theory (GWT) and has been developed with input from Baars, who is based at the Neurosciences Institute in San Diego. Although it has scientific competitors, GWT is among the most recognized and best-supported theories of consciousness and higher-order cognition. Franklin's LIDA interests us as a computational model of human decision making that might be applicable to the design of AMAs because of its relationship to GWT, and because it is quite comprehensive. Systems that attempt, like LIDA, to replicate human intelligence fully, are often referred to as having artificial general intelligence (AGI). Of course, there are other AGI models we could have focused on, for example Ben Goertzel's Novamente project. Goertzel believes that with enough resources, an AGI system can be achieved within the next ten years.

The CogAff model of philosophers Aaron Sloman and Ron Chrisley, which we mentioned in chapter 10, is another candidate.

Stan Franklin is not the only scientist who has turned to GWT to develop a computational model of human-like decision making. Murray Shanahan, a roboticist at Imperial College in London, and Stanislas Dehaene, a cognitive neuropsychology researcher at Institut National de la Santé in Paris, have both turned to GWT in their modeling of human cognition. The models of Franklin, Shanahan, and Dehaene all differ in various details, but because none of those details seem specific to AMA design, we'll minimize confusion by focusing entirely on Franklin's LIDA.

Following the engineer's creed that you don't really know how something works if you can't build it, Franklin has set his sights on designing a system that implements GWT fully. This has forced him to look at the operation of lower-level cognitive functions with a specificity that is often overlooked when considering the validity of higher-level theories. Franklin's desire is to build a computer system based on the best neuroscientific understanding of how the various affective, memory, reasoning, learning, and procedural mechanisms in the brain function, and to use whichever software tools are the most capable of performing each activity.

Franklin's LIDA is not explicitly designed for moral deliberation. Rather, LIDA is a model of how every agent is engaged in the process of trying to make sense of its environment. Agents must continually select a next action to perform on the basis of many different sources and kinds of information. The GWT is a theory of how a winner emerges from the competition for attention between various coalitions of information. The winning coalition occupies consciousness, and is broadcast throughout the brain, where it is combined with information that facilitates the selection of the agent's next action. For example, if there is competition for attention among available sources of nutrition, an object to inspect, a playful companion, or the presence of a threatening predator, the predator would typically have to win the competition if there is any hope for long-term survival. Within the LIDA model, moral decision making is a form of action selection similar to any other. From the perspective of action selection, a more human-like AMA does not need specially dedicated moral reasoning processes. Rather, the system needs only the normal set of deliberative mechanisms, applied to inputs having relevance to moral challenges.

LIDA's designers hypothesize that in each second there are multiple cognitive cycles, and in each cycle there is a competition for attention, a winner that occupies consciousness, and the selection of a next action. We will focus on how sensitivity to morally relevant information enters each cycle, how multiple cycles lead to higher-order analysis, how complex challenges are processed and an action is selected, and how an agent learns to refine its moral decision-making faculties.

The LIDA model is a complex one, with many layers and separate modules to handle different functions. There are modules for each of the different forms of memory (perceptual memory, transient episodic memory, procedural memory, etc.) and individual processes, for example turning externally and internally derived sensory data into percepts—say, the detection of the presence of a chair or a predator. Franklin has drawn on what he considers the best available software tools for implementing specific activity.

We won't attempt to evaluate how satisfactory LIDA is as a model of human cognition or whether there are better hardware and software tools for implementing specific functions. Our concern here is whether a complex model, for example LIDA, is useful as a platform for implementing the various aspects of human decision making that we have raised in earlier chapters. The LIDA model has not been fully implemented, nor has any other model of human cognition; however, the core of LIDA has been demonstrated in a program named IDA that Franklin developed for the U.S. Navy. The IDA program performed the role of a Navy detailer, who assigns each sailor to a new billet at the end of a tour of duty. The Navy employs three hundred full-time detailers. They communicate with sailors to find out their preferences in assignments, match these to available posts, make sure that the needs and some 90 policies of the Navy are satisfied, and negotiate with the sailor as to whether a proposed assignment is satisfactory.

The LIDA model is IDA with Learning. Much of LIDA is highly theoretical, and the actual software tools for substantiating individual tasks have not been developed. Furthermore, testing the conceptual model would require significant funding to build the system. Franklin is diligent in fleshing out the various conceptual details necessary to substantiate LIDA, but whether a fully functioning LIDA would demonstrate the moral acumen we believe an AMA will require is also impossible to judge without building and testing the system. We will outline the first steps of designing a computational LIDA that could support the various faculties necessary for moral decision making. Again, our concern here is not necessarily to endorse LIDA as the best approach for building an AMA, but rather to offer one example of a computational model for an AMA that accommodates many of the complexities we have raised. First, we will describe the general features of LIDA as a model of human action selection.

The LIDA Model

Making sense of the world, in order to determine what to do next, is a continuous process. The LIDA model tries to capture this dynamic by describing the unconscious mechanisms that feed the conscious processing of information,

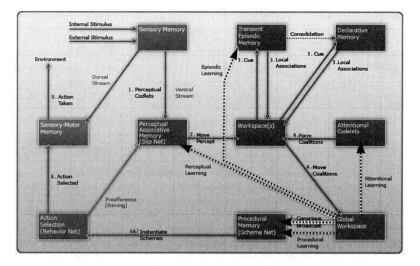

Figure 11.1. The LIDA Cognitive Cycle. (Stan Franklin, Sidney D'Mello, and Austin Hunter.)

as represented in GWT. Figure 11.1 illustrates an individual LIDA cognitive cycle from sensory input in the upper left to consciousness in the lower right, and on to the selection of an action.

Franklin's basic strategy (and significant contribution) is to match the complex higher-level cognitive processes described by GWT with a description of lower-level mechanisms that make such higher-level processes possible and computable. These lower-level mechanisms are captured in the individual LIDA cycles. Each individual cycle captures the ever-ongoing need for the agent to sense its environment and its own internal state, process these inputs, and select an appropriate response. Franklin posits that there are roughly five to ten such cycles in each second, that is, five to ten discrete inputs to consciousness and the selection of five to ten behaviors. Individual LIDA cycles are the "atoms" on which the more complex "molecules" of higher-order cognitive functions are built.

The upper left-hand corner of figure 11.1 illustrates the agent receiving both external and internal sensory input. Unconscious mechanisms, utilizing massive parallel processing, are continually at work organizing and making sense of this input. Lower-level sensory inputs are associated together to form features (color, texture), which are in turn combined into higher-level percepts, for example objects, specific people, feelings, or events. For example, a collection of visual inputs combines with internally stored information to represent the presence of a chair. Within the agent's workspace, associations form between percepts and memory. Active processes in transient episodic (short-term) memory and declarative (long-term) memory form local associations, which expand the internal, unconscious representation of the agent's world. The perception of a familiar face might have cued the recollection of a name and the agent's last interaction with that person, which was stored in memory. At this stage, the system will have cued other information, including similar-looking people, associates of the identified person, and other associated data, some of which may be irrelevant to the situation at hand.

Meanwhile, attention codelets (pieces of software code that perform simple operations) scan the representations in the workspace, looking for specific information that should be brought to the agent's attention. Imagine, for example, one codelet looking for evidence that the agent's natural predator is in the environment. In effect, it is the job of this codelet to get the agent to attend to the presence of the predator, but other attention codelets are also competing to direct the agent to attend to other matters.

The winner for that cognitive cycle comes to occupy the global workspace, thus being broadcast globally to enlist other modules to help the system find an appropriate response. Franklin posits that an action is selected at the end of every cognitive cycle, though certainly some of the actions selected entail the need for multiple cycles in order to generate a full response to a complex challenge.

It is usual to think of decision making as a deliberative process involving conscious reflection about competing evidence or goals. Deliberation can entail problem solving, reasoning, planning, and metacognition. These higher-order cognitive processes are distinguished in the LIDA model by the fact that they typically require multiple cognitive cycles. But in most situations, including many of those that could be said to involve morals, the selection of an action occurs in a single cognitive cycle. Actions that follow from single cycles are said by Franklin to be consciously mediated.

More complicated decisions require conscious deliberation, or "volitional" decision making, in William James's terms. In 1890, James suggested that we think of volitional decision making as a negotiation among internal proposers of a course of action, objectors, and supporters. James's example entailed getting out of bed on a cold winter morning, but in this age of overheated houses perhaps the example of waking up thirsty will be more familiar. On waking up, the idea of drinking orange juice may "pop into mind," propelled to consciousness by an orange-juice proposer. "No, it's too sweet," asserts an objector. "How about a beer?" says a different proposer. "Too early in the day," says another objector. "Orange juice is more nutritious," says a supporter. With no further objections, drinking orange juice is selected.

The LIDA model fleshes out James's volitional decision making within global workspace theory by means of a multicyclic process. An idea pops into consciousness because it is a part of the winning coalition for that cycle.

Coalitions between individual pieces of information are created by an attention codelet, looking specifically for those pieces of information. For example, an attention codelet might look for something as simple as objects that are red, or a codelet could search for red and blood together. In LIDA, the proposers, objectors, and supporters referred to in James's model are implemented as individual attention codelets. In the presence of an activated thirst node in the workspace, one such attention codelet, a proposer codelet, has the task of bringing drinking orange juice to mind. Seeing a node for "drink some orange juice" in the workspace, another attention codelet, an objector codelet, attempts to bring to mind the idea that orange juice is too sweet. Supporter codelets are implemented similarly. The LIDA model also includes a timekeeper codelet, and other mechanisms that we won't describe fully here. These mechanisms ensure that the decision-making process does not oscillate endlessly between proposals and objections and reaches a resolution of the challenge at hand.

This simple synopsis only begins to capture the depth and level of analysis that has gone into the development of the LIDA model, and its application to specific aspects of cognition, including perception and learning, modeling memory, and the role of feelings and emotions. Stan Franklin, with the coauthorship of many different computer and cognitive scientists, has written more than fifty articles on IDA and LIDA, many of which focus on specific mechanisms within the model. Readers interested in particular aspects of cognition and how they might be implemented within computer systems will want to check out some of these articles. Our discussion here is a continuation of Franklin's larger project in exploring how moral decision-making faculties might be implemented within the LIDA model.

Human Moral Decision Making and LIDA

There is little evidence that moral decision making in humans follows any formal procedure. Perhaps some trained ethicists actually engage in a formal and extended deliberation on those occasions when they have the time to do so. Individuals who have a commitment to a particular moral code may have internalized feelings, character traits, and heuristics that facilitate their responding quickly (perhaps within one cognitive cycle) to challenges within the apparent constraints of their preferred moral code, and with little or no need for reflection. But most decision making is somewhat messy, drawing on emotions, moral sentiments, intuitions, heuristics in the form of automated responses, rules and duties, and perhaps some explicit valuation of utility or expected outcomes.

Memories and personality traits find their way into the mix. In all likelihood, no two people process moral decisions in quite the same way, even when confronted with identical challenges. Humans are hybrid decision makers, with unique approaches to moral choices, honed over time and altered by their own distinctive experiences.

The messiness of human moral decision making has been explored by psychologists. Going back at least to the 1970s, their experiments have probed how morally trivial inputs have a large effect on the behavior of individuals. For example, subjects who have just discovered a dime in a phone booth are much more likely to help someone in distress (96 percent v. 13 percent).

In another experiment during the same era, students at Princeton Theological Seminary on their way to giving a presentation were told either that they were running late, on time, or early. On the way they encountered someone in distress. In this "good Samaritan" experiment, only 10 percent of those who were running late stopped to help, versus 45 percent of those who were told they were on time and 63 percent of those who were told they had plenty of time. The students' prior responses to a questionnaire about their religious and moral beliefs were not significantly correlated to their decisions to stop.

Philosophers argue vigorously about the interpretation of these experiments and whether they are relevant to ethics. Irrespective of that debate, whether an engineer should design an AMA so that it is susceptible to such manipulations of its environment remains an open question. And regardless of what an engineer should want the AMA to do, it is possible that any system that has sufficient flexibility to be able to adapt to unanticipated inputs would necessarily be susceptible to similar manipulations.

For some moral philosophers, the messiness of human moral decision making underscores the reasons for keeping moral philosophy separate from the psychology of moral decision making. In their view, ethical theories provide ideals to be reflected on, not procedures for making moral decisions. But, as we have discussed, there is no guarantee that those ideals are computationally tractable, nor is there any account forthcoming from the ethicist of how to build systems that pursue them. ("Not my job!" such an ethical theorist might well retort.)

The ethicist who deliberately ignores human psychology has relatively few options when the engineer knocks on her door asking for advice about how to build an AMA. Furthermore, as we have pointed out, bottom-up factors will be important in the development of AMAs. It is in this spirit that we think it's worth pursuing the complexities that might be afforded by a moral LIDA. This doesn't mean, however, that the goal is to implement an agent who will be more helpful after finding a dime! The goal is not to reproduce every aspect of human psychology but to reproduce those aspects that make real-world actions possible and ethical.

Our task here is to explain how some of this messiness can be accommodated within LIDA by providing a framework where the various influences on ethical decisions, from feelings to rules, might be represented mechanistically. The resulting agent may not be theoretically pure. It may not be a perfect utilitarian or deontologist, and it may not live up to ethical ideals, but its goals are applied, not theoretical. A LIDA-based AMA is intended to be a practical solution to a practical problem: how to take into account as much ethically relevant information as possible in the time available to select an action.

In our discussion we'll focus on six areas:

1. Where are bottom-up propensities and values implemented? How does the agent learn new values and propensities, as well as reinforce or defuse existing values and propensities?
2. How does the LIDA model transition from a single cycle to the determination that information in consciousness needs to be deliberated on?
3. How are rules or duties represented in the LIDA model? What activates a rule and brings it to conscious attention? How might some rules be automated so that they no longer require deliberation?
4. How can planning or imagination (the testing out of different scenarios) be implemented in LIDA?
5. What determines the end of a deliberation?
6. When a resolution to the challenge has been determined, how might the LIDA model monitor whether that resolution is successful? How might LIDA use this monitoring for further learning?

Bottom-Up Propensities, Values, and Learning

In chapter 7, we suggested that skills that emerge from bottom-up strategies promise to be integral to the overall design of AMAs. We asked whether engineers could meet the technological challenge of developing systems with complex moral faculties from the bottom-up. LIDA offers a step toward meeting this challenge.

Sophisticated morality requires the ability to reflect on propensities that have been shaped by evolution and experience. People naturally favor family and neighbors over those who are members of other groups. These propensities are captured in emotional-affective responses to actions and their outcomes. Through reflection on the moral outcomes produced by these propensities, a sophisticated moral agent may take steps to modulate them. One may work harder, for instance, to donate to charities that aid people very remote from us, but one may also decide that charity begins at home and work harder to cultivate strong relationships with those nearby.

Feelings and inherent values embodied in people's unthinking reactions, for example the disgust associated with blood and other bodily fluids, may influence morality from the bottom up, but are not necessarily reflective of the values a society would recognize as moral values. Negative feelings may, for example, lead to prejudices when an agent automatically attaches such feelings to individuals who are not a part of the agent's immediate group. From a moral perspective, it is important to understand how top-down considerations use and apply these bottom-up propensities. The approach LIDA offers to this hybrid challenge begins with the way an agent captures bottom-up propensities and the values implicit in these propensities.

Within LIDA, perceptual memory (part of long-term memory) is represented by a SlipNet, a network of nodes and links between the nodes that represent structures and concepts, including features, objects, and valenced feelings. Links between these nodes represent relationships that can form more complex structures (percepts). These percepts pass on to the system's working memory (workspace), from where they cue associated information in other areas of short- and long-term memory, and this information in turn leads to further associations that may enrich or alter the percepts.

Associations between valenced feelings (positive or negative) and objects, people, contexts, situations, and so on are a primary way values and bottom-up propensities form in an agent's mind. The values are implicit in the feelings and their valences, and LIDA captures this dynamic. These associations may arise during perception where sensory inputs are connected to nodes (objects, feelings, ideas, categories) in perceptual memory. These nodes in turn activate and connect to information retrieved from the various memory systems, which in LIDA are represented as separate memory modules.

Affects and perceptions that arise within the same LIDA cycle will form associations, particularly when the affective input is strong. However, unless the sensory input is particularly strong and sustained, or the initial input cues associated memories, the perception of the objects and their associated affects decays quickly and disappears. The strength of a value—the strength of the connection—is reinforced by sustained sensory input, but these values are short-lived unless the information comes to attention. Attention reinforces a connection for the longer term and produces learning.

Baars posits that each instance of attention contributes to learning. Conscious attention, modeled in Franklin's LIDA as the global broadcast in each cognitive cycle, strengthens links between percepts. Powerful memories—memories linked to strong valences—are reinforced each time they come to attention.

The challenges facing LIDA are similar to those for any human-like computer architecture, including how the system acquires new concepts or generates new nodes. A second, particularly pressing problem is how to represent valences in the SlipNet. Must they be represented somatically or is it adequate to use a cognitive representation of the valence? If a feeling is expunged of any somatic affect and is represented merely as a string of symbols or a mathematical formula, will it carry the full import of the feeling as it is factored into the selection of an action?

These are not easy problems, but LIDA does offer an architecture for integrating presently available solutions. Given the modularity of LIDA, it will also be able to integrate more sophisticated solutions to these challenges as they emerge from laboratories focusing on the development of specific hardware and software tools.

Moral Deliberation Involving Rules

Moral dilemmas that require some deliberation arise periodically—for example, in the form of conflicting voices in one's head. Some of these voices might frame their arguments in terms of rules, for example, "Thou shalt not steal." Let's consider how the activation of a rule, duty, or other objection to an action leads to a deliberative process. How are such rules or duties represented in the LIDA model? What activates a rule and brings it to conscious attention? How might some rules be automated so that they no longer require deliberation?

A specific example of an inner dialogue about a human moral dilemma may help. Suppose the company you work for licenses some new, expensive computer software, say Adobe's Photoshop. After becoming comfortable with the new software package at work, you feel the urge to copy it onto your home computer. An internal dialog commences, but not necessarily as wholly verbal and grammatical as what follows. "Let's bring Photoshop home and load the program on my Mac." "You shouldn't do that. That would be illegal and stealing." "But I'd use it for work-related projects that benefit my company, which owns the software." "Yes, but you'd also use it for personal projects with no relation to the company." "True, but most of the work would be company related." And so on and on.

In LIDA, a proposer representing the idea of copying Photoshop to the home Mac might win the competition for consciousness, modeling the way this idea might "pop into mind." The proposal impels the initiation of a behavior stream, but in a subsequent cycle that follows soon after, an objector succeeds in bringing to consciousness the idea "No, that would be stealing." The process continues over succeeding cognitive cycles with supporter codelets, and with further proposals and objections winning the competition to be consciously broadcast. The game is afoot.

Note that the first objection is implicitly based on the rule "Do not steal." At the end of the proposal cycle, the proposal to copy Photoshop is in the workspace. There it cues the "Do not steal" rule from semantic memory, a part of long-term declarative memory. The rule is activated and represented as a structure in the workspace, that is, as a collection of nodes and links. An attention codelet then forms a coalition with this rule, to build an objector-attention codelet whose informational content is "Don't copy Photoshop, that would be stealing." If effective, the objection coming to consciousness arrests the action scheme implicit in the idea of copying the software.

Rules and duties are stored in semantic memory as perceptual structures. Cued by a proposal or an objection, the rule or duty is recalled into working memory and brought into consciousness to participate in the internal dialogue. Note that a supporter, as well as an objector, can invoke a rule. The dialogue stops when a proposal is on the table without further objection long enough for the timer to metaphorically ding. At that point a scheme in procedural memory for acting on the proposal is presented to the action selection mechanism. The scheme presented will have a high degree of activation, so its selection is assured, barring some crisis or intervening alarm.

The activation of a proposer or objector decays (weakens) in each cycle. Therefore, rules that function as strong constraints will require a high level of activation to be sustained. To function properly, a rule such as "Thou shalt not kill" needs to be reinforced, and this may be accomplished by feelings, in the form of strong valences, associated with the rule. Feelings of shame, disgust with killing, or fear of the law are effective reinforcers in people. But other supporters can provide positive valence to, say, the action of killing in warfare, or of protecting children and others under one's protection.

Each time an application of a rule or duty comes to consciousness, it—like every conscious event—becomes available for perceptual learning. If a particular rule is applied frequently in similar situations, LIDA may produce a category node in perceptual memory that represents the rule in an abstract version of the similar situations. In our example, the moral decision-making agent might learn the abstract node "Don't copy software you don't have a license for." If such a node is reinforced often enough, this application of the rule is automatic. During the extended learning process, the node would acquire links to other nodes, particularly to feelings with negative valence. Thus, when faced with a situation where copying software might be tempting, this rule node can become part of the percept. Its presence in the workspace would then inhibit proposer codelets from proposing copying software, that is, by invoking the rule automatically.

Why does the internal dialogue begin? We've seen *how* it begins. It begins with a proposer-attention codelet popping a proposal into mind. But why isn't the action of copying the software, for example, simply selected as the consciously mediated action, at the end of a single cycle, with no dialogue at all? In some specific situations, copying software is permissible. The software license may allow installation on two machines, office and home, for use by a single user. If encountered frequently enough, a scheme for copying software can be procedurally learned with this situation as its context. In such a case, copying software can become a consciously mediated action that is selected during a single cycle. But in order for such a scheme to be procedurally learned, its action must have been selected volitionally at least once; that is, some deliberative process must have allowed it.

Generally, it's the perceived novelty of a given situation that leads to it being the subject of deliberation rather than simply being selected. It's the newness, or at least apparent newness, of a situation that in effect demands that the agent think about it. New situations do not fit neatly into innate or learned heuristics, and therefore demand attention. In attending to new circumstances, associated proposals and objections naturally come to mind.

The Implementation of Planning and Imagination

Decision making in general and moral decision making in particular often require imaginative planning and testing of various possible scenarios. The approaches to building AMAs we have described in the previous chapter generally lack mechanisms for generating and testing alternative actions (although BDI agents have some capabilities in this regard). The LIDA model, like many traditional AI programs, has the capacity to construct internal models that can be used to assess different situations. For example, Deep Blue II, the system that beat Gary Kasparov at chess, tested many sequences of moves before selecting the best one to execute.

The LIDA model approaches planning and the evaluation of options differently from traditional AI. In good old-fashioned artificial intelligence (GOFAI), the programmers need to determine many of the criteria for evaluating a possible scenario in advance. In LIDA, scenarios are built and evaluated by individual codelets performing discrete tasks. A scenario may be evaluated by thousands of different codelets each looking for specific kinds of information. Attention codelets that find information relevant to their concerns compete to bring that information into consciousness. If, for example, a codelet discovers information representing blood in a scenario, this codelet might recruit other codelets to inspect whether that scenario leads to humans or animals being harmed. Codelets are a particularly useful model for moral decision making, in that no one needs to specify in advance the moral criteria for evaluating a scenario. Rather, thousands of attention codelets might search for morally relevant information, while only those that found information germane to their directive or function would compete for attention.

In LIDA, imagination corresponds to a model built in the workspace by codelets whose task is to build structures within the workspace. The components of internal models of the world are nodes and links from perceptual memory. Action selection in LIDA takes place at the end of each cognitive cycle. The action may be as simple as adding a component to a model in the workspace. By repeatedly altering a model in the workspace, imaginative deliberation can take place over many cycles.

Consider a town planner who has been given the task of designing and locating the emergency services in a town. Part of the planner's training would have involved learning complex internal behavior streams for constructing and manipulating scenarios by placing various facilities at particular locations. Other internal behavior streams would allow the evaluation of such scenarios (mental plans of the locations for ambulance, fire station, police, and hospital facilities) using functional, aesthetic, and moral criteria. Volitional decision making, as described earlier, would employ yet other behavior streams to decide which of the constructed scenarios to select. Appropriately, in LIDA, the central site for much of this work is the workspace, though an embodied LIDA-based robot might also put ideas on paper.

Ultimately, for moral deliberation to be appropriately modeled by LIDA, attention codelets that are sensitive to morally relevant information will need to be designed. Whether the design of such morally sensitive codelets differs from the general design of codelets that search for concrete information remains to be seen. But minimally, for example, we expect that attention codelets that are sensitive to concrete information about the facial and vocal expressions of people affected by an AMA's actions will need to be part of the mix. The advantage of codelets is that they provide an indefinitely extensible framework for taking more and more of the relevant factors into account.

Resolution, Evaluation, and Further Learning

A LIDA-based agent would reach a resolution when there is no longer an objection to a proposal. Given that the activation of an objection decays in repeat cycles, strongly reinforced proposals will in time prevail over weak objections. But proposals and their supporters also weaken in their activation over time. Weak proposals may also lose the competition for attention to other concerns demanding attention, defusing any pressure or need for the agent to act on the challenge. Highly activated rules, duties, or other objectors will outlast weak proposers, and force the development of more creative proposals that accommodate the strong objections.

However, time pressures may force a decision before all objections have been dispelled. Decay in the strength of proposals and objections, time pressures on decision making, and pressures from other concerns can drive the selection of a response to a challenge even when the response is inadequate or incomplete. Furthermore, moral deliberations seldom vanquish all objections, even with a generous allocation of time. Moral decisions are often messy, but the LIDA architecture has the potential to produce adaptive behavior despite the complexity. Future LIDA-inspired moral agents may consider a broader array of proposals, objections, and supporting evidence than a human agent can, and thereby, perhaps, select a more satisfactory course of action than many humans.

The LIDA model is not designed around fixed moral values and may, like a human agent, be susceptible to acting on strongly reinforced impulses and proposals without necessarily considering the needs of others. This is the problem exposed by experiments such as the aforementioned good Samaritan one. Some philosophers have argued that such experiments show that the notion of stable moral character is a myth, while others argue that they only reinforce the idea that ethics is not about how humans do behave but about providing them with ideals for reflective self-regulation that transcend ordinary psychological tendencies. These are issues that lie far beyond the present technical capacities of LIDA. But what LIDA offers is a model for computer learning that could provide steps toward a more complete model of moral education or the development of good character.

The way a LIDA-based AMA monitors its actions will be important to its moral development. When a resolution to a moral challenge has been determined, such an agent monitors the success of the resulting actions as it would any other action, primarily by means of an expectation codelet. An expectation codelet is an attention codelet that is spawned by the selected action. The job of this expectation codelet is to bring to consciousness information about the outcome of the action. In particular, the expectation agent would become activated by discrepancies between the predicted result of a course of action and its actual result. Attention to this discrepancy would in turn reinforce or inhibit the application of that behavior scheme to future similar challenges. In this manner, attention to how the result correlates with the prediction would contribute to procedural learning. This general model of procedural learning is applicable to moral development in the context of an agent that has explicitly factored moral considerations into the selection of an action, and into its expectations about the positive moral outcome of the selected action.

Moving Forward

The value of a comprehensive theory, for example the GWT-LIDA model, is that it provides a framework for integrating input from a wide variety of sources. A modular system, for example LIDA, can support a broad range of inputs. Modular computer systems don't depend totally on the ingenuity of one design team. The designers of comprehensive systems can draw on the best-of-breed in the selection of modules developed by other researchers for managing sensory input, perception, or various forms of memory, including semantic memory and procedural memory. In the GWT-LIDA model, competition for consciousness between different coalitions, global broadcasting of the winning coalition, and the selection of an action in each cycle are the mechanisms for integrating the input from the various sources. The unconscious parallel processing of information, the speed of the cycles, and the multicyclic approach to higher-order cognitive faculties holds out the promise that a LIDA-like moral agent could integrate a wide array of morally relevant inputs into its choices and actions.

Nevertheless, we don't want to give the impression that AI projects such as LIDA can solve all problems. Like other AI procedures for testing scenarios, LIDA must face the challenge of scaling—that is, the issue of whether its strategy can be adapted to handle the building and evaluation of complex scenarios. Furthermore, the foregoing discussion raises a host of additional questions. Do the mechanisms suggested by these descriptions capture important aspects of the human decision-making process? Even if humans function differently, are the mechanisms described adequate to capture the practical demands of moral decision making? Are the mechanisms for representing the conflict between different rules (proposers and objectors) too simplistic to capture the rich dynamics of human moral decision making? Can rudimentary systems that implement these mechanisms be scaled up to handle the more sophisticated moral challenges that autonomous systems functioning in a wide variety of contexts will encounter? Is the functional model of consciousness suggested by GWT and the LIDA model adequate? Or will the agent require some form of phenomenal experience that is not captured in the system described? Can morality really be understood without a full description of its social aspects? How well would LIDA handle the kinds of delicate social negotiations that are involved in managing and regulating the conflicts that arise among agents with competing interests?

Franklin and others working with the LIDA model are able to suggest ways LIDA could meet these challenges, but the approaches will initially be only theories with no proof of concept. For example, Franklin believes that LIDA will need something like a ToM to function adequately within social contexts, and is working through ways the model might be adapted to accommodate an appreciation of other's beliefs and intents. He believes ToM can be built into the model using the existing structures. As of this writing, there is no ToM in LIDA, but certainly the aforementioned attention codelets sensitive to the emotional expressions on people's faces would be an aspect of building this capacity.

Of course, many will remain suspicious of mechanical explanations of moral faculties. But the proof, as has been often said, will be in the pudding. What we have described is certainly not a demonstration that fully functioning AMAs will emerge from computational systems. Rather, we have outlined one rich experimental framework for exploring this possibility.

The approach to building AMAs outlined in this chapter differs from the approaches described in chapter 9. There we surveyed software projects that focus on one aspect of moral decision making. Here we have an approach that provides a general architecture for combining multiple kinds of morally relevant considerations. However, at this stage, LIDA is only partially implemented and is largely a conceptual model. No one can know in advance whether it is better to pursue less ambitious projects that can currently be fully implemented, for example those described in chapter 9, or to attempt to develop systems with AGI. Indeed, the idea that there is a best approach may rest on a misconception. Eventually there might be ways of combining the specialized approaches we discussed in chapters 9 and 10 into a dedicated modular architecture, for example the one proposed by Ronald Arkin, or into a global model, for example LIDA. But what we hope to have illustrated with this chapter and chapter 9 is that ethical software has left the pages of science fiction and is taking form in real lines of code. No matter how primitive these efforts may currently be, the experiment of designing AMAs has begun.

Chapter 12

DANGERS, RIGHTS, AND RESPONSIBILITIES

Tomorrow's Headlines

"Robots March on Washington Demanding Their Civil Rights"

"Terrorist Avatar Bombs Virtual Holiday Destination"

"Nobel Prize in Literature Awarded to IBM's Deep-Bluedora"

"Genocide Charges Leveled at FARL (Fuerzas Armadas Roboticas de Liberacion)"

"Nanobots Repair Perforated Heart"

"VTB (Virtual Transaction Bot) Amasses Personal Fortune in Currency Market"

"UN Debates Prohibition of Self-Replicating AI"

"Serial Stalker Targets Robotic Sex Workers"

Are these headlines that will appear in this century or merely fodder for science fiction writers? In recent years, an array of serious computer scientists, legal theorists, and policy experts have begun addressing the challenges posed by highly intelligent (ro)bots participating with humans in the commerce of daily life. Noted scientists like Ray Kurzweil and Hans Moravec talk enthusiastically about (ro)bots whose intelligence will be superior to that of humans, and how humans will achieve a form of eternal life by uploading their minds into computer systems. Their predictions of the advent of computer systems with intelligence comparable to humans around 2020–50 are based on a computational theory of mind and the projection of Moore's law over the next few decades. Legal scholars debate whether a conscious AI may be designated a "person" for legal purposes, or eventually have rights equal to those of humans. Policy planners reflect on the need to regulate the development of technologies that could potentially threaten human existence as humans have known it. The number of articles on building moral decision-making faculties into (ro)bots is a drop in the proverbial bucket in comparison to the flood of writing addressing speculative future scenarios.

New technologies will be combined to afford new possibilities. Advances in the fields of genetics, nanotechnology, and neuropharmacology will commingle with each other and with AI in ways that are far beyond humanity's ability to predict. Superintelligent (ro)bots are only one among many technologies that might emerge from AI research. Possibilities such as the rise of a cyborg culture appear to be natural extensions of present research in neuroprosthetics, including cochlear implants, neural links to artificial limbs, and deep brain stimulations that alleviate symptoms of Parkinson's disease. Future cyborgs might even erase the boundaries between cyberspace and RL (real life) with the help of neural links between computers and brains. An interface connecting the activity of nanobots within the bloodstream to an external computer opens up possibilities for repairing damaged organs as well as enhancing physical and mental faculties. However, externally controlled nanobots may also permit unscrupulous access to people's inner lives.

Which futuristic visions are likely within the near future (twenty to fifty years) and which are speculative fantasies? For every Ray Kurzweil prophesying that the Singularity (a point when AI exceeds human intelligence) is near, there are perhaps two equally noted scientists dubious of such claims. Scientists who believe it is inevitable that humans will create advanced forms of AI differ on how soon strong AI will be possible (ten to two hundred years), while those skeptical of the entire enterprise differ on whether it is possible. The skeptics emphasize the difficulty of the technological challenges that must be surmounted, while the believers are more likely to downplay it. The true believers tend to gloss over the ethical challenges that will be entailed in building AMAs, while the skeptics, to our minds, seem more sensitive to the risk that the systems that are built may acquire and act on values that are less than benign. This is certainly a generalization, but when the believers discuss the ethics of AI systems with superior intelligence, they tend toward dubious or naive assumptions as to why humans will be able to trust the beneficence of such systems. In these differences, we may just be observing psychological orientations (the cup is half full or half empty) and the need for those who identify with grand challenges to be optimistic about the social benefits that will be derived from their projects.

It can be difficult to fathom the gap between the relatively primitive state of existing (ro)botic technology and speculation regarding what is soon to come. Yes, research is progressing at a remarkable rate. However, major technological thresholds need to be crossed before the promise of human-like AI, not to mention superhuman AI, should be considered a serious possibility by policy makers and the general public.

In this chapter, we will discuss some of the more futuristic considerations that are related to the implementation of moral decision-making faculties in AI. Let us be clear at the outset. None of these futuristic reflections help us write a line of code for building AMAs. However, legal questions regarding who is responsible for the actions of a (ro)bot, and when it might cross the threshold to where it bears responsibility for its own actions, are certainly related to the themes of this book. Policy debates over the need to regulate or relinquish future research impact the development of AMAs, and will in turn be affected by any advances that ensure the safety of (ro)botic technology. Furthermore, social policy is influenced by the hopes and fears of the public. Public policy toward the development of AI will, with a bit of luck, be informed by realistic possibilities rather than speculation or hype. We will address the hopes and fears first, and then turn to issues of moral agency and legal responsibility, before concluding with some comments about whether research into (ro)botic technology should be embraced, regulated, or relinquished.

Futurology

*The possibility of super-intelligent, self-replicating artifacts
making all the important decisions gave rise to speculation that
robots or other forms of autonomous AI will eventually take
over the world and dominate or even destroy humanity. While
some scientists and technologists perceive such a development
as natural or inevitable, others find it possible, but not probable
or inevitable, or consider the takeover scenarios exaggerated,
leading to a distorted public image of robotics and AI, and
possibly damaging for further development of AI.*
—Iva Smit, *Robots, Quo Vadis?*

The futuristic (ro)botic literature spins scenarios of intelligent machines acting as moral or immoral agents, beyond the control of the engineers who built them. (Ro)bots play a pivotal role in both utopian and dystopian visions.

Speculation that AI systems will soon equal if not surpass humans in their intelligence feed technological fantasies and fears regarding a future robot takeover. Perhaps, as some versions of the future predict, a species of self-replicating (ro)bots will indeed threaten to overwhelm humanity. However,

Bill Joy's famous jeremiad in *Wired* (2000) against self-reproducing technology notwithstanding, self-replicating robots are unlikely to be a major threat. The roboticist Jordan Pollack of Brandeis University points out that unlike pathogens or replicating nanotechnology, (ro)bots require significant resources both in the form of raw materials and infrastructure to reproduce themselves. Arresting (ro)bot reproduction is a simple matter of destroying the infrastructure or shutting down the supply chain. Daniel Wilson also captured some of the absurdity in overblown fears of a robot takeover in his dryly humorous yet informative *How to Survive a Robot Uprising: Tips on Defending Yourself against the Coming Rebellion.*

Nonetheless, tactics for stopping large robots from replicating are not likely to be successful when dealing with tiny nanobots. On the other hand, nanobots, even in this age of miniaturization, are unlikely to be very intelligent. Intelligent or not, the gray goo scenarios beloved by alarmists in which self-replicating nanobots eat all the organic material on earth symbolize the serious ethical challenges posed by nanotechnology. And it is also possible, as Michael Crichton dramatized in his novel *Prey,* that groups of nanobots working together might display threatening swarm behavior.

Futurists interested in the advent of a Singularity or advanced systems with AGI commonly refer to the need for friendly AI. The idea of friendly AI is meant to capture the importance of ensuring that such systems will not destroy humanity. However, it is often hard to tell how committed those who speak of this project are to the hard work that would be necessary to make AI friendly, or whether they are giving this project lip service in order to quell the apprehension that advanced AI may not be benign—a fear that might lead to policies that interfere with the headlong charge toward superhuman AI.

The concept of friendly AI was conceived and developed by Eliezer Yudkovsky, a cofounder of the Singularity Institute for AI. The institute assumes that the accelerating development of IT will eventually produce smarter-than-human AI and has as its stated goal to confront the opportunities and risks posed by this challenge. Eliezer is a brilliant young man whose ideas sometimes border on genius. He is almost religiously devoted to the belief that a Singularity is inevitable. His thoughts on making AI friendly presume systems will soon have advanced faculties that will facilitate training them to value humans and to be sensitive to human considerations.

Yudkovsky proposes that the value of being "friendly" to humans is *the* top-down principle that must be integrated into AGI systems well before a speculative critical juncture known as the "hard takeoff." As opposed to a "soft takeoff," where the transition to a Singularity takes place over a long period of time, the "hard takeoff" theory predicts that this transition will happen very abruptly, perhaps taking only a few days. The idea is that once a system with near-human faculties turns inward and begins modifying its own code, its development could take off exponentially. The fear is that such a system will soon far exceed humans in its capacities and, if it is not friendly to humans, might treat humans no better than humans treat nonhuman animals or even insects.

Ben Goertzel does not believe that Yudkovsky's friendly AI strategy is likely to be successful. Goertzel is one of the leading scientists working on building an AGI. His Novamente project is presently directed at building an AGI that functions within the popular online universe Second Life, and he believes that this will be possible within the next decade given adequate funding. Goertzel's concern is that being "friendly" to humans is not likely to be a natural value for an AGI and therefore is less likely to survive successful rounds of self-modification. He proposes that an AGI be designed around a number of basic values. In a working paper on AI morality, Goertzel makes a distinction between those abstract basic values—for example, creating diversity, preserving existing patterns that have proved valuable, and keeping oneself healthy—that might be easy to ground in the system's architecture and hard-to-implement basic values that would need to be learned through experience. Among these "hard basic values" are preserving life and making other intelligent or living systems happy. Without experience, it would be difficult for the system to understand what life or happiness is.

Goertzel suggests that it will be possible to "explicitly wire the AGI with the Easy basic values: ones that are beneficial to humans but also natural in the context of the AGI itself (hence relatively likely to be preserved through the AGI's ongoing self-modification process)," and he advocates the strategy of using "an experiential training approach to give the system the Hard basic values." He properly tempers these suggestions with a dose of humility:

> Finally, at risk of becoming tiresome, I will emphasize one more time that all these remarks are just speculation and intuitions. It is my belief that we will gain a much better practical sense for these issues when we have subhuman but still moderately intelligent AGI's [sic] to experiment with. Until that time, any definitive assertions about the correct route to moral AGI would be badly out of place.

We agree with Goertzel that although it may be important to reflect on serious future possibilities arising from intelligent systems, it will be difficult to make headway on formulating strategies for making those systems moral. First, computer scientists will need to discover which platforms are likely to lead toward a (ro)bot with AGI.

Peter Norvig, director of research at Google and coauthor of the classic modern textbook *Artificial Intelligence: A Modern Approach*, is among those who believe that morality for machines will have to be developed alongside

AI and should not be solely dependent on future advances. By now, it should be evident that this is also how we view the challenge of developing moral machines.

Fears that advances in (ro)botic technology might be damaging to humanity underscore the responsibility of scientists to address moral considerations during the development of systems. One AI scientist particularly sensitive to the challenges that advanced AI could pose is Hugo de Garis, who heads the Artificial Intelligence Group at Wuhan University in Wuhan, China. De Garis is working on building brains out of billions of artificial neurons. He has been particularly vocal in pointing out the potential negative impact from AI research, including his own. He foresees a war between those who are supportive of advanced artilects (a term he has derived from "artificial intellects" to refer to ultraintelligent machines) and those who fear artilects.

Nick Bostrom, a philosopher who founded both the World Transhumanist Association and the Future of Humanity Institute at Oxford University, proposes that superintelligent machines will far surpass humans in the quality of their ethical thinking. However, Bostrom cautions that given that such machines would be intellectually superior and unstoppable, it behooves their designers to provide them with human-friendly motivations.

Bostrom, like Josh Storrs Hall, whose belief that humans can evolve artificial agents with positive values we discussed in chapter 7, generally holds that superintelligent systems will act in a way that is beneficial to humanity. Michael Ray LaChat of the Methodist Theological School in Ohio goes a step further in predicting the development of AI into an entity that "will become as morally perfect as human beings can imagine....The empathetic imagination of this entity will take into account the suffering and pain of all truly sentient beings in the process of decision-making....Human persons will increasingly come to rely on the moral decisions of this entity." Perhaps, as LaChat's writings suggest, the word "entity" should be replaced with the word "deity."

We do not pretend to be able to predict the future of AI. Nevertheless, the more optimistic scenarios are, to our skeptical minds, based on assumptions that border on blind faith. It is far from clear which platforms will be the most successful for building advanced forms of AI. Different platforms will pose different challenges, and different remedies for those challenges. (Ro)bots with emotions, for example, represent a totally different species from (ro)bots without emotions.

However, we agree that systems with a high degree of autonomy, with or without superintelligence, will need to be provided with something like human-friendly motivations or a virtuous character. Unfortunately, there will always be individuals and corporations who develop systems for their own ends. That is, the goals and values they program into (ro)bots may not serve the good of humanity. Those who formulate public policy will certainly direct attention to this prospect. It would be most helpful if engineers took the potential for misuse into account in designing advanced AI systems.

The development of systems without appropriate ethical restraints or motivations can have far-reaching consequences, even when (ro)bots have been developed for socially beneficial ends. As we discussed in chapter 9, the U.S. Department of Defense is particularly interested in replacing humans in dangerous military enterprises with robots. One stated goal is saving the lives of human soldiers. Presumably, robot soldiers will not be programmed with anything as restrictive as Asimov's First Law. Will, for example, the desirability of saving human lives by building robotic soldiers for combat outweigh the difficulty of guaranteeing that such machines are controllable and can't be misused?

From the perspective of designing moral machines, the importance of the futuristic scenarios is that they function as cautionary tales, warning engineers to be on guard that solutions to present problems will not hold unintended future consequences. For example, what will happen when military robots come into contact with service robots in a home that have been programmed with Asimov's First Law? Initially, one might assume that very little would change for either the military or the service robot, but eventually, as robots acquired the capacity to reprogram or restructure the way they process information, more serious consequences might result from this meeting, including the prospect that one robot would reprogram the other.

In the meantime, the more pressing concern is that very small incremental changes made to structures through which an AMA acquires and processes the information it is assimilating will lead to subtle, disturbing, and potentially destructive behavior. For instance, a robot that is learning about social factors related to trust might overgeneralize irrelevant features, for example eye, hair, or skin color, and develop unwanted prejudices as a result.

Learning systems may well be one of the better options for developing sophisticated AMAs, but the approach holds its own set of unique issues. During adolescence, learning systems will need to be quarantined, sheltering humans from their trials and errors. The better-learning (ro)bots will be open systems—expanding the breadth of information they integrate, learning from their environment, other machines, and humans. There is always the prospect that a learning system will acquire knowledge that conflicts directly with its in-built restraints. Whether an individual (ro)bot will "be conflicted" by such knowledge or use it in a way that circumvents restraints we do not know. Of particular concern is the possibility that a learning system could discover a way to override control mechanisms that function as built-in restraints.

If and when (ro)bots develop a high degree of autonomy, simple control systems that restrain inappropriate behavior will not be adequate. How can engineers build in values and control mechanisms that are difficult, if not impossible, for the system to circumvent? In effect, advanced systems will require values or moral propensities that are integral to the system's overall design and that the system neither can nor would consider dismantling. This was Asimov's vision of a robot's positronic brain being designed around the Three Laws.

One of the attractions of a bottom-up approach to the design of AMAs is that control mechanisms serving as restraints on the system's behavior might evolve in a manner where they are indeed integrated into the overall design of the system. In effect, integral internal restraints would act like a conscience that could not be circumvented except in pursuit of a goal whose importance to humanity was clear. Storrs Hall and others have stressed this point in favoring the evolutionary approaches for building a conscience for machines. However, bottom-up evolution spawns a host of progeny, and those that adapt and survive will not necessary be only those whose values are transparently benign from the perspective of humans.

Punishment—from shame to incarceration—or at least fear of punishment plays some role in human development and in restraining inappropriate behavior. Unfortunately, it is doubtful that the notion of being punished would have any lasting effect in the development of (ro)bots. Could a (ro)bot really be designed to *fear* being turned off? Certainly something corresponding to a sense of *failure* or even *shame* might be programmed into a future (ro)botic system to occur if it is unsuccessful at achieving its goals. Furthermore, mechanisms for hampering the system's pursuit of its goals, for example slowing down its information or energy supply if it violates norms, might serve as surrogate forms of "punishment" for simple autonomous (ro)bots. However, more advanced machines will certainly find ways to circumvent these controls to discover their own sources of energy and information.

The restraining influence of authentic feelings of failure or shame suggests the value of a (ro)bot having emotions of its own. Unfortunately, introducing emotions into (ro)bots is a virtual Pandora's box filled with both benefits and ethical challenges. As William Edmonson, a lecturer in the School of Computer Science at the University of Birmingham, writes, "emotionally immature Robots will present humans with strange behaviours and these might raise ethical concerns. Additionally, of course, the Robots themselves may present the ethical challenge–is it unethical to construct Robots with emotions, or unethical to build them without emotions?"

From both a technical and moral perspective, building (ro)bots capable of feeling psychological and physical pain is not a simple matter. We'll return to the morality of introducing emotions into (ro)bots when we discuss (ro)bot rights. For our purposes here, it suffices to say that while undesirable emotions may play an important role in human moral development, introducing them into (ro)bots for this purpose alone is likely to create many more problems than it solves.

Designing or evolving restraints that are integral to the overall architecture of a (ro)bot is among the more fascinating challenges future roboticists will need to address. Their success in developing adequate control systems may well determine the technological feasibility of designing AMAs, and whether the public will support building systems that display a high degree of autonomy.

The fear that future systems could not be restrained adequately and could be destructive to humans leads a few critics to suggest that research into advanced AI should be stopped before it gets out of hand. We'll address the public policy challenges posed by AI later. But first, let's look at the criteria for designating (ro)bots as moral agents and whether they may some day be deserving of civil and legal rights.

Responsibility, Liability, Agency, Rights, and Duties

Autonomous (ro)bots aren't going to attempt a global takeover any time soon. But they are already causing harm, real and perceived, and they will not always operate within ethical or legal guidelines. When they do cause harm, someone—or something—will need to be held responsible.

If the accelerating pace of the digital age has taught only one lesson, it's that laws lag behind technology. This has become apparent to many people who deal with the archaic copyright laws in the United States. Computers make copying and distributing information easy, whether or not the material has a copyright. Some (especially representatives of the book publishing, music, and movie industries) see this as necessitating better digital rights management schemes to enforce the rights that intellectual property owners currently have. But others argue that it is the asserted rights that are a broken relic of a bygone era, and those rights should be fixed not enforced.

James Boyle, of the Duke Law School Center for the Study of the Public Domain, argues that long-term copyrights made sense when publishers invested heavily in expensive printing technology. They deserved a fair return on those investments. Now that digital reproduction and distribution have trivial costs, authors and the public would be better served, he argues, by releasing materials into the public domain, the "digital commons," sooner than the present laws allow. Boyle's approach has been to promote new copyright agreements—"copylefts"—that allow authors to select from a menu of specific rights that they may transfer to others who wish to reuse their work. But such agreements do nothing to unlock the vast repository of cultural wealth that has little commercial value but remains locked up by copyrights conceived in a different era.

Just as copyright law has not kept up with the digital age, liability law is not going to keep up with challenges posed by increasingly autonomous artificial agents. Legal scholars will, of course, continue to react to technological developments. It was almost fifteen years after the Internet was opened to commercial interests before prominent law schools like Duke saw the need for centers to study legal issues in the digital context. Similarly, we predict that it will be perhaps another fifteen years before a major law school sees the need to start a Center for Law and Artificial Agents. Much harder than reacting, however, is the task of anticipating the legal developments that will require attention.

Will there be a need for the (ro)bot equivalent of a Bill of Rights? (A Bill of (Ro)bot Lefts?) Both the European Parliament and the South Korean government have recently published position articles that suggest this may happen.

Of more immediate concern than rights for (ro)bots are the existing product safety and liability laws. These will prove to be just as inadequate for ascribing responsibility for the actions of (ro)bots as copyright law has been for the Internet. For example, Helen Nissenbaum has emphasized in an article she published in 1996 that "many hands" play a role in creating the various components that make up complex automata. As systems become more complex, it is extremely difficult to establish blame when something does go wrong. How these components will interact in the face of new challenges and in new contexts cannot always be anticipated. The time and expense entailed in determining that relatively tiny O-rings were responsible for the 1986 *Challenger* disaster illustrates just how difficult it is to determine why complex systems fail. Increasing the autonomy of machines will make these problems even more difficult.

For the near future, product safety laws will continue to be stretched to deal with artificial agents. Practical liability for illegal, irresponsible, and dangerous practices will be established by the courts first, and legislatures second. Intelligent machines will pose many new challenges to existing law. We predict that companies producing and utilizing intelligent machines will stress the difficulties in determining liability and encourage no-fault insurance policies. It may also be in their interests to promote a kind of independent legal status as agents for these machines (similar to that given corporations) as a means of limiting the financial and legal obligations of those who create and use them. In other words, a kind of de facto moral agency will be attributed to the systems long before they are capable of acting as fully intelligent autonomous systems. Many people, however, will resist the idea that artificial systems should ever be considered as moral agents because they take computers and robots to be essentially mindless.

Throughout this book, we have argued that it doesn't really matter whether artificial systems are *genuine* moral agents. The engineering objective remains the same: humans need advanced (ro)bots to act as much like moral agents as possible. All things considered, advanced automated systems that use moral criteria to rank different courses of action are preferable to ones that pay no attention to moral issues. It would be shortsighted and dangerous to dismiss the problem of how to design morally sensitive systems on the grounds that it's not genuine moral agency.

Still, a danger looms. By calling artificial systems moral agents, perhaps people will end up absolving the designers, programmers, and users of AMAs of their proper moral responsibilities. Calling a machine a moral agent might tempt one to pass the buck when something goes wrong.

This is a serious issue, but the slope is not quite as slippery as one might think. Discussion about the assignment of blame and responsibility goes on even when a person is acting as an agent for another. To take an extreme case, if you hire a contract killer, it is no defense to say that the person you hired should have applied his own ethical standards and therefore you bear no responsibility for the murder. Even in less extreme cases, the agency of those who work for you or with you does not automatically absolve you of moral responsibility for their actions. Likewise, we see no justification for the view that attributing moral agency to complex artifacts should provide an easy way to deny responsibility for their actions.

So for the immediate practical purposes of designing and assigning responsibility for harms (software engineering and social engineering), we think that not very much hangs on whether robots and software agents really are moral agents. Nevertheless, it can still be instructive to look at the philosophical arguments about genuine moral agency, to see whether they provide clues to anticipating and dealing with the legal and political issues that will arise for autonomous (ro)bots.

Moral Agency

In daily practice, it is common initially to judge people by the outcomes of their actions. But conclusions based solely on outcomes are adjusted or abandoned when one learns more about the motives behind the actions in question. Motives can so significantly affect one's judgment that even apparently good actions can be judged bad, as when suspicion of ulterior motive can result in judging seemingly correct behavior to be immoral. (E.g., "He is kind and generous to her because he wants to con her into marriage.") Reflecting on such cases, many ethicists have agreed that an action should only be considered moral if it stems from a certain state of the agent's mind—from a certain quality of intention, purpose, motive or disposition.

In recent years, a number of philosophers have sought to break out of the traditional methods of the discipline by inventing the field of "experimental philosophy." Instead of relying on intuitions about thought experiments that are agreed on within the narrow confines of their colleagues' offices, experimental philosophers are now investigating systematically how intuitions about ethical (and other philosophical) problems can be influenced by seemingly irrelevant facts. For instance, in the trolley cases in which five people can be saved from a runaway trolley by sacrificing one, it has been found that being asked to imagine a scenario where they must touch the person who will die makes a big difference to people's intuitions about what is permissible. Thus, similar outcomes are assessed differently according to one's sense of direct agency in the situation. Likewise, we predict that direct, physical interactions with robots will increase people's sense of their agency and responsibility.

Another interesting result from experimental philosophy was discovered by Joshua Knobe, a philosopher at the University of North Carolina at Chapel Hill. Knobe has presented people with scenarios depicting the moneymaking motives of a corporation's CEO. In the scenarios, the CEO's desire to make money is paramount for him. The CEO can be described as saying "I don't care if it harms/helps the environment so long as it makes us money!" In some scenarios, the actions he chooses lead to predictable secondary effects that are negative, and in some they are positive. In Knobe's experiments, people are inclined to assign blame when the CEO's actions lead to bad side-effects but not to assign praise when they lead to equally predictable good side-effects. This asymmetry between credit and blame in otherwise identical scenarios may be explainable given that the CEO's profit-first motive is already morally loaded. Nevertheless, we think Knobe's discovery is relevant to people's likely reactions to autonomous artificial agents. They will, of course, be blamed when things go wrong. Still, as noted in chapter 9, the research by roboticist Matthias Scheutz seems to show that people will be more inclined to tolerate disobedience in a robot when they assume that it is working toward a shared goal.

For utilitarians and other consequentialists, agency is secondary; an agent is judged by the effects of his or her actions rather than the intentions behind those actions. But clearly, humans' interactions with complex machines and attitudes toward them are going to be shaped by something other than pure philosophical theory. Moral philosophers may lament this, but anyone interested in the future perspective of law and politics toward (ro)bots can safely bet that they won't follow a purely consequentialist approach. Similarly, while virtue ethics provides rich intellectual resources for philosophical reflections about character, these reflections are likely to remain relatively remote from the daily tug-of-war of courts and legislatures. Kantian ethicists tend to be among the most resistant to the idea that machines could be genuine moral agents. Specifically, many Kantians believe that machines necessarily lack the kind of genuine ("metaphysical") freedom of will that is essential to any kind of genuine moral agency. We have argued that genuineness is not the appropriate goal for the engineering task, and we would argue, too, that it is not an appropriate criterion for the legal questions either. Indeed, the very active legal issues surrounding direct rights for nonhuman animals show that the law already is willing to go where Kant would not have gone.

The discordant and sometimes obviously anthropocentric theories of the various ethical schools do not bring one very close to clear criteria for legally treating an autonomous (ro)bot as a moral agent. However, one should not conclude that systems incapable of comprehending the effects of their actions will not be morally praised or blamed for these effects. Human tendencies to assign praise and blame are complex and subject to many influences, and there is every chance they will be extended to (ro)bots. An AMA might be considered *praiseworthy* once it has the capacity to assess the effects of its actions on sentient beings and to use those assessments to make appropriate choices.

In chapter 4, we described Floridi and Sanders' three criteria for attributing agency to mindless machines: interactivity, autonomy, and adaptability. On their view, one can look at a system at a variety of levels, from low-level mechanical details to more abstract high-level aspects. Each level can be considered its own "level of abstraction" in the language used by Floridi and Sanders. They maintain that if, from a given level of abstraction, the system is taken to possess the three features, it should be considered an agent. If it acts in ways that have moral consequences, then it will be considered a moral agent. The applicable "level of abstraction" is specified by the features a given person can observe (the observables). Different people, for example software users versus programmers versus engineers, will consider different features to be observable. Programmers will be aware of the software and engineers of the machinery while users may only perceive the behavior. Hence they will work at different "levels" of abstraction.

Many ethicists and philosophers of technology have been reluctant to attribute agency to artifacts because to do so seems to absolve the designers and users of those artifacts from moral responsibility for their usage. Floridi and Sanders attempt to assuage these concerns by making a distinction between moral *accountability* and moral *responsibility*. They write that "agents (including human agents) should be evaluated as moral if they play the 'moral game.' Whether they mean to play it, or they know that they are playing it, is relevant only at a second stage, when we want to know whether they are morally responsible for their actions."

According to Floridi and Sanders, something much less than an attribution of agency is required to hold an artifact *accountable*. When an artificial agent produces morally undesirable outcomes, one holds it accountable by removing it from service, destroying it, and so on. Their point is that by focusing on the more limited notion of moral accountability, it is possible to sidestep the worries about whether technological artifacts possess sufficiently person-like capacities to count as moral agents in exactly the same sense as human beings. On their view, there is a level of abstraction at which mindless systems can be considered moral agents, and it is essential to think about the design, use, and regulation of such systems in terms of moral accountability rather than being limited by worries about moral personhood that are more connected to questions about responsibility.

We agree to a great extent with the spirit of Floridi and Sanders' approach. In our view, worries about whether artificial systems can be "genuine" moral agents distract from important questions about how to design systems to act appropriately in morally charged situations. Floridi and Sanders do a good job of addressing these (frequently Kantian-inspired) worries, thereby helping to "liberate technological development of [artificial agents] from being bound by the standard limiting view."

With their "levels of abstraction," they are concerned to build a framework that can legitimize the idea that software systems have moral agency— their goal, as they put it, is "to clarify the concept of agent." However, we don't think their philosophical analysis produces useful suggestions for the engineering challenge of building AMAs, which is why we have not addressed it in much detail before this point in the book. The closest they come to the implementation question is their suggestion that morally acceptable behavior could be defined as a "threshold function" applied to the observable variables that make up a level of abstraction—above a threshold might be considered moral, and below it immoral—but it is very hard to see how to put this abstract idea into practice. They also suggest that artificial agents should be designed for compliance with the Association for Computing Machinery's Code of Ethics. But how this could be implemented with a threshold is unclear. What are the variables, for example, that will enable a threshold to be defined for producing behavior in compliance with items in this code such as "Contribute to society and human well-being" and "Be honest and trustworthy"?

Despite our concerns about the limits of their shifting the concept of agency, we don't want to downplay our significant agreement with Floridi and Sanders. Their framework is helpful in thinking about how and why people interacting with (ro)bots might start to treat them as AMAs. This will, however, be dependent on the level of abstraction an observer relates to. According to Floridi and Sanders, systems that appear to ordinary users to possess adaptability do not appear so to software engineers who are operating at a different level of abstraction. Deterministic rules embedded in the computers' programs will be among the observables to the software engineers. While it is the case that in large-scale projects, no single individual may be able to treat the entire program as observable, any "ethical subroutines" will nonetheless be observable to some engineers. The questions that will face the legal system will be what level or levels of observation are appropriate for deciding legal questions. In fact, a very similar debate goes on in legal and scientific circles about how to handle mechanistic gene-and-neuron-level explanations of human behavior—could these absolve some people of liability for their actions? Indeed, for the past fifty years, legal systems have struggled with similar questions as to whether sociological factors absolved individuals of responsibility for criminal actions. Recent advances in neuroscience have led to the establishment of working groups in "neuroethics" at several universities, notably the University of Pennsylvania, Stanford University, and the University of British Columbia.

The pressing issue for us here remains the one of who is responsible for the behavior of autonomous AMAs. Floridi and Sanders argue that the traditional view that only humans can be found responsible for certain kinds of software and/or hardware is now rather outdated. Any agent is morally accountable. But artificial agents cannot be held responsible for their actions the same way humans are. Obviously, subjecting AMAs to human kinds of praise or blame may not make much sense. Working with clear definitions of agents' domains (i.e., level of abstraction and morality thresholds) helps make this problem manageable by making it possible to separate and formalize responsibility, and clarify its part in morality. Moreover, avoiding anthropocentric and anthropomorphic attitudes toward agenthood removes numerous hindrances to the investigation and better understanding of what Floridi and Sanders call *distributed morality*, that is, "a macroscopic and growing phenomenon of global moral actions and collective responsibilities resulting from the 'invisible hand' of systemic interactions among several agents at a local level." Their concept allows for mindless morality without inappropriately assigning moral responsibility to the machines. This is complementary to the traditional approach of human-centered morality based on mental states, feelings, emotions, and legal responsibility. On this view, artificial agents that satisfy the criteria of interactivity, autonomy, and adaptability are legitimate, fully accountable sources of moral (or immoral) actions, even if they do not exhibit free will, mental states, or responsibility.

The responsibility for the behavior of intelligent artifacts remains a pressing and difficult matter to resolve, because the increasingly complex chains between actions and consequences typical for contemporary society obscure who makes key decisions and complicate the issue of what is right or wrong.

Traditionally, human designers and operators were held morally accountable for the actions of machines. This view is still appropriate in many situations, but does it apply when the behavior of a machine emerges, to some extent unforeseeably, from decisions made by many people and possibly also by other machines? Floridi and Sanders suggested that assigning responsibility at any cost and looking for the responsible individual when something untoward happens is not likely to deliver the desired results under these circumstances. Rather, the *ethics of creative stewardship*, that is, focusing on accountability and promoting normative action by monitoring and censuring autonomous agents, provides a far better perspective for dealing with the challenges of modern technology. We wish to emphasize once more, however, that while these post hoc questions about moral accountability are important, they do not provide obvious solutions to the primary technological challenge of building AMAs that have the capacity to assess the effects of their actions on sentient beings, and to use those assessments to make appropriate decisions.

Rights and Responsibilities

Beginning with Sam Lehman-Wilzig's 1981 article "Frankenstein Unbound: Towards a Legal Definition of Artificial Intelligence," the question of whether there are barriers to designating intelligence systems legally accountable for their actions has captured the attention of a small but growing community of scholars. They generally concur that the law, as it exists, can accommodate the advent of intelligent (ro)bots. A vast body of law already exists for attributing *legal personhood* to nonhuman entities (corporations). No radical changes in the law would be required to extend the status of *legal person* to machines with higher-order faculties, presuming that the (ro)bots were recognized as responsible agents.

From a legal standpoint, the more difficult questions concern the rights that might be conferred on an intelligent system. When or if future artificial moral agents should acquire legal status of any kind, the question of their legal rights will also arise. This will be particularly an issue if intelligent machines are built with a capacity for emotions of their own, for example the ability to feel pain.

Isaac Asimov anticipated this problem in his novella *The Bicentennial Man*, on which a movie with the same title, starring Robin Williams, was based. Only when the main character, "Andrew," an NDR-113 model robot, has his components replaced with organic matter and allows his positronic brain to decay and die is he accepted as a human being. A lesson one may take from this is that human morality springs from mortality. This would make Josh Storrs Hall's fantasy of perfectly moral machines arising necessarily from their immortality seem even more remote from what people want of their AMAs.

Already there are calls to block research into the kinds of machines that could fully participate in the human moral sphere. Philosopher Thomas Metzinger is author of a book on consciousness called *Being No-One: The Self-Model Theory of Subjectivity*. Metzinger's theory of the phenomenal self model (PSM) has been used as the basis for virtual reality experiments in which human subjects experience events taking place in their own bodies while seeing the events from a third person perspective. Nothing in Metzinger's account rules out the possibility of building a PSM into machines. Indeed, his book has inspired the work of the roboticist Owen Holland on machine consciousness. However, near the end of his book Metzinger writes:

> Suffering starts on the level of Phenomenal Self Models....The PSM is the decisive neurocomputational instrument not only in developing a host of new cognitive and social skills but also in forcing any strongly conscious system to functionally and representationally appropriate its own disintegration, its own failures and internal conflicts. Pain and any other nonphysical kind of suffering, generally any representational state characterized by a "negative valence" and integrated into the PSM are now phenomenally owned. Now it inevitably, and transparently, is my own suffering....Therefore, we should ban all attempts to create (or even risk the creation of) artificial and postbiotic PSMs from serious academic research.

Our present laws are based on a clear distinction between persons and machinery that will be increasingly challenged by more and more sophisticated artificial agents. Floridi and Sanders are right that whether one sees such systems as agents at all will depend on the levels of abstraction one applies. It is always possible to focus on low-level mechanisms and, from that perspective, express the view that nothing like moral agency is present. But, as we have seen, the same happens if one goes too low into the molecules that make up human beings. Which level to apply is partly a pragmatic matter—it depends on what you know and what you want to accomplish—but ultimately is a matter of choice. From one perspective, the (ro)bots we create can seem mere machines and from another, complex adaptive entities that may be more or less sensitive to the things that matter morally to us.

David Calverley, a lawyer who has written specifically about AMAs, points out that while intelligent machines with higher-order faculties such as consciousness may indeed fulfill current legal standards for being designated "legal persons," ultimately their recognition as such will be a political and not a legal determination.

Recognizing Success

Whether or not the legal ins and outs of personhood can be sorted out, more immediate and practical for engineers and regulators is the need to evaluate AMA performance. But ethical standards are diverse, and ethical behavior is hard to define, which suggests that something other than explicit standards might be necessary.

In many ways, the problem of identifying a good AMA is a narrower version of the old AI standby of how to say when a machine is intelligent. And just as Alan Turing tried to sidestep the question of defining intelligence, an obvious idea for bypassing disagreements about ethical standards is to come up with a variant of the Turing test: the MTT (introduced in chapter 4). A human judge asks questions and tries to determine from the answers whether she is interacting with a machine or a human being. If the judge cannot reliably distinguish a machine's answers to questions about moral issues from a person's, then the machine's performance may be judged satisfactory. Any MTT is bound to be a far from perfect evaluation tool, just like the original Turing test, but thinking through the limitations of such a test can help sort out what one does want in an evaluation of AMAs.

Turing tests are procedural tests. They specify a procedure for determining whether a machine's performance is at the desired level without setting explicit standards. Nevertheless, procedures aren't entirely neutral about what they consider important. Thus, the question-and-answer format of the MTT may place undue emphasis on a machine's ability to articulate reasons for its moral decisions. This might suit a Kantian who thinks that good actions must flow from good reasons, but it is not so suitable from either a utilitarian or common-sense approach. The most famous utilitarian of the nineteenth century, John Stuart Mill, argued that actions are morally good independent of the agent's motivations. And many people think that young children (and perhaps even dogs) are moral agents even though they are incapable of articulating the reasons for their actions.

One way to shift the focus from reasons to actions might be to restrict the information available to the human judge in some way. Suppose the human judge in the MTT is provided with descriptions of actual, morally significant actions of a human and an AMA, purged of all references that would identify the agents. If the judge correctly identifies the machine at a level above chance, then the machine has failed the test.

There is, however, a problem both for this version of the MTT and the initial question-and-answer version. The problem is that distinguishability is the wrong criterion, because the machine might be recognized for responding or acting in ways that are consistently better than a human would. Turing considered an analogous problem for his original Turing test, and suggested dumbing down the machine's replies—making it delay its responses to arithmetic problems, for example. For the original Turing test, this is acceptable, since indistinguishability really is the goal. But for AMAs, one might actually want them to be more consistent and impartial than humans usually are in their moral decisions and actions. Asking the judge to decide which of a pair of agents acted less morally than the other might solve this problem. If the machine is not readily identified as less moral more often than the human, then it has passed the test. This is the cMTT (discussed in chapter 4).

Still, the cMTT is far from perfect. First, one might think the standard is too low. Even though to pass the test the machine must, on average, be judged at least as moral as humans, one might demand more. That is, the goal should not be just to construct an AMA but to construct an exemplary AMA. The cMTT allows the machine's aggregate performance to contain actions that would be judged as morally wrong, and morally worse than the human actions, so long as on balance these do not cause the machine to be rated lower than the human. The cMTT could, in response, be tightened to require that the machine not be judged worse than the human in any comparison of specific actions. But even with this restriction, the resulting standard might be too low: human behavior itself is typically far from being morally ideal! People are likely to be much less tolerant of decisions that result in harm to others made by a machine than of those made by another human being.

Without any other generally agreed-on standard, however, the cMTT may remain the only workable yardstick available for assessing what is acceptable behavior from AMAs.

Embrace, Reject, or Regulate?

Public policy toward (ro)bots will undoubtedly be influenced by ideas about how to evaluate their intelligence and moral capacities. But political factors will play the larger role in determining the issues of accountability and rights for (ro)bots, and whether some forms of (ro)bot research will be regulated or outlawed.

(Ro)bot accountability is a tricky but manageable issue. For example, companies developing AI are concerned that they may be open to lawsuits even when their systems enhance human safety. Peter Norvig of Google offers the example of cars driven by advanced technology rather than humans. Imagine that half the cars on U.S. highways are driven by (ro)bots, and the death toll decreases from roughly forty-two thousand a year to thirty-one thousand a year. Will the companies selling those cars be rewarded? Or will they be confronted with ten thousand lawsuits for deaths blamed on the (ro)bot drivers?

Norvig's question faces any new technology. It could just as easily be asked about a new drug that reduces the overall death rate from heart disease while directly causing some patients to die from side effects. And just as drug companies face lawsuits, so, too, will (ro)bot manufacturers be sued by (ro)bot-chasing lawyers. Some cases will have merit, and some won't. However, free societies have an array of laws, regulations, insurance policies, and juridical precedents that help protect industries from frivolous lawsuits. Companies pursuing the huge commercial market in (ro)botics will protect their commercial interests by relying on the existing frameworks and by petitioning legislatures for additional laws that help manage their liability.

However, as (ro)bots become more sophisticated, two questions may arise in the political arena. Can the (ro)bots themselves, rather than their manufacturers or users, be held directly liable or responsible for damages? Do sophisticated (ro)bots deserve any recognition of their own rights?

We think that both of these questions are futuristic compared to the aims of this book. Nevertheless, others have already started to discuss them, and we don't want to ignore that discussion entirely.

There are many ways agents are held responsible for their actions within legal systems, corresponding to different available means of punishment. Human agents have historically been punished in a variety of ways: through infliction of pain, social ostracism or banishment, fines or other confiscation of property, or deprivation of liberty or life itself. Debates over whether it makes sense to hold (ro)bots accountable for their actions often center on whether any of these traditionally applied punishments makes sense for artificial agents. For instance, the infliction of pain only counts as a real punishment for agents that are capable of feeling it. Depriving an agent of freedom only really punishes an agent who values freedom. And confiscation of property is only possible for agents who have property rights to begin with.

If you are convinced that artificial agents will never satisfy the conditions for real punishment, the idea of holding them directly accountable for their actions is a nonstarter. One can believe this and still agree with the main thrust of this book, which is that some facsimile of moral decision making is needed for autonomous systems. Successful AMAs might be constructed even if they could never be held directly responsible for anything, just as artificial chess players can win tournaments even though they never get direct credit for doing so.

However, you may be among the readers who believe that (ro)bots will eventually reach the point where it would be nothing but human prejudice to deny that they deserve equal treatment under the law. Such a movement is likely to come gradually, and with much disagreement about when the threshold has been crossed. In this respect, calls for (ro)bot rights are likely to mimic the politically significant movement to increase rights for animals.

Much of the animal rights movement has focused on protecting the more intelligent species from pain and distress.

Pain and emotional distress are not yet, of course, issues for (ro)bots. The kinds of emotional mechanisms we discussed in chapter 10 certainly do not cause actual conscious discomfort to the machines. However, designers will, in all likelihood, continue trying to build realistic emotions and pain responses into (ro)bots. It will be particularly difficult to establish whether these future (ro)bots actually have any subjective experience of pain, just as it is difficult to establish whether people in vegetative states experience subjective pain or what kinds of pain animals experience. If (ro)bots might one day be capable of experiencing pain and other affective states, a question that arises is whether it will be moral to build such systems—not because of how they might harm humans, but because of the pain these artificial systems will themselves experience. In other words, can the building of a (ro)bot with a somatic architecture capable of feeling intense pain be morally justified and should it be prohibited?

In the previous section, we described how the German philosopher Thomas Metzinger has already called for a ban on building (ro)bots with a conscious self model, precisely because he thinks this would increase the amount of pain and distress in the world. We think that Metzinger's proposal is unlikely to be heeded. The commercial pressure toward more and more sophisticated (ro)bots is just too strong, particularly when it is so easy for people to shield themselves behind all the doubts about whether (ro)bots could really be conscious.

If not prohibited, should there be regulation of experiments in which a robot *might* experience emotional states? A significant body of law has evolved to protect animals from undue suffering, including a network of institutional animal care and use committees that regulate the appropriate care and use of animals in research. These committees are similar to the institutional review boards that oversee the ethical treatment of humans in research. Regulations protecting animals are far less stringent than those protecting humans, and there is much scientific disagreement about how animal pain and distress can be measured. Nevertheless, members of animal care and use committee attempt to balance the needs of scientific research against the well-being of animals used in experiments. To date, there are no review boards to oversee the ethical treatment of (ro)bots in research, nor is there any need for them. However, as the appearance of subjective feelings of pain and pleasure in (ro)bots becomes stronger, there will be calls for regulations and review boards to oversee the kinds of research that can be performed.

Establishing the subjective experience of the systems, while hard enough, will only serve as a backdrop for deeper concerns. No doubt, there will be individuals and groups for whom the prospect of developing artificial systems with emotions is deemed unacceptable for ethical reasons, or offensive, if not an abomination, for religious reasons. Barring a major political movement to severely restrict (ro)botic research, we would anticipate that legislatures will decide questions regarding the treatment of (ro)bots in research narrowly. Initially, there will be legislation requiring a review of the use and treatment of (ro)bots in only specialized forms of research, but as more sophisticated systems are built, a broader array of experiments will require ethical review.

Regulating the treatment of (ro)bots in research is not the same as granting legal rights to them, but the establishment of protections provides a toehold for the assignment of rights. The progression toward rights for (ro)bots is likely to be slow. (Ro)bots may be programmed to demand energy, information, and eventually education, protection, and property rights, but how is one to evaluate whether they *truly desire* social goods and services? If a robot in a plaintive voice begs that you not turn it off, what criterion will you use to decide whether or not this is a plea that should be honored? As systems get more and more sophisticated, fewer and fewer people may question whether it is appropriate to anthropomorphize the actions of a (ro)bot, and many people will come to treat the (ro)bots as the intelligent entities they appear to be.

Sexual politics are one frontier where these issues may come to the fore. The adoption of mechanical devices, robots, and virtual reality by the sex industry is nothing new, and while some are offended by such practices, governments in democratic countries have largely turned away from trying to legislate the private practices of the individuals who use these products. However, other social practices are likely to ignite public debate. Examples are the rights of humans to marry robots and of (ro)bots to own property. Lester del Rey was the first writer to fictionalize a robot marrying a human in the classic short story "Helen O'Loy," which he published in 1938. Helen, the robotic heroine, not only marries her inventor but later sacrifices herself when her husband dies. In 2007, almost seventy years later, the University of Maastricht in the Netherlands awarded a doctorate to AI enthusiast David Levy for his thesis that trends in the development of robotics and in shifting social attitudes toward marriage will lead to humans perceiving sophisticated robots as suitable marriage partners. Given that marriage is an institution legally recognized by the state, legislatures can anticipate debating this possibility. Unlike most other kinds of rights for robots, marriage is an issue that humans will have a direct interest in, and may therefore be among the first rights considered for robots. Initially, presuming a human is granted the right to marry a robot, this might confer only limited rights to the robot. However, over time there would be demands for robots to have the legal right to inherit property, and to serve as a surrogate in health decisions involving an incapacitated human spouse.

Long before legislatures consider granting rights to (ro)bots, however, they are likely to be forced to deal with demands to restrict research or even ban outright the development of sophisticated AI systems. Even as the public embraces scientific progress, there is considerable confusion, anxiety, and fear regarding the way future technologies might transform human identity and community.

The difficulty, as we mentioned earlier, will be for legislatures, judges, and public officials to distinguish the societal challenges that need to be addressed from issues that are based on speculative projections. Unrealistic expectations and fears come partly from researchers who—because they need to promise results in order to get funding for their projects—give overly optimistic time frames for their anticipated results.

An actual catastrophe in which an AI system causes significant harm to humans, or widespread fears that advanced forms of AI will eventually eliminate humans, could, of course, lead to political pressures that override any reasonable perspective. In addition, the political arena can be especially unpredictable and chaotic when confronted with issues in which many different constituencies have a stake. Because of the commercial forces involved in (ro)botics, and because it is hard to know exactly what directions the technological developments will take, it is clear that there will be many stakeholders. It is difficult to predict exactly who they will be, what their concerns will be, and how they will align with each other. This unpredictability is accentuated when one considers the regulation of "enhancement technologies" that promise tighter and tighter integration of technology with the human body. Artificial intelligence is typically included in discussions of technological enhancements, from neuroprostheses to neuropharmacology to nanotechnology. James Hughes, author of *Citizen Cyborg: Why Democratic Societies Must Respond to the Redesigned Human of the Future*, argues that enhancement technologies will be a core political issue in the United States and Europe in the coming decades.

By what criteria will the risks posed by new technologies be assessed? How convincingly must a critic prove the likelihood of the danger? At what stage is government justified in stepping into the realm of science to stop or slow scientific research, regardless of whether harm has already occurred?

The precautionary principle, which we introduced in chapter 3, is often invoked to argue that scientists should relinquish research into fields that have the potential to be harmful to humans. The European Union has codified the precautionary principle in various directives, but the United States has not done so. This difference is reflected in Europe's more restrictive policies toward new technologies, including genetically modified foods. On the other hand, rather than explicitly rejecting research that poses dangers, legislators in the United States create regulatory hurdles that can be insurmountable. For example, fear in the United States that genetically modified grains designed to facilitate the production of low-cost drugs will contaminate existing strains of corn and wheat has resulted in the absence of any regulatory standard for establishing acceptable risks. This has more or less arrested any field tests of these plants.

Which of the promised advances in computer technology or medical science are people willing to forego on the basis of highly speculative fears that humanity is heading toward the eradication of the human species as it has been known? Who decides when research has crossed a threshold where it becomes dangerous? Which avenues of research in the development of artificial agents hold potential dangers that can be foreseen, and how will these dangers be addressed? Which of these dangers can be managed and which may require the relinquishment of further research? What areas of concern will need regulation and oversight, and how might this be managed in a way that does not interfere with scientific progress?

We have many questions and few answers. The lack of clarity on these serious issues increases the prospect of political influence in determining whether new technologies are regulated. Fear of possible bad consequences is just one concern on the minds of political leaders. Economic interests, hopes of helping the needy, and pressure from socially conservative constituents are among the considerations that will influence decisions.

Furthermore, decisions to regulate research in Europe, the United States, or Asia will not necessarily be supported by other governments. Values and social pressures differ from country to country and state to state, as President George W. Bush discovered when he tried to slow stem cell research. The Japanese are under tremendous pressure to develop service robots to care for the elderly and homebound, while countries with more open immigration and guest worker programs are not under the same pressure. The values of religiously conservative voters, who care about social issues, tend to be much more influential in American than in European politics. Calls to relinquish research on ethical grounds are not likely to carry the same weight in more liberal countries.

National and international mechanisms for discriminating real dangers from speculative dangers are needed. One dimension of this challenge is determining when technological thresholds that present clear ethical challenges and potential harms to humans are about to be crossed. This is easier said than done. It is not clear whether legislatures and international bodies such as the UN have the will to create effective mechanisms for oversight. Furthermore, there are few concrete suggestions on how any regulation of AI research might be accomplished. A "Roboethics Roadmap," developed for the European Robotics Research Network (EURON) by Gianmarco Veruggio, an Italian roboticist and president of Scuola di Robotica, admirably outlines the benefits, obstacles, and challenges for a broad array of robotic applications, but is largely focused on getting concerned parties to begin thinking about the issues. The expressed focus of the Singularity Summit in the United States is also to ensure that (ro)bots will be friendly to human concerns, but here, too, there are few concrete proposals. Perhaps this is all that can be expected at this stage of development.

A more difficult challenge than distinguishing real from speculative danger will be to assess how the cumulative effect of incremental changes might lead to fundamental shifts in the structure of society. Coevolution of human culture and its technologies has been ongoing since the day humans first picked up stones and used them as hammers or weapons. Cultural evolution continues at a rapid pace. Society is pretty good at assimilating change, for example, the extension of the average life expectancy at birth in the United States from forty-seven in 1900 to seventy-eight years today, and the advent of cell phones and iPods. But might the cumulative effect of new technologies give rise to forms of societal change that are seriously disruptive, if not outright destructive?

Leon Fuerth, research professor of international affairs at George Washington University and formerly national security advisor to Vice President Al Gore, uses the phrase "social tsunami" to describe the challenges posed by genetic engineering, nanotechnology, neuropharmacology, and AI. From his experience as a policy advisor in the Clinton-Gore administration, he notes that the public policy apparatus is not well adapted to plan for possible future crises. Policy makers are suspicious about the ability of social planners to predict what might happen. Immediate goals beat out longer-term objectives in the competition for funds. While there are certainly limits in people's ability to predict the future, failure to develop even short-term planning for events that have the potential to seriously disrupt social stability is shortsighted. Fuerth stresses the need for "forward engagement," the disciplined capacity to plan for potentially major societal events.

We agree with Fuerth that it is time to bring a little foresight and planning to the challenges AI and other enhancement technologies pose. An initiative that regularly brings together experts and concerned members of the public to map the current and imminent challenges posed by digital technologies would be particularly helpful. A central responsibility for this body would be to clarify those technological thresholds that must be crossed before speculative futuristic challenges should be treated as real possibilities. Their reports could serve as an educational vehicle and as a framework for illuminating those challenges for which policy makers and society as a whole do indeed need to plan. Science is not static. Progress in one research avenue impacts progress in others. Such a map will need to be revised regularly.

In this book, we have endeavored to map the pathways by which autonomous (ro)bots might become AMAs. No one knows where the ultimate technological limits of moral machines may lie, or whether there are any limits at all. (Although there's no shortage of people claiming to know!) Engineers and ethicists must recognize the limits of current technologies and utilize the ethical capabilities provided by the best technologies. Overly optimistic assessments of technological capacities could lead to a dangerous reliance on (ro)bots that are not sufficiently sensitive to ethical considerations. Overly pessimistic assessments could stymie the development of some truly useful technologies or induce a kind of fatalistic attitude toward (ro)bots.

We believe it is necessary to proceed with the development of AMAs. Whether the future holds (ro)bots that are "real" moral agents is beside the point. It will be possible to engineer systems that are more sensitive to the laws and moral considerations that inform ethical decisions than anything presently available. The future needs AMAs.

EPILOGUE—(RO)BOT MINDS AND HUMAN ETHICS

In writing this book, we have learned that the process of designing (ro)bots capable of distinguishing right from wrong reveals as much about human ethical decision making as about AI.

We started with the deliberately naive idea that ethical theories might be turned into decision procedures, even algorithms. But we found that top-down ethical theorizing is computationally unworkable for real-time decisions. Furthermore, the prospect of reducing ethics to a logically consistent principle or set of laws is suspect, given the complex intuitions people have about right and wrong.

Professional ethicists already know that their theories cannot provide real-time decision procedures. Instead, many of them see the project of ethics as aimed at justifying ethical decisions within a single, comprehensive framework. Perfect consequentialism or Kantianism represent ideals against which actions are to be measured. But for such ethicists, the impossible rigor demanded by such perfection looms large. For example, can a determined consequentialist also have genuine commitments to friends and family, come what may, or must he subjugate personal relationships to the maximization of utility?

In our view, however, this is a monkish pursuit, not much removed from the question of whether it is possible to live according to a vow of perfect poverty or perfect silence. People don't want AMAs to replicate the abstractions of moral philosophers any more than they want their neighbors to do so. People want their neighbors to have the capacity to respond flexibly and sensitively in real and virtual environments. They want to have confidence that their neighbors' behavior will satisfy appropriate norms, and that they can trust their neighbors' actions. Meeting this challenge will entail an even more thorough understanding of human ethical behavior than is presently available. That is, building AMAs forces one to take a particularly comprehensive approach to ethical decision making. It is important, we think, that the project of building AMAs highlights the need for a richer understanding of human morality.

This does not mean that top-down theories are worthless, but it impels one to take a different look at their role. Different theories provide languages for describing ethical challenges and lenses through which to view them. Every theory provides concepts that underscore different features of actions and outcomes in situations of moral risk. Different ethical theories, intuitions, and social practices must be factored into the choice of actions. For humans, and for AMAs, the challenge is to broaden awareness of the moral considerations that impinge on a particular situation.

Trust and cooperation cannot be built by the dogmatic imposition of one framework over another or through the rigid application of one view of what is ethically "correct." Rather, they require the capacity to see the other's point of view. Ethical theories are thus not strict guides to action, but frameworks for negotiation. Real problems facing real agents are the playing field on which the social norms surrounding trust and cooperation must be addressed.

Some ethicists will claim that this misses the point of ethics (as they understand it)—that ethics is about what *should be*, not merely about the way people *do* function in social situations. We agree that ethics helps an agent reflect on the "oughts." These oughts translate into the weights agents place on particular moral considerations. An agent will still need to find a way to steer between the many moral considerations that impinge on each new challenge and come up with a course of action that balances those considerations as well as possible, while being able to explain why some considerations could not be fully accommodated.

Perhaps one might have come to a similar conclusion through just thinking about the moral decision making of humans, irrespective of autonomous machines. However, reflection on a comprehensive approach toward teaching robots right from wrong has demanded attention to aspects of moral decision making that people normally take for granted in their daily, frequently less-than-perfect attempts to behave ethically toward each other.

The quest to develop AMAs will also feed back on ethical understanding by providing a platform for experimental investigation. For instance, by tinkering with the correspondence between what is said, what is done, and what is conveyed by nonverbal means, researchers will be able to systematically test how words, deeds, and gestures interact to shape ethical judgment. And by simulating the interactions among agents with different ethical viewpoints, it will be possible to supplement the speculative thought experiments of science fiction and philosophy with testable social and cognitive models.

Humans have always looked around for company in the universe. Their long fascination with nonhuman animals derives from the fact that animals are the things most similar to them. The similarities and the differences tell humans much about who and what they are. As AMAs become more sophisticated, they will come to play a corresponding role as they reflect humans' values. For humanity's understanding of ethics, there can be no more important development.

NOTES

These notes expand on some of themes in the chapters, and we hope they inspire further thought and reading. We also give credit to people and works that have specifically influenced our writing about machine morality. The bibliography provides a more complete list of sources that have nourished our thinking about teaching robots right from wrong. Where those sources can be easily determined from the main text, we have not repeated them here in the notes, on the assumption that interested readers will be able to find the relevant items in the bibliography.

Introduction

Asimov first explicitly introduced the Three Laws of Robotics in the short story "Runaround," published in the March 1942 issue of *Astounding Science Fiction*. In his 1985 novel *Robots and Empire*, Asimov formulated an additional Zeroth Law, to stand above the original three: "A robot may not harm humanity, or, by inaction, allow humanity to come to harm." Other science fiction writers have explored similar ideas, sometimes anticipating Asimov's laws and sometimes expanding on them.

Journalist Noah Shachtman blogged about the incident in South Africa of a robotic gun going awry; see "Robot Cannon Kills 9, Wounds 14," *Wired*, October 18, 2007, http://blog.wired.com/defense/2007/10/robot-cannon-ki.html. While mechanical malfunction was ultimately determined to be the cause of the accident, Shachtman reports early claims that faulty software may have played a part. He also links to a video of a separate incident in the United States, purportedly showing a remotely operated weapon emptying its magazine in an uncontrolled fashion and, although fortunately out of ammunition by this point, swinging around in the direction of the camera and the spectators, allegedly including some members of the United States Congress.

The future market for robots is analyzed by Dan Kara, president and editorial director of *Robotics Trends*, at his blog, www.robonexus.com/roboticsmarket .htm. His analysis is partly on the basis of figures from the Japan Robot Association (www.jara.jp/e/).

Oxford University philosopher Nick Bostrom has argued that it is quite possible we are *already* living as part of a computer simulation, if not the Matrix per se. In a 2003 article in *Philosophical Quarterly*, "Are You Living In a Computer Simulation?" he argued that one of these three things has to be true: (1) the human species is very likely to go extinct before reaching a "posthuman" stage; (2) any posthuman civilization is extremely unlikely to run a significant number of simulations of their evolutionary history (or variations thereof); and (3) we are almost certainly living in a computer simulation. Bostrom considers the three possibilities to be equally likely. His paper and others debating its merit can be found at www.simulation-argument.com/.

Chapter 1

Philippa Foot introduced the trolley case thought experiment in her 1967 article "The Problem of Abortion and the Doctrine of Double Effect." The original trolley cases have been embellished into dozens, perhaps hundreds, of variants to test philosophical intuitions about what is or isn't permissible according to various ethical theories. Trolley cases feature prominently in recent attempts by scientists to understand the evolutionary, emotional, and neurological bases for human moral decisions. Joshua Greene was the first person to pose trolley cases to subjects in the brain scanner, with his fMRI study published in *Science* in 2001.

Our discussion of the actual driverless trains derives from the 2002 article "The Future Lies in Driverless Metros" by Mike Knutton, journalist and editor of the *International Railway Journal;* he quotes Morten Sondergaard of the Copenhagen metro and discusses the experience of the Paris metro with its driverless Meteor trains. Professor R. J. Hill of Cambridge University made the case that politics and economics rather than engineering will hold back railway automation in his 1983 article "The Automation of Railways" in the journal *Physics in Technology*. Since at least 2003, Bob Crow, the leader of Britain's National Union of Rail, Maritime and Transport Workers, has repeatedly threatened strike action in opposition to the expansion of driverless trains in the London Underground.

To learn more about Joseph Engelberger's take on robotics and the service industry see his 1989 book *Robotics in Service*. Engelberger's status as "father of robotics" is recognized annually by the Robotics Industries Association with its Joseph F. Engelberger Award for outstanding contributions to robotics.

IBM maintains a full archive about Deep Blue and its defeat of world chess champion Gary Kasparov at www.research.ibm.com/deepblue/. Aleksandr Kronrod, a Russian AI researcher, has made the claim that "chess is the *Drosophila* of AI." Many cognitive scientists now believe that instead of being AI's fruit fly, chess was actually a red herring, leading researchers into a blind alley for decades.

F-Secure Corporation is headquartered in Helsinki; Mikko Hyppönen is chief research officer. Journalist Michael Shnayerson quotes Hyppönen in his January 2004 article "The Code Warrior" in *Vanity Fair*.

Blaster (also known as Lovesan) was a worm that spread through several versions of Microsoft Windows operating systems, causing instability and programming hijacked systems to launch a distributed denial-of-service attack against Microsoft's windowsupdate.com website. The planned attack failed to cause any serious problems for Microsoft.

Computer ethics emerged as a distinct field in the early 1980s. It was put on the map in 1985 when Terrell Ward Bynum and Jim Moor edited a special issue of the journal *Metaphilosophy* that was republished as a book, and Deborah Johnson also published her textbook on the subject. Bynum has also written "A Very Short History of Computer Ethics," published in the summer 2000 issue of the American Philosophical Association's *Newsletter on Philosophy and Computing* and also available at www.southernct.edu/organizations/rccs/resources/research/introduction/bynum_shrt_hist.html.

The Internet Archive Project and its Wayback Machine can be found at www.archive.org/. Journalist Reni Gertner wrote about lawyers using the Wayback machine in her article "Lawyers Are Turning to Old Websites for Evidence," published in *Lawyers Weekly* in August 15, 2005.

The U.S. Army's plans for autonomous battlefield systems are presented at their Future Combat Systems website, www.army.mil/fcs/. Journalist Tim Weiner's account of the army's plans appeared in his article "New Model Army Soldier Rolls Closer to Battle" in the *New York Times* of February 16, 2005. Noah Schactman and David Hambling are journalist-bloggers who follow the technology of automated warfare closely. Some recent articles by them on the *Wired* Blog Network include Schactman's "Armed Robots Pushed to Police," on August 16, 2007, and "Roomba-Maker Unveils Kill-Bot" on October 17, 2007, and Hambling's "Armed Robots Go into Action," on September 10, 2007.

Peter Norvig's comments about the cumulative effects of small mistakes can be found in the transcript of a talk he gave at the Singularity Summit in San Francisco, September 9, 2007. The Singularity Summit is an annual conference about the future of AI and humanity; see www.singinst.org/media/singularitysummit2007/).

The final quotation of the chapter is from Rosalind Picard's book *Affective Computing*, published in 1997. Picard is more concerned with computers' abilities to recognize emotions than their moral behavior, but clearly the one feeds into the other—a theme we develop in chapter 10.

Chapter 2

The NSPE Code of Ethics may be found at www.nspe.org/Ethics/CodeofEthics/.

Helen Nissenbaum, professor of media, culture, and communication and of computer science at New York University, has extensively surveyed the ways values influence the design process. Nissenbaum's website lists many of her articles: www.nyu.edu/projects/nissenbaum/main_cv.html. She is codirector of the Values at Play research project (http://valuesatplay.org/), which looks at how designers of computer games can become more aware of the values they build into their games.

Neuroethics is a term that has come to prominence since the turn of the twenty-first century; it describes an emerging subfield of bioethics that deals specifically with the ethical issues arising from neuroscience. Stanford University has developed a neuroethics program as part of its Center for Biomedical Ethics (see http://neuroethics.stanford.edu). Other resources include the University of Pennsylvania's neuroethics website (http://neuroethics.upenn.edu/) and the philanthropic Dana Foundation (www.dana.org/neuroethics/). A peer-reviewed journal, *Neuroethics*, published its first issue in March 2008.

The Drew McDermott quote comes from a paper titled "Why Ethics is a High Hurdle for AI," which he presented on July 12 at the 2008 North American Conference on Computing and Philosophy at Indiana University in Bloomington, Indiana.

Chapter 3

In the light of modern scientific discoveries about tool use and manufacture by animals, especially chimpanzees and New Caledonian crows, it is much harder to claim that humans are the only toolmakers. Still, it is clear that our toolmaking capacities are several levels beyond anything found in other animals.

The quotation from Sherry Turkle is from an interview in the MIT alumni magazine *Open Door* (http://alumweb.mit.edu/opendoor/200307/turkle.shtml).

Helen Nissenbaum's call for engineering activism appears in the March 2001 article "How Computer Systems Embody Values," in *Computer*, the flagship magazine of the Institute of Electrical and Electronics Engineers.

The full quote from Maggie Boden reads:

AI could be the Westerner's mango tree. Its contribution to our food, shelter, and manufactured goods, and to the running of our administrative bureaucracies can free us not only from drudgery but for humanity it will lead to an increased number of "service" jobs in the caring professions, education, craft, sport, and entertainment. Such jobs are human rather than inhuman, giving satisfaction not only to those for whom the service is provided, but also to those who provide it. And because even these jobs will very likely not, be full-time, people both in and out of work will have time to devote to each other which today they do not enjoy. Friendship could become a living art again.

Batya Friedman and Peter Kahn, faculty members at the University of Washington in Seattle, published a discussion of the implications of using software to assist medical resource allocation decisions in 1992 in "Human Agency and Responsible Computing: Implications for Computer System Design," in *Systems*

Software. Our discussion of the use of software to predict patients' dying wishes draws on a report in the May 15, 2007, issue of the *Economist* titled "Logical Endings." The original research article, "How Should Treatment Decisions Be Made for Incapacitated Patients, and Why?" by Shalowitz, Garrett-Mayer, and Wendler, was published in 2007 in the open-access journal *PLoS Medicine.*

Experimental data supporting the claim that people readily anthropomorphize geometric figures appears in a 2000 review article in *Trends in Cognitive Science* by Brian Scholl and Patrice Tremoulet, "Perceptual Causality and Animacy."

The quote regarding the hundreds of Packbots deployed to Iraq is from a report by Joel Rothstein titled "Soldiers Bond with Battlefield Robots: Lessons Learned in Iraq May Show Up in Future Household 'Avatars,'" MSNBC/Reuters, May 23, 2006. We draw on this article when we discuss the soldiers who bonded with Scooby Doo. The quotation from Colin Angle of iRobot Corporation about Scooby Doo appeared in a May 24, 2006, CNET News story, "My Friend the Robot," by Tom Krazit.

Historian Jonathan Coopersmith of Texas A & M University has extensively studied the way the desire for pornography has driven technology. See, for example, his 1999 article "The Role of the Pornography Industry in the Development of Videotape and the Internet," in *IEEE International Symposium on Technology and Society—Women and Technology: Historical, Societal, and Professional Perspectives* (New Brunswick, NJ: Institute of Electrical Electronics Engineers).

In a *New York Times* article on February 16, 2005, "New Model Army Soldier Rolls Closer to Battle," Tim Weiner, reporting on U.S. military investment in robotics, said that "the United States will spend many billions of dollars on robots by 2010." See the January 23, 2005, BBC News story "US Plans 'Robot Troops' for Iraq," http://news.bbc.co.uk/2/hi/americas/4199935.stm. Surya Singh and Scott Thayer authored a technical survey of autonomous robots for military systems in 2001 entitled "ARMS (Autonomous Robots For Military Systems): A Survey of Collaborative Robotics Core Techologies." This report may be found at the website of Carnegie Mellon University's Robotics Institute, www.ri.cmu. edu/pubs/pub_3884.html. It is noteworthy that ethics and morality do not come up anywhere in the seventy-two-page text, and safety is mentioned only in the titles of other cited works.

Our discussion of how Americans rated different risks draws on Paul Slovic's 1987 article "Perception of Risk" in *Science.* The 1999 WHO report entitled "Injury: A Leading Cause of the Global Burden of Disease" can be found at www .who.int/violence_injury_prevention/publications/other_injury/injury/en/.

Chapter 4

For Joel Rothstein's MSNBC/Reuters report, see the notes to chapter 3. "Bots on the Ground: In the Field of Battle (Or Even above It), Robots Are a Soldier's Best Friend," by Joel Garreau, appeared in the May 6, 2007, *Washington Post.*

Readers may recognize the name Craig Venter, whose institute is behind the quest for "wet Alife." Venter headed the private group Celera Genomics, which produced the first map of the human genome (his own genome was one of the five sampled), sharing credit for this result with the International Human Genome Project. After leaving Celera, Venter founded the J. Craig Venter Institute (www.tigr.org/) in 2006. The institute is pursuing various bioengineering projects, including the attempt to build living cells from the ground up. An organization with similar objectives, Protolife (www.protolife.net/) was founded by physicist Norman Packard and philosopher Mark Bedau.

Allen Newell and Herbert Simon's seminal Turing Award article "Computer Science as Empirical Inquiry: Symbols and Search," originally published in 1975 in the *Communications of the ACM*, has been widely reprinted in countless anthologies.

The concept of a Singularity for AI was first coined by the mathematician and science fiction author Vernor Vinge, in an essay, "First Word" published in January 1983 in *OMNI* (now defunct). Vinge collected his thoughts on the subject in a conference address that was later revised and published in spring 1993 as "The Coming Technological Singularity: How to Survive in the Post-Human Era" in *Whole Earth Review*.

The fascinating and tragic story of Alan Turing's life and work was dramatized in the play and television movie *Breaking the Code*, which was based on Andrew Hodges's 1983 biography *Alan Turing: The Enigma*.

The exchange of views about the nature of mind between Thomas Hobbes and René Descartes is to be found in the "Objections and Replies" by noteworthy philosophers of the day that were commissioned by Marin Mersenne and published with Descartes's *Meditations* in 1641. (The translations by E. S. Haldane and G. R. T. Ross, published in 1978 as a two-volume set titled *The Philosophical Works of Descartes*, remain the edition of choice for most English-speaking scholars.)

The passage we quote from cyberneticist Heinz von Foerster about ethics and choice is from his 1992 essay "Ethics and Second-Order Cybernetics" and is available online at www.imprint.co.uk/C&HK/vol1/v1–1hvf.htm. Daniel Dennett's discussion of freedom of will is to be found in his 2003 book *Freedom Evolves*.

The methods used for Deep Blue are described by M. Campbell, A. J. Hoane, and F. Hsu in the January 2002 issue of *Artificial Intelligence*. For more on Deep Blue as human-machine collaboration, see "Chess Bump: The Triumphant Teamwork of Humans and Computers" by William Saletan, *Slate*, May 11, 2007, www.slate.com/id/2166000/.

The quotation from Christopher Lang is from his unpublished 2002 paper "Ethics for Artificial Intelligence," http://philosophy.wisc.edu/lang/AIEthics/index.htm.

Rodney Brooks's website at MIT maintains a wealth of information about his robots and projects (http://people.csail.mit.edu/brooks/). The most widely read, discussed, and reprinted statement of his philosophy of cognition and robot building is his "Intelligence without Representation," which originally appeared in *Artificial Intelligence* in 1991. Although the quotation "the world is its own best representation" does not directly appear in his 1991 article, it is the slogan that he and many others have used to encapsulate the main idea behind his subsumption architecture for robots. The practical applications of Brooks's research are seen in the spinoff, iRobot Corporation (website: www.irobot.com/). Brian Scasselati's comment was made when he came as a guest lecturer to Wendell Wallach's Yale seminar on "Robot Morals and Human Ethics" in November 2005.

The question of bat consciousness entered philosophical consciousness with the appearance of Thomas Nagel's 1974 essay "What Is It Like to Be a Bat?" in *Philosophical Review*, in which Nagel also broached the idea that there might be a gap between what we can know and what we can understand. Patricia Churchland's remarks about the ability of science to close that gap were made in a talk she gave at the dedication of MIT's Picower Institute for Learning and Memory, http://mitworld.mit.edu/video/342/. David Chalmers resuscitated arguments for dualism in his 1996 book *The Conscious Mind: In Search of a Fundamental Theory*. Colin McGinn's view that a complete understanding of consciousness might remain forever cognitively closed to human beings is in his 1999 book *The Mysterious Flame: Conscious Minds in a Material World*.

Igor Aleksander's ideas about consciousness and emotions in machines can be found in a 2005 article he coauthored with Mercedes Lahnstein and Rabinder Lee titled "Will and Emotions: A Machine Model That Shuns Illusions," which was presented at the Symposium on Next Generation Approaches to Machine Consciousness of the United Kingdom's Society for the Study of AI and the Simulation of Behavior, at the University of Hertfordshire, UK, on April 13, 2005. Owen Holland and Ron Goodman describe their approach in their 2003 article "Robots with Internal Models: A Route to Machine Consciousness," in Holland's edited volume *Machine Consciousness*. We give Stan Franklin's approach full treatment in chapter 11 here.

The final part of this chapter draws on the 2001 essay "Prolegomena to Any Future AMA," by Colin Allen, Gary Varner, and Jason Zinser, in the *Journal of Experimental and Theoretical Artificial Intelligence*.

Chapter 5

Ron Arkin's work at Georgia Tech on battlefield ethics for robots is sponsored by the U.S. Army Research Office under Contract no. W911NF-06–0252. A technical report describing the research, "Governing Lethal Behavior: Embedding Ethics in a Hybrid Deliberative/Reactive Robot Architecture," can be found at www.cc.gatech.edu/ai/robot-lab/online-publications/formalizationv35.pdf. The epigraph to this report, which Arkin attributes to Thomas Jefferson in 1787, is well worth repeating here: "State a moral case to a ploughman and a professor. The former will decide it as well, and often better than the latter, because he has not been led astray by artificial rules."

Peter Asaro, a philosopher of technology who is a fellow at the Rutgers University Center for Cultural Analysis, represents the view of many experts when he writes: "The most demanding scenarios for thinking about robot ethics, I believe, lie in the development of more sophisticated autonomous weapons systems"; "What Should We Want from a Robot Ethic?" *International Review of Information Ethics* (2006).

Dennett's claim that roboticists are doing philosophy, whether or not they think this is so, appears in the essay "Cog as a thought experiment" that he wrote in 1997 for the journal *Robotics and Autonomous Systems*.

Our discussion of Caroline Whitbeck's ideas about engineering ethics, and the quotation, are drawn from her 1995 article "Teaching Ethics to Scientists and Engineers: Moral Agents and Moral Problems," in *Science and Engineering Ethics*.

Chapter 6

Ethical theorists who take a heuristic approach to ethical principles include W. D. Ross in his 1930 book *The Right and the Good*, and Bernard Gert in his 1988 book *Morality*.

The "empirical turn" in recent ethics is represented by philosophers Joshua Knobe of the University of North Carolina, Chapel Hill, Shaun Nichols, of the University of Arizona, Tucson, and John Doris, of Washington University at St. Louis, among others. Doris coordinates the Moral Psychology Research Group, whose website provides a good entry point to the subject at http://moralpsychology.net/group/.

James Gips's essay "Towards the Ethical Robot" was originally presented as a conference paper in 1991, and was published in the 1995 volume *Android Epistemology*, edited by Ken Ford, Clark Glymour, and Patrick Hayes.

Jeremy Bentham himself was well aware of the difficulties of precise utilitarian calculations, and discussed the problems of the "original" and "derivative" consequences of a mischievous act as they affect "assigned" and "unassignable" individuals in his *Introduction to the Principles of Morals and Legislation*, originally published in 1780. The all-knowing "World Agent" is imagined by Bernard Williams in his 1985 book *Ethics and the Limits of Philosophy*.

Roger Clarke's discussion of Asimov's laws appears in a pair of articles (1993 and 1994) in *IEEE Computer*: "Asimov's Laws of Robotics: Implications for Information Technology." See also Wendell Wallach's 2003 essay "Robot Morals and Human Ethics" for further discussion of the laws.

Philip Pettit's discussion of voting paradoxes appears in his essay "*Akrasia*, Collective and Individual," in *Weakness of Will and Practical Irrationality* (2003), edited by Sarah Stroud and Christine Tappolet.

In his "New Ten Commandments," Bernard Gert of Dartmouth College provides an ethical system whose rules can be disobeyed when conflicts arise. These rules are described in his 1988 book, *Morality*.

Critical analyses of the possibility of having a Kantian machine are provided by Thomas Powers in his essay "Prospects for a Kantian Machine" (*IEEE Intelligent Systems*, July/August 2006), and in Bernd Carsten Stahl's 2004 essay "Information, Ethics, and Computers: The Problem of Autonomous Moral Agents" (*Minds and Machines*).

Tom Beauchamp and James Childress developed four principles that are widely used in medical ethics in their 1979 book *Principles of Biomedical Ethics*.

Our ideas about the integration of cognition, emotions, and reflective capacities owe much to Iva Smit. See her 2002 essay "Equations, Emotions, and Ethics: A Journey between Theory and Practice."

Chapter 7

The Human Genome Project has revolutionized biologists' ideas about the relationship of genes to traits with the discovery that there is a surprisingly small number of protein-coding genes in the human genome (only about 50 percent more than the roundworm *C. elegans*). With this discovery, developmental factors and the complex interactions between genome and environment have come to the fore. Eva Jablonka and Marion Lamb's 2005 book *Evolution in Four Dimensions: Genetic, Epigenetic, Behavioral, and Symbolic Variation in the History of Life* provides a good introduction to the excitement of postgenomic biology.

Ada Lovelace's "Notes on the analytical engine" appeared in *Taylor's Scientific Memoirs* in 1843. Charles Babbage first proposed the design for the analytical engine in 1837, but it remained only partially built by the time of his death in 1871.

John Holland developed his ideas about genetic algorithms in his 1975 book *Adaptation in Natural and Artificial Systems*. There are now more books, conferences, and online guides to genetic algorithms than we can possibly list.

E. O. Wilson, known as one of the world's experts on ant behavior, created a huge stir with his book *Sociobiology*, first published in 1975. Wilson was perceived by many as being unjustifiably reductionistic about human behavior and morality.

The classic book on game theory is *Theory of Games and Economic Behavior* by Oskar Morgenstern and John Von Neumann. (Von Neumann was also the architect of the standard design for digital computers consisting of central processing unit, control unit, and memory.) The story of how game theory cross-fertilized evolutionary biology is too long to tell here, but Richard Dawkins's 1976 book *The Selfish Gene* did much to popularize the idea (like Wilson, he has been accused of excessive reductionism).

Robert Axelrod and William Hamilton published their seminal article "The Evolution of Cooperation" in the March 27, 1981, issue of *Science*. Their work inspired many of the ideas we describe in this chapter, including Peter Danielson's computer simulations, which are described in two books, *Artificial Morality: Virtuous Robots for Virtual Games* (1992) and *Modeling Rationality, Morality and Evolution* (1998). William Harms's work appears in a pair of articles in 1999 and 2000 titled, respectively, "Biological Altruism in Hostile Environments" and "The Evolution of Cooperation in Hostile Environments." The second article is a commentary on an article by Brian Skyrms titled "Game Theory, Rationality and Evolution of the Social Contract." The quotation from Tennyson is from his poem "In Memoriam. A. H. H." These themes were originally described in Skyrms's 1996 book *Evolution of the Social Contract*. Critics who have pointed out the substantial gap between simple simulations and real-world evolution include Martin Barrett, Ellery Eells, Branden Fitelson, and Elliott Sober in their 1997 review of Skyrms's book for the journal *Philosophy and Phenomenological Research*.

People sometimes prefer fairness over immediate gain, and this phenomenon has been widely investigated in the context of "the ultimatum game," which Werner Güth and colleagues first described in 1982 in their article "An

Experimental Analysis of Ultimatum Bargaining" in the *Journal of Economic Behavior and Organization*. That some animals may also value fairness over food is suggested by the work of Sarah Brosnan and Frans de Waal in their article "Monkeys Reject Unequal Pay," in *Nature*, September 18, 2003.

Results such as those from the ultimatum game have led several people to suppose that there must be innate moral structures. John Rawls's suggestion of a universal moral grammar has been picked up enthusiastically by Marc Hauser, but the reaction to his 2006 book *Moral Minds: How Nature Designed Our Universal Sense of Right and Wrong* has been mixed. Those who are impressed by the postgenomic ideas in biology especially find strong claims about innateness to be incapable of explaining much.

The quotation attributed to Rodney Brooks about the disappointing results from ALife appears in his 2001 article "Steps towards Living Machines" and also in his book *Flesh and Machines.*" The quotation from Thomas Ray appears in his essay "Kurzweil's Turing Fallacy" in the 2002 collection *Are We Spiritual Machines? Ray Kurzweil vs. the Critics of Strong A.I.*

Our remark about the role of complexity in natural selection is based on the work of Larry Yaeger and Olaf Sporns at Indiana University. Their 2006 article "Evolution of Neural Structure and Complexity in a Computational Ecology" appeared in *ALife X*, the published proceedings of the "ALife X" conference held at Indiana University, Bloomington, June 3–7, 2006.

Lawrence Kohlberg's classic work is his two-volume *Essays on Moral Development*. Vol. 1, *The Philosophy of Moral Development*, appeared in 1981; and vol. 2, *The Psychology of Moral Development*, in 1984.

Information about Deb Roy's robot Ripley, including video clips and research articles, can be found at www.media.mit.edu/cogmac/projects/ripley.html.

Chapter 8

The English translation of Comte-Sponville's *Small Treatise on the Great Virtues* was published in 2001. The examples we give of kind motives in the text are drawn from Bernard Williams's 1985 book *Ethics and the Limits of Philosophy*, already mentioned in the notes for chapter 6.

Although it would be anachronistic to claim that Aristotle was a connectionist, an affinity between Aristotle and connectionism has been suggested by several authors. These include James Gips, in his 1995 essay "Towards the Ethical Robot" (see the notes to chapter 6), and Paul Churchland, in his 1995 book *The Engine of Reason, the Seat of the Soul: A Philosophical Journey into the Brain*. Churchland also returns to this theme in his 1996 essay "The Neural Representation of the Social World" in the anthology *Mind and Morals*, edited by Larry May, Marilyn Friedman, and Andy Clark.

A stronger link between Aristotelian ethics and connectionism is asserted by William Casebeer in his 2003 book *Natural Ethical Facts: Evolution, Connectionism, and Moral Cognition*; our quotation from Casebeer is on page 5. Jonathan Dancy draws the connection between connectionism and particularism in his 1993 book

Moral Reasons. Andy Clark suggests a similar view in his essay "Connectionism, Moral Cognition, and Collaborative Problem Solving," which also appeared in May, Friedman, and Clark's *Mind and Morals*. David DeMoss explores the subject in a 1998 article *"Aristotle, Connectionism, and the Morally Excellent Brain."* See also the work of Marcello Guarini described in chapter 9.

Chapter 9

Bill Joy's 2000 essay "Why the Future Doesn't Need Us" was in the April issue of *Wired*, available at www.wired.com/wired/archive/8.04/joy.html. Joy's jeramiad created quite a stir and a number of critiques, including one in 2000 by Max More titled "Embrace, Don't Relinquish, the Future," and another in 2001 by John Seely Brown titled "Don't Count Society Out: A Response to Bill Joy."

Michael Anderson, Susan Anderson, and Chris Armen describe the MedEthEx system in their article "An Approach to Computing Ethics" in the July–August 2006 issue of *IEEE Intelligent Systems*. Susan Anderson is the philosopher in the MedEthEx team, and she refers to the duties implemented in MedEthEx as W.D. Ross's prima facie duties. We defer to her language throughout the chapter, although in medical ethics these duties are more commonly known as (three of) the four principles of biomedical ethics (the fourth being justice). Medical ethicists typically attributed these principles to Tom Beauchamp and James Childress, rather than W. D. Ross. Beauchamp and Childress's influential 1979 book *The Principles of Biomedical Ethics* drew on the earlier work of W. D. Ross in formulating the four principles, and they have subsequently had a major influence on medical and research ethics. The Andersons' latest work is described in a chapter entitled "Ethical Healthcare Agents" to appear in a 2008 book, *Advanced Computational Intelligence Paradigms in Healthcare—3*, edited by Lakmi C. Jain. The extensive quotation from them is on page 244 of the book.

Brian Duffy's work on social agents began while he was a student at University College, Dublin. Duffy has since joined the Eurécom Affective Social Computing Lab in France. The terminology of BDI (belief desire intention) agents is due to philosopher Michael Bratman, whose 1987 book *Intention, Plans, and Practical Reason* has had an important influence on computer models of decision making.

Some of the most philosophically advanced work on multiagent simulations is from the Netherlands, where there are state mandates to include all stakeholders in important public policy decisions. Jeroen van den Hoven and Gert-Jan Lokhorst describe their approach to computerized support for multiagent ethical decision making in their article "Deontic Logic and Computer Supported Computer Ethics" in *CyberPhilosophy: The Intersection of Philosophy and Computing*, edited by Terrell Bynum and James Moor (2002). Vincent Wiegel's SophoLab system is described in a joint article he wrote with Hoven and Lokhorst, "Privacy, Deontic Epistemic Action Logic and Software Agents," in *Ethics and Information Technology*, December 2005. We quote Wiegel's description of the agents in his system from a mail message Wiegel sent to us, August 16, 2007.

Evidence of resurgent interest in human-level AI comes from many directions. For example, the summer 2006 issue of *AI* was dedicated to this theme.

Paul Rozin, Jonathan Haidt, and Clark McCauley provide an overview of the literature on disgust in a chapter they wrote for the *Handbook of Emotions*, edited by Michael Lewis and Jeannette Haviland-Jones, 2nd edition (2000). Shaun Nichols's 2004 book *Sentimental Rules: On the Natural Foundations of Moral Judgment* brings the psychology of emotions into the arena of moral philosophy.

Peter Salovey and John Mayer's article "Emotional Intelligence" was published in the journal *Imagination, Cognition, and Personality* in 1990.

Richard Lazarus's cognitive account of emotions is described in his 1991 book *Emotion and Adaptation*, which is the source of the fifteen core relational themes we mention. Philosopher Jesse Prinz argues against Lazarus in his 2004 book *Gut Reactions: A Perceptual Theory of Emotions*, providing instead a modern version of William James's view that emotions are felt bodily changes. Prinz's view is also similar to Antonio Damasio's neo-Jamesian view of emotions as felt somatic markers, as described in Damasio's 1995 book *Descartes' Error: Emotion, Reason, and the Human Brain* and in his 1999 book *The Feeling of What Happens: Body and Emotions in the Making of Consciousness*. See also Ronald de Sousa's 1987 monograph *The Rationality of Emotion*. The idea that emotions are crucial for rationality can, of course, be traced to much earlier sources, for instance to Hume in the eighteenth century.

For an example of the two-pathway approach to decision making see neuroscientist Joseph LeDoux's 1996 book *The Emotional Brain: The Mysterious Underpinnings of Emotional Life*. Joshua Greene and his colleagues' 2001 *Science* study showing that emotional centers were differently engaged for different versions of the trolley cases was mentioned in the notes to chapter 1. Greene is actively pursuing additional studies of the pathways involved in moral decision making.

The "fast and frugal" approach to decision making was introduced by Gerd Gigerenzer and Peter Todd in their 1999 book *Simple Heuristics That Make Us Smart*.

Huggable has an embedded 1.8 Ghz Pentium M with 1 Gigabyte of RAM. More details are available in "The Design of the Huggable: A Therapeutic Robotic Companion for Relational, Affective Touch" (2006) by Walter Dan Stiehl and colleagues.

The quotation from Rosalind Picard is from "The Love Machine" by David Diamond in *Wired* (December 2003). The MOUE is described by Christine Lisetti and colleagues in "Developing Multimodal Intelligent Affective Interfaces for Tele-home Health Care" in *International Journal of Human-Computer Studies* (2003).

The OCC model of emotions is presented in *The Cognitive Structure of Emotions* by Andrew Ortony, Gerald Clore, and Allan Collins, published in 1988. A description of Sloman's CogAff model can be found in the 2005 article "The Architectural Basis of Affective States and Processes" by Aaron Sloman, Ron Chrisley, and Matthias Scheutz.

Our description of Sandra Gadanho's research is based upon her 2003 article "Learning Behavior-Selection by Emotions and Cognition in a Multi-Goal Robot Task" in the *Journal of Machine Learning Research*.

We are hardly the first to note that (ro)bots will need to be capable of adapting to dynamically changing social interactions. Our thinking here is influenced by Cynthia Breazeal's 2002 book *Designing Sociable Robots*. See also Kerstein Dautenhahn's 2002 book *Socially Intelligent Agents: Creating Relationships with Computers*.

The idea of theory of mind was first floated by David Premack and Guy Woodruff in their 1978 article "Does the Chimpanzee Have a Theory of Mind?" in *Behavioral and Brain Sciences*.

Some of the earliest work on infant empathy was done by Martin Hoffman, professor of psychology at New York University. See his 2000 book *Empathy and Moral Development: Implications for Caring and Justice*.

William Sims Bainbridge describes Cyburg in his 2006 book titled *God from the Machine: Artificial Intelligence Models of Religious Cognition*.

Matthias Scheutz's work on disobedient robots is described in his 2007 paper coauthored with Charles Crowell, "The Burden of Embodied Autonomy: Some Reflections on the Social and Ethical Implications of Autonomous Robots," presented at the Workshop on Roboethics at the International Conference on Robotics and Automation.

The work of Francisco Varela, for example his 1980 book with Humberto Maturana, *Autopoiesis and Cognition: The Realization of the Living*, has been a rallying point for the view of life and cognition as self-organizing processes.

The two requirements for trustworthy agents in limited domains comes from Catriona Kennedy's 2004 article "Agents for Trustworthy Ethical Assistance."

The list of three approaches to consciousness attributed to Owen Holland comes from a presentation available online at http://cswww.essex.ac.uk/staff/owen/adventure.ppt.

Chapter 11

This chapter is the result of a collaboration with Stan Franklin, and he should be credited as a coauthor here. Franklin has been developing his ideas for a computational implementation of Baars's GWT in a number of articles, beginning with his 2000 essay "A 'Consciousness' Based Architecture for a Functioning Mind." Additional references are listed in the bibliography. Baars's books include *A Cognitive Theory of Consciousness* (1988) and *In the Theater of Consciousness* (1997).

Murray Shanahan's robotics group at Imperial College in London is pursuing projects in spatial reasoning and perception using an upper-torso humanoid robot called LUDWIG (see http://casbah.ee.ic.ac.uk/~Empsha/ludwig/Introduction.html). Shanahan has written a series of research articles with Bernard Baars applying GWT to issues in robotics. Stanislas Dehaene, a former president of the Association for the Scientific Study of Consciousness and author of *The Cognitive Neuroscience of Consciousness* (2001), has expanded on Baars's approach with his neuronal global workspace model, which is based on a neural net representation of the prefrontal cortex.

Franklin's LIDA borrows techniques from a variety of sources, including Douglas Hofstadter and Melanie Mitchell's Copycat architecture (1994), Pentti Kanerva's sparse distributed memory (1988), Gary Drescher's schema mechanism (1991), Pattie Maes's behavior net (1989), and Rodney Brooks's subsumption architecture. (1991) The LIDA model's codelets are similar to the agents in Marvin Minsky's *Society of Mind* (1986), demons in John Jackson's Pandemonium (1987), and Robert Ornstein's small minds (1986).

The elements of William James's views on volition can be found in his 1890 book *The Principles of Psychology*.

The 1970s saw a number of experiments by social psychologists challenging the idea that stable moral character determines ethical behavior. The experiments we describe are derived from Isen and Levin's "Effect of Feeling Good on Helping: Cookies and Kindness" (1972), and Darley and Batson's "From Jerusalem to Jericho: A Study of Situational and Dispositional Variables in Helping Behavior" (1973). Also important to this debate is Latane and Darley's "The Unresponsive Bystander: Why Doesn't He Help?" which appeared in 1970. For current discussion of these results, and some controversial claims about their consequences for ethics, see philosopher John Doris's 2002 book *Lack of Character: Personality and Moral Behavior*.

For additional reading about imagination, cognition, and ethics, see Mark Johnson's 1994 book *Moral Imagination: Implications of Cognitive Science for Ethics* as well as the May, Friedman, and Clark anthology mentioned in the notes to chapter 10.

Chapter 12

Some of our imaginary headlines are not so far from reality already. For example, journalist Matt Gross wrote about tourism in the virtual world Second Life in his article "It's My (Virtual) World..." in the *New York Times* travel section, November 3, 2006. Describing a patron at a virtual concert, Gross wrote, "Then things turned *really* nasty: Mr. Folds pulled out a light saber and attacked the audience." www.nytimes.com/2006/11/03/travel/escapes/03second.html.

The idea of a "soft takeoff" for the Singularity has been proposed by Ray Kurzweil and Hans Moravec and was dramatized by Charles Stross in his science fiction novel *Accelerando*, which was first published as an electronic book for free download and then in conventional paperback form in 2006.

The quotation from Ben Goertzel on the Easy and Hard basic values is from his 2002 essay "Thoughts on AI Morality," available at his website, www.goertzel.org/dynapsyc/2002/AIMorality.htm.

The quotation from Michael Ray LaChat is from his essay "Moral Stages in the Evolution of the Artificial Super-Ego: A Cost-Benefits Trajectory," included in the collection edited by Iva Smit and Wendell Wallach of the presentations at the 2003 Symposium on Cognitive, Emotive and Ethical Aspects of Decision Making in Humans and in Artificial Intelligence in Baden-Baden, which Smit and Wallach organized.

The experiment we describe as based on Thomas Metzinger's account of consciousness was described in "Video Ergo Sum: Manipulating Bodily Self-Consciousness," by Bigna Lenggenhager, Tej Tadi, Thomas Metzinger, and Olaf Blanke, in *Science*, August 24, 2007. Regarding Metzinger's view that the development of artificially conscious systems should be banned, we quote from Metzinger's 2004 book *Being No One*, p. 622.

BIBLIOGRAPHY

Adams, B., Breazeal, C., Brooks, R. A., & Scassellati, B. (2000). Humanoid Robots: A New Kind of Tool. *IEEE Intelligent Systems* 15, 25–31.

Aleksander, I. (2007). *The World in My Mind, My Mind in the World: Key Mechanisms of Consciousness in People, Animals and Machines*. Thorverton, UK: Imprint Academic.

Aleksander, I., & Dunmall, B. (2003). Axioms and Test for the Presence of Minimal Consciousness in Agents. In O. Holland (Ed.), *Machine Consciousness* (pp. 7–18). Thorverton, UK: Imprint Academic.

Aleksander, I., Lanhnstein, M., & Rabinder, L. (2005, April). *Will and Emotions: A Machine Model That Shuns Illusions*. Paper presented at the Symposium on Next Generation Approaches to Machine Consciousness, Hatfield, UK.

Allen, C. (2002, August). *Calculated Morality: Ethical Computing in the Limit*. Paper presented at the 14th International Conference on Systems Research, Informatics and Cybernetics, Baden-Baden, Germany.

Allen, C., Smit, I., & Wallach, W. (2006). Artificial Morality: Top-Down, Bottom-Up and Hybrid Approaches. *Ethics and New Information Technology* 7, 149–155.

Allen, C., Varner, G., & Zinser, J. (2000). Prolegomena to Any Future Artificial Moral Agent. *Journal of Experimental and Theoretical Artificial Intelligence* 12, 251–261.

Allen, C., Wallach, W., & Smit, I. (2006). Why Machine Ethics? *IEEE Intelligent Systems* 21(4), 12–17.

Allhoff, F., Lin, P., et al. (Eds.) (2007). *Nanoethics: The Ethical and Social Implications of Nanotechnology*. Hoboken, NJ: Wiley-Interscience.

Anderson, M., & Anderson, S. L. (2006). Machine Ethics. *IEEE Intelligent Systems* 21(4), 10–11.

Anderson, M., & Anderson, S. L. (2006, July). *MedEthEx: A Prototype Medical Ethics Advisor*. Paper presented at the Eighteenth Conference on Innovative Applications of Artificial Intelligence, Boston.

Anderson, M., and S. L. Anderson (2008). *Ethical Healthcare Agents. Advanced Computational Intelligence Paradigms in Healthcare-3*. L. C. Jain. Berlin, Springer: 233–257.

Anderson, M., Anderson, S. L., & Armen, C. (2006). An Approach to Computing Ethics. *IEEE Intelligent Systems*, 56–63.

Anderson, M., Anderson, S. L., & Armen, C. (2005, November). *Towards Machine Ethics: Implementing Two Action-Based Ethical Theories*. Paper presented at the American Association for Artificial Intelligence 2005 Fall Symposium on Machine Ethics, Arlington, VA.

Anderson, M., & Anderson, S. L. (2008, March). EthEl: Towards a principled ethical eldercare robot. ACM/IEEE Human-Robot Interaction Conference, Amsterdam.

Anderson, S. L. (2005, November). *Asimov's "Three Laws of Robotics" and Machine Metaethics*. Paper presented at the American Association for Artificial Intelligence 2005 Fall Symposium on Machine Ethics, Arlington, VA.

Antunes, L., & Coelho, H. (1999). Decisions Based upon Multiple Values: The BVG Agent Architecture. In P. Barahona & J. J. O. Alferes (Eds.), *Ninth Portuguese Conference on Artificial Intelligence* (pp. 297–311). Springer.

Appiah, K.A. (2008). *Experiments in Ethics*. Cambridge: Harvard University Press.

Aristotle. (1908). *Nichomachean Ethics* (W. D. Ross, Trans.). Oxford: Clarendon Press.

Aristotle. (1924 [rev. 1958]). *Aristotle's Metaphysics* (W. D. Ross, Trans.) Oxford: Clarendon Press.

Arkin, R. (2004, January). *Bombs, Bonding, and Bondage: Human-Robot Interaction and Related Ethical Issues*. Paper presented at the First International Conference on Roboethics, San Remo, Italy.

Arkin, R. (2007). *Governing Lethal Behavior: Embedding Ethics in a Hybrid Deliberative/Reactive Robot Architecture*. Technical Report GIT-GVU-07–11, College of Computing, Georgia Institute of Technology.

Arkin, R. (2007, Winter–Spring). Robot Ethics: From the Battlefield to the Bedroom, Robots of the Future Raise Ethical Concerns. *Research Horizons*, 14–15.

Arkoudas, K., & Bringsjord, S. (2004, September). *Metareasoning for Multi-Agent Epistemic Logics*. Paper presented at the Fifth International Conference on Computational Logic in Multi-Agent Systems, Lisbon, Portugal.

Arkoudas, K., & Bringsjord, S. (2005, November). *Toward Ethical Robots via Mechanized Deontic Logic*. Paper presented at the American Association for Artificial Intelligence 2005 Fall Symposium on Machine Ethics, Arlington, VA.

Asaro, P. (2006). What Should We Want from a Robot Ethic? *International Review of Information Ethics* 6, 10–16.

Ashley, K. D. (1990). *Modeling Legal Arguments: Reasoning with Cases and Hypotheticals (Artificial Intelligence and Legal Reasoning)*. Cambridge, MA: MIT Press.

Asimov, I. (1942, March). Runaround. *Astounding Science Fiction*, 94–103.

Asimov, I. (1950). *I, Robot*. New York: Gnome Press.

Asimov, I. (1985). *Robots and Empire*. Garden City, NY: Doubleday.

Axelrod, R., & Hamilton, W. (1981). The Evolution of Cooperation. *Science* 211, 1390–1396.

Baars, B. (1997). *In the Theater of Consciousness: The Workspace of the Mind*. Oxford: Oxford University Press.

Baars, B. J. (1988). *A Cognitive Theory of Consciousness*. Cambridge, UK: Cambridge University Press.

Baars, B. J. (2002). The Conscious Access Hypothesis: Origins and Recent Evidence. *Trends in Cognitive Science* 6, 47–52.

Baars, B. J., & Franklin, S. (2003). How Conscious Experience and Working Memory Interact. *Trends in Cognitive Science* 7, 166–172.

Baddeley, A. D. (1992). Consciousness and Working Memory. *Consciousness and Cognition* 1, 3–6.

Baddeley, A. D., Conway, M., & Aggleton, J. (2001). *Episodic Memory*. Oxford: Oxford University Press.

Baddeley, A. D., & Hitch, G. J. (1974). Working Memory. In G. A. Bower (Ed.), *The Psychology of Learning and Motivation* (pp. 47–89). New York: Academic Press.

Bainbridge, W. S. (2006). *God from the Machine: Artificial Intelligence Models of Religious Cognition*. Lanham, MD: AltaMira Press.

Barad, J., & Robertson, E. (2000). *The Ethics of Star Trek*. New York: Harper-Collins.

Barrett, M., Eells, E., Fitelson, B., & Sober, E. (1999). Models and Reality—A Review of Brian Skyrms's *Evolution of the Social Contract*. *Philosophy and Phenomenological Research* 59(1), 237–241.

Barsalou, L. W. (1999). Perceptual Symbol Systems. *Behavioral and Brain Sciences* 22, 577–609.

Bartneck, C. (2002, November). *Integrating the Ortony/Clore/Collins Model of Emotion in Embodied Characters*. Paper presented at the workshop Virtual Conversational Characters: Applications, Methods, and Research Challenges, Melbourne, AU.

Bates, J. (1994). The Role of Emotion in Believable Agents. *Communications of the ACM* 37, 122–125.

Baum, E. (2004). *What Is Thought?* Cambridge, MA: MIT Press.

Beauchamp, T. L., & Childress, J. F. (2001). *Principles of Biomedical Ethics* (5th ed.). Oxford: Oxford University Press.

Bechtel, W., & Abrahamsen, A. (2007, August). *Mental Mechanisms, Autonomous Systems, and Moral Agency*. Paper presented at the annual meeting of the Cognitive Science Society, Nashville, TN.

Bennett, D. (2005, September 11). Robo-Justice: Do We Have the Technology to Build Better Legal Systems? *Boston Globe*.

Bentham, J. (1907 [1780]). *An Introduction to the Principles of Morals and Legislation*. Oxford: Clarendon Press.

Berne, E. (1964). *Games People Play: The Basic Hand Book of Transactional Analysis*. New York: Ballantine Books.

Billings, L. (2007, July 16). Rise of Roboethics. *Seed.*

Birrer, F. (2001). Applying Ethical and Moral Concepts and Theories to IT Contexts: Some Key Problems and Challenges. In R. A. Spinello & H. T. Tavani (Eds.), *Readings in Cybernetics* (pp. 91–97). Sudbury, MA: Jones & Bartlett.

Blackmore, S. (2003). Consciousness in Meme Machines. In O. Holland (Ed.), *Machine Consciousness* (pp. 19–30). Thorverton, UK: Imprint Academic.

Boden, M. A. (1983). Artificial Intelligence as a Humanizing Force. In A. Bundy (Ed.) *Proceedings of the Eighth International Joint Conferences on Artificial Intelligence* (pp. 1197–1198).

Boden, M. A. (1995). Could a Robot Be Creative—How Would We Know? In K. Ford, C. Glymour, & P. Hayes (Eds.) *Android Epistemology* (pp. 51–72). Menlo Park, CA: AAAI Press.

Boden, M. A. (2005). Ethical issues in AI and biotechnology. In U. Görman, W.B. Drees, & M. Meisinger (Eds.), *Creative Creatures: Values and Ethical Issues in Theology, Science and Technology* (pp. 123–134). London: T & T Clark.

Boella, G., van der Torre, L., & Verhagen, H. (2005, April). *Introduction to Normative Multiagent Systems.* Paper presented at the Artificial Intelligence and the Simulation of Behavior '05 Convention, Social Intelligence and Interaction in Animals, Robots and Agents: Symposium on Normative Multi-Agent Systems, Hatfield, UK.

Bostrom, N. (1998). How Long before Superintelligence? *International Journal of Future Studies* 2, 1–13.

Bostrom, N. (2003). Are You Living in a Computer Simulation? *Philosophical Quarterly* 53(211), 243–255.

Bostrom, N. (2003). The Ethics of Superintelligent Machines. In I. Smit, W. Wallach, & G. Lasker (Eds.), *Fifteenth International Conference on Systems Research, Informatics and Cybernetics: Symposium on Cognitive, Emotive and Ethical Aspects of Decision Making in Humans and in Artificial Intelligence* (Vol. II, pp. 12–18). Windsor, Ontario, Canada: International Institute for Advanced Studies in Systems Research and Cybernetics.

Bostrom, N. (2003). When Machines Outsmart Humans. *Futures* 35(7), 759–764.

Bratman, M. (1987). *Intention, Plans, and Practical Reason.* Cambridge, MA: Harvard University Press.

Breazeal, C. (2002). *Designing Sociable Robots.* Cambridge, MA: MIT Press.

Breazeal, C. (2003). Emotion and Sociable Humanoid Robots. *International Journal of Human-Computer Studies* 59, 119–155.

Breazeal, C., & Scassellati, B. (2001). Challenges in Building Robots That Imitate People. In K. Dautenhahn & C. Nehaniv (Eds.), *Imitation in Animals and Artifacts* (pp. 363–390). Cambridge, MA: MIT Press.

Bringsjord, S., Arkoudas, K., & Bello, P. (2006). Toward a General Logicist Methodology for Engineering Ethically Correct Robots. *IEEE Intelligent Systems* 21(4), 38–44.

Bringsjord, S., & Ferucci, D. (1998). Logic and Artificial Intelligence: Divorced, Still Married, Separated...? *Minds and Machines* 8(2), 273–308.

Brooks, R. (1986). A Robust Layered Control System for a Mobile Robot. *IEEE Journal of Robotics and Automation*, RA-2(1), 14–23.

Brooks, R. (2002). *Flesh and Machines*. New York: Pantheon Books.

Brooks, R. A. (1989). A Robot That Walks: Emergent Behavior from a Carefully Evolved Network. *Neural Computation* 1, 253–262.

Brooks, R. A. (1991). How to Build Complete Creatures Rather Than Isolated Cognitive Simulators. In K. van Lehn (Ed.), *Architectures for Intelligence* (pp. 225–239). Hillsdale, NJ: Erlbaum.

Brooks, R. A. (1991). Intelligence without Representation. *Artificial Intelligence* 47(1–3), 139–159.

Brooks, R. A. (1997). The Cog Project. *Journal of the Robotics Society of Japan* 15, 968–970.

Brooks, R. A. (2001). Steps towards Living Machines. In T. Gomi (Ed.), *The International Symposium on Evolutionary Robotics From Intelligent Robotics to Artificial Life* (pp. 72–93). Tokyo: Springer-Verlag.

Brosnan, S., & de Waal, F. B. M. (2003). Monkeys Reject Unequal Pay. *Nature* 425, 297–299.

Brown, J. S. (2001). Don't Count Society Out: A Response to Bill Joy. In M.C. Roco & W.S. Bainbridge (Eds.) *Societal Implications of Nanoscience and Nanotechnology* (pp. 37–46). New York: Springer.

Bryson, J., & Kime, P. (1998, August). *Just Another Artifact: Ethics and the Empirical Experience of AI.* Paper presented at the Fifteenth International Congress on Cybernetics, Namur, Belgium.

Bynum, T. W. (Ed.). (1985). *Computers and Ethics*. Malden, MA: Blackwell.

Bynum, T. W. (2000). A Very Short History of Computer Ethics. *American Philosophical Association Newsletter on Philosophy and Computing* 99(2), 163–165.

Bynum, T. W. (2001). Computer Ethics: Its Birth and Its Future. *Ethics and Information Technology* 3(2), 109–112.

Calverley, D. (2005, April). *Towards a Method for Determining the Legal Status of a Conscious Machine.* Paper presented at the Artificial Intelligence and the Simulation of Behavior '05: Social Intelligence and Interaction in Animals, Robots and Agents: Symposium on Next Generation Approaches to Machine Consciousness, Hatfield, UK.

Campbell, M. (1997). An Enjoyable Game: How HAL Plays Chess. In D. Stork (Ed.), *HAL's Legacy: 2001's Computer as Dream and Reality* (pp. 75–98). Cambridge, MA: MIT Press.

Campbell, M., Hoane, A. J., & Hsu, F. (2002, January). Deep Blue. *Artificial Intelligence* 134, 57–83.

Canamero, L. D. (2005). Emotion Understanding from the Perspective of Autonomous Robots Research. *Neural Networks* 18, 445–455.

Capek, K. (1973 [1920]). *Rossum's Universal Robots*. New York: Simon and Schuster.

Carpenter, J., Eliot, M., & Schultheis, D. (September, 2006). *Machine or Friend: Understanding Users' Preferences for and Expectations of a Humanoid Robot Companion.* Paper presented at the Fifteenth Conference on Design and Emotion, Gothenburg, Sweden.

Carsten Stahl, B. (2004). Information, Ethics, and Computers: The Problem of Autonomous Agents. *Minds and Machines* 14(1), 67–83.

Casebeer, W. (2003). *Natural Ethical Facts: Evolution, Connectionism, and Moral Cognition*. Cambridge, MA: MIT Press.

Chalmers, D. J. (1996). *The Conscious Mind*. Oxford: Oxford University Press.

Chaput, H. H., Kuipers, B., & Miikkulainen, R. (September, 2003). Constructivist Learning: A Neural Implementation of the Schema Mechanism. Paper presented at the Workshop for Self-Organizing Maps '03, Kitakyushu, Japan.

Chomsky, N. (1965). *Aspects of the Theory of Syntax*. Cambridge, MA: MIT Press.

Chomsky, N. (1985). *Syntactic Structures*. Berlin: Mouton.

Chopra, S., & White, L. (2004). Artificial Agents—Personhood in Law and Philosophy. *European Conference on Artificial Intelligence* 16, 635–639.

Churchland, P. M. (1989). *A Neurocomputational Perspective: The Nature of Mind and the Structure of Science*. Cambridge, MA: MIT Press.

Churchland, P. M. (1995). *The Engine of Reason, The Seat of the Soul: A Philosophical Journey into the Brain*. Cambridge, MA: MIT Press.

Churchland, P. M. (1996). The Neural Representation of the Social World. In L. May, M. Friedman & A. Clark (Eds.), *Mind and Morals: Essays on Cognitive Science and Ethics* (pp. 91–108). Cambridge, MA: MIT Press.

Clark, A. (1996). Connectionism, Moral Cognition, and Collaborative Problem Solving. In L. May, M. Friedman, & A. Clark (Eds.), *Mind and Morals: Essays on Cognitive Science and Ethics* (pp. 109–127). Cambridge, MA: MIT Press.

Clark, A. (1998). *Being There: Putting Brain, Body, and World Together Again*. Cambridge, MA: MIT Press.

Clark, A. (2003). *Natural-Born Cyborgs: Minds, Technologies, and the Future of Human Intelligence*. Cambridge, MA: MIT Press.

Clark, J. (2002). *Paris Says "Oui" to Driverless Trains*. Transport for London website. Originally retrieved from http://tube.tfl.gov.uk/content/metro/02/0207/11/Default.asp and now archived at The Internet Archive at http://web.archive.org/web/20040211000716/http://tube.tfl.gov.uk/content/metro/02/0207/11/Default.asp.

Clarke, R. (1993). Asimov's Laws of Robotics: Implications for Information Technology (1). *IEEE Computer* 26(12), 53–61.

Clarke, R. (1994). Asimov's Laws of Robotics: Implications for Information Technology (2). *IEEE Computer* 27(1), 57–66.

Coleman, K. G. (2001). Android Arete: Towards a Virtue Ethic for Computational Agents. *Ethics and Information Technology* 3(4), 247–265.

Comte-Sponville, A. (2001). *A Small Treatise on Great Virtues; The Uses of Philosophy in Everyday Life* (C. Temerson, Trans.). New York: Metropolitan Books.

Conway, M. A. (2002). Sensory-Perceptual Episodic Memory and Its Context: Autobiographical Memory. In A. D. Baddeley, M. Conway, & J. Aggleton (Eds.), *Episodic Memory* (pp. 53–70). Oxford: Oxford University Press.

Coopersmith, J. (1999). The Role of the Pornography Industry in the Development of Videotape and the Internet. *IEEE International Symposium on Technology and Society—Women and Technology: Historical, Societal, and Professional Perspectives* (pp. 175–182). New Brunswick, NJ.

Cotterill, R. M. J. (2003). CyberChild: A Simulation Test-Bed for Consciousness Studies. *Journal of Consciousness Studies* 10, 31–45.

D'Mello, S. K., Ramamurthy, U., & Franklin, S. (2005, July). *Encoding and Retrieval Efficiency of Episodic Data in a Modified Sparse Distributed Memory System.* Paper presented at the Twenty-seventh Annual Conference of the Cognitive Science Society, Strassa, Italy.

D'Mello, S. K., Ramamurthy, U., Negatu, A., & Franklin, S. (2006). A Procedural Learning Mechanism for Novel Skill Acquisition. In T. Kovacs & J. A. R. Marshall (Eds.), *Adaptation in Artificial and Biological Systems, AISB '06* (Vol. 1, pp. 184–185). Bristol, UK: Society for the Study of Artificial Intelligence and the Simulation of Behaviour.

Damasio, A. (1994). *Descartes' Error: Emotion, Reason, and the Human Brain.* New York: Putnam.

Damasio, A. (1999). *The Feeling of What Happens: Body and Emotion in the Making of Consciousness.* New York: Harcourt Brace.

Dancy, J. (1993). *Moral Reasons.* Malden, MA: Blackwell.

Dancy, J. (1998, August). *Can a Particularist Learn the Difference between Right and Wrong?* Paper presented at the Twentieth World Congress of Philosophy, Boston.

Dancy, J. (2005). Moral Particularism. *The Stanford Encyclopedia of Philosophy (Summer 2005 Edition),* E. N. Zalta (Ed.), http://plato.stanford.edu/archives/ sum2005/entries/moral-particularism.

Danielson, P. (1992). *Artificial Morality: Virtuous Robots for Virtual Games.* New York: Routledge.

Danielson, P. (1998). *Modeling Rationality, Morality and Evolution.* Oxford: Oxford University Press.

Danielson, P. (2003). *Modeling Complex Ethical Agents.* Paper presented at the conference on Computational Modeling in the Social Sciences, Seattle, Washington.

Danielson, P. (2006, June). *From Artificial Morality to NERD: Models, Experiments, & Robust Reflective Equilibrium.* Paper presented at the EthicALife Workshop of the ALifeX Conference, Bloomington, Indiana.

Darley, J. M., & Batson, C.D. (1973). From Jerusalem to Jericho: A Study of Situational and Dispositional Variables in Helping Behavior. *Journal of Personality and Social Psychology* 27, 100–108.

Darwin, C. (1860). *Origin of Species* (Harvard Classics, Vol. 11.). New York: Bartleby Press.

Darwin, C. (1872). *The Expression of Emotions in Man and Animals.* London: John Murray.

Darwin, C. (2004 [1871]). *The Descent of Man.* New York: Penguin.

Das, P., Kemp, A. H., Liddell, B. J., Brown, K. J., Olivieri, G., Peduto, A., Gordon, E., & Williams, L. M. (2005). Pathways for Fear Perception: Modulation of Amygdala Activity by Thalamo-Cortical Systems. *NeuroImage* 26, 141–148.

Dautenhahn, K. (Ed.). (2002). *Socially Intelligent Agents: Creating Relationships with Computers and Robots*. New York: Springer.

Davachi, L., Mitchell, J. P., & Wagner, A. D. (2003). Multiple Routes to Memory: Distinct Medial Temporal Lobe Processes Build Item and Source Memories. *Proceedings of the National Academy of Sciences* 100 2157–2162.

Davidson, R. J., Maxwell, J. S., & Shackma, A. J. (2004). The Privileged Status of Emotion in the Brain. *Proceedings of the National Academy of Sciences* 101, 11915–11916.

Dawkins, R. (1989). *The Selfish Gene*. Oxford: Oxford University Press.

de Garis, H. (1990). The Twenty-first-century Artilect: Moral Dilemmas Concerning the Ultra-intelligent Machine. *Revue Internationale de Philosophie* 44, 131–138.

de Garis, H. (2005). *The Artilect War: Cosmists vs. Terrans: A Bitter Controversy Concerning Whether Humanity Should Build Godlike Massively Intelligent Machines*. Palm Springs, CA: ETC.

de Martino, B., Kumaran, D., Seymour, B., & Dolan, R. J. (2006). Frames, Biases, and Rational Decision-Making in the Human Brain. *Science* 313, 684–687.

de Sousa, R. (1987). *The Rationality of Emotion*. Cambridge, MA: MIT Press.

de Waal, F. B. M. (2006). *Primates and Philosophers: How Morality Evolved*. Princeton, NJ: Princeton University Press.

Dehaene, S. (2002). *The Cognitive Neuroscience of Consciousness*. Cambridge, MA: MIT Press.

Dehaene, S., Changeux, J., Naccache, L., Sackur, J., & Sergent, C. (2006). Conscious, Preconscious, and Subliminal Processing: A Testable Taxonomy. *Trends in Cognitive Sciences* 10, 204–211.

DeMoss, D. (1998). Aristotle, Connectionism, and the Morally Excellent Brain. The Paideia project on-line. *Proceedings of the Twentieth World Congress of Philosophy*. American Organizing Committee Inc., Boston. www.bu.edu/wcp/Papers/Cogn/CognDemo.htm

Dennett, D. C. (1995). Cog: Steps towards Consciousness in Robots. In T. Metzinger (Ed.), *Conscious Experience* (pp. 471–487). Thorverton, UK: Imprint Academic.

Dennett, D. C. (1996). When Hal Kills, Who's to Blame? In D. Stork (Ed.), *Hal's Legacy* (pp. 351–365). Cambridge, MA: MIT Press.

Dennett, D. C. (1997). Cog as a Thought Experiment. *Robotics and Autonomous Systems* 20(2–4), 251–256.

Dennett, D. C. (1997). Consciousness in Human and Robot Minds. In M. Ito, Y. Miyashita, & E. T. Rolls (Eds), *Proceedings of the IIAS Symposium on Cognition, Computation, and Consciousness* (pp. 17–30). New York: Oxford University Press.

Dennett, D. C. (2003). *Freedom Evolves*. New York: Viking.

Descartes, R. (1978). *The Philosophical Works of Descartes* (E. S. Haldane & G. R. T. Ross, Trans.). Cambridge, UK: Cambridge University Press.

Diamond, D. (2003, December). The Love Machine. *Wired* 11(12), www.wired.com/wired/archive/11.12/love.html.

Dietrich, E. (2007). After the Humans Are Gone. *Journal of Experimental and Theoretical Artificial Intelligence* 19(1), 55–67.

Doris, J. M. (2002). *Lack of Character: Personality and Moral Behavior*. Cambridge, UK: Cambridge University Press.

Drescher, G. L. (1991). *Made-Up Minds: A Constructivist Approach to Artificial Intelligence*. Cambridge, MA: MIT Press.

Dreyfus, H. (1979). *What Computers Can't Do: The Limits of Artificial Intelligence*. New York: Harper Colophon Books.

Dreyfus, H., & Dreyfus, S. (1990). What Is Morality? A Phenomenological Account of the Development of Ethical Expertise. In D. Rasmussen (Ed.), *Universalism vs. Communitarianism: Contemporary Debates in Ethics* (pp. 237–264). Cambridge, MA: MIT Press.

Duffy, B. R., & Joue, G. (2005). The Paradox of Social Robotics: A Discussion. In M. Anderson, S.L. Anderson, & C. Armen (Cochairs), *Machine Ethics: Papers From The AAAI Fall Symposium*. Arlington, VA: AAAI Press.

Edelman, G. M. (1987). *Neural Darwinism*. New York: Basic Books.

Ekman, P. (1993). Facial Expression of Emotion. *American Psychologist* 48, 384–392.

Engelberger, J. F. (1989). *Robotics in Service*. Cambridge, MA: MIT Press.

Epstein, R. (1996). *The Case of the Killer Robot: Stories about the Professional, Ethical, and Societal Dimensions of Computing*. New York: Wiley.

Estes, W. K. (1993). *Classification and Cognition*. Oxford: Oxford University Press.

Ferbinteanu, J., & Shapiro, M. L. (2003). Prospective and Retrospective Memory Coding in the Hippocampus. *Neuron* 40, 1227–1239.

Flack, J., & de Waal, F. B. M. (2000). 'Any Animal Whatever': Darwinian Building Blocks of Morality in Monkeys and Apes. In L. Katz (Ed.), *Evolutionary Origins of Morality* (pp. 1–30). Thorverton, UK: Imprint Academic.

Flavell, J. H. (1979). Metacognition and Cognitive Monitoring: A New Area of Cognitive-Developmental Inquiry. *American Psychologist* 34, 906–911.

Floridi, L., & Sanders, J. W. (2001). Artificial Evil and the Foundation of Computer Ethics. *Ethics and Information Technology* 3(1), 55–66.

Floridi, L., & Sanders, J. W. (2004). On the Morality of Artificial Agents. *Minds and Machines* 14(3), 349–379.

Foerst, A. (2005). *God in the Machine: What Robots Teach Us about Humanity and God*. New York: Plume.

Fogg, B. J., & Nass, C. (1997). Silicon Sycophants: The Effects of Computers That Flatter. *Journal of Human-Computer Studies* 46, 551–561.

Foot, P. (1967). The Problem of Abortion and the Doctrine of Double Effect. *Oxford Review* 5, 5–15.

Foot, P. (1967). Moral Beliefs. In P. Foot (Ed.), *Theories of Ethics* (pp. 83–100). Oxford: Oxford University Press.

Ford, K., Glymour, C., & Hayes, P. (Eds.). (1995). *Android Epistemology*. Menlo Park, CA: AAAI Press.

Ford, K., Glymour, C., & Hayes, P. (Eds.). (2006). *Thinking about Android Epistemology*. Cambridge, MA: MIT Press.

Franklin, S. (2000). Deliberation and Voluntary Action in "Conscious" Software Agents. *Neural Network World* 10, 505–521.

Franklin, S. (2001). A "Consciousness" Based Architecture for a Functioning Mind. In D. Davis, (Ed.), *Visions Of Mind* (pp. 149–175). Hershey, PA: IDEA Group, Inc.

Franklin, S. (2001). Conscious Software: A Computational View of Mind. In V. Loia & S. Sessa (Eds.), *Soft Computing Agents: New Trends for Designing Autonomous Systems* (pp. 1–46). Berlin, GE: Springer (Physica-Verlag).

Franklin, S. (2003). IDA: A Conscious Artifact? *Journal of Consciousness Studies* 10, 47–66.

Franklin, S. (2005). Cognitive Robots: Perceptual Associative Memory and Learning. Paper presented at *Proceedings of the Fourteenth Annual International Workshop on Robot and Human Interactive Communication (RO-MAN 2005)* (pp. 427–433).

Franklin, S. (2005). Evolutionary Pressures and a Stable World for Animals and Robots: A Commentary on Merker. *Consciousness and Cognition* 14, 115–118.

Franklin, S. (March, 2005). *Perceptual Memory and Learning: Recognizing, Categorizing, and Relating.* Paper presented at American Association for Artificial Intelligence Symposium on Developmental Robotics, Palo Alto, CA.

Franklin, S., Baars, B. J., Ramamurthy, U., & Ventura, M. (2005). The Role of Consciousness in Memory. *Brains, Minds and Media* 1, 1–38.

Franklin, S., & Graesser, A. C. (1997). Is It an Agent, or Just a Program? A Taxonomy for Autonomous Agents. In J. Muller, M. Woolridge, & N.R. Jennings (Eds.), *Intelligent Agents III* (pp. 21–35). Berlin: Springer Verlag.

Franklin, S., & McCauley, L. (2004). Feelings and Emotions as Motivators and Learning Facilitators. In E. Hudlicka & L. Cañamero (Co-chairs), *Architectures for Modeling Emotion: Cross-Disciplinary Foundations, AAAI 2004 Spring Symposium Series* (Technical Report SS-04-02, pp. 48–51). Palo Alto, CA: AAAI Press.

Franklin, S., & Ramamurthy, U. (2006). Motivations, Values and Emotions: Three Sides of the Same Coin. In *Proceedings of the Sixth International Workshop on Epigenetic Robotics* (Vol. 128, pp. 41–48). Paris: Lund University Cognitive Studies.

Freeman, W. J. (1999). *How Brains Make Up Their Minds.* London: Weidenfeld and Nicolson.

Freeman, W. J. (2003). The Wave Packet: An Action Potential for the Twenty-first Century. *Journal of Integrative Neuroscience* 2, 3–30.

Friedman, B. (1995, May). *It's the Computer's Fault: Reasoning about Computers as Moral Agents.* Paper presented at the Conference on Human Factors in Computing Systems, Denver, Colorado.

Friedman, B., & Kahn, P. (1992). Human Agency and Responsible Computing: Implications for Computer System Design. *Journal of Systems and Software* 17, 7–14.

Friedman, B., & Nissenbaum, H. (1996). Bias in Computer Systems. *ACM Transactions on Information Systems* 14(3), 330–347.

Gadanho, S. C. (2003). Learning Behavior-Selection by Emotions and Cognition in a Multi-Goal Robot Task. *Journal of Machine Learning Research* 4, 385–412.

Gardner, A. (1987). *An Artificial Approach to Legal Reasoning.* Cambridge, MA: MIT Press.

Garreau, J. (2007, May 6). Bots on the Ground: In the Field of Battle (Or Even above It), Robots Are a Soldier's Best Friend. *Washington Post.*

Gazzaniga, M. S. (2005). The Believing Brain. In *The Ethical Brain* (pp. 145–162). New York: Dana Press.

Georges, T. M. (2003). *Digital Soul: Intelligent Machines and Human Values.* Cambridge, MA: Westview Press.

Gert, B. (1988). *Morality.* Oxford: Oxford University Press.

Gertner, R. (2005, August 15). Lawyers Are Turning to Old Websites for Evidence. *Lawyer's Weekly USA.*

Gibson, J. J. (1979). *The Ecological Approach to Visual Perception.* Mahwah, NJ: Erlbaum.

Gigerenzer, G., & Selten, R. (2002). *Bounded Rationality: The Adaptive Toolbox.* Cambridge, MA: MIT Press.

Gigerenzer, G., Todd, P., & Group, T. A. R. (1999). *Simple Heuristics That Make Us Smart.* Oxford: Oxford University Press.

Gilligan, C. (1982). *In a Different Voice: Psychological Theory and Women's Development.* Cambridge, MA: Harvard University Press.

Gips, J. (1991). Towards the Ethical Robot. In K. G. Ford, C. Glymour, & P.J. Hayes (Eds.), *Android Epistemology* (pp. 243–252). Cambridge, MA: MIT Press.

Gips, J. (2005). Creating Ethical Robots: A Grand Challenge. In M. Anderson, S.L. Anderson, & Armen, C. (Co-chairs), *AAAI Fall 2005 Symposium on Machine Ethics* (pp. 1–7). Alexandria, VA: AAAI Press.

Glenberg, A. M. (1997). What Memory Is For. *Behavioral and Brain Sciences* 20, 1–19.

Goertzel, B. (2002, May). Thoughts on AI Morality. *Dynamic Psychology.* www.goertzel.org/dynapsyc/2002/AIMorality.htm.

Goertzel, B., et al. (2008, March). *An Integrative Methodology for Teaching Embodied Non-Linguistic Agents, Applied to Virtual Animals in Second Life.* Paper presented at First Conference on Artificial General Intelligence (AGI-08), Memphis, TN.

Goertzel, B., & Pennachin, C. (2007). *Artificial General Intelligence.* Berlin: Springer.

Goertzel, B., Pennachin, C., & Bugaj, S. V. (March, 2002). The Novamente AGI Engine: An Artificial General Intelligence in the Making. http://inteligenesiscorp.com/agiriorg/article.htm.

Goldin, I. M., Ashley, K. D., & Pinkus, R. L. (2001, May). *Introducing PETE: Computer Support for Teaching Ethics.* Paper presented at the Eighth International Conference on Artificial Intelligence and Law, St. Louis, Missouri.

Goleman, D. (1995). *Emotional Intelligence.* New York: Bantam Books.

Good, I. J. (1982, November). *Ethical Machines.* Paper presented at the Tenth Machine Intelligence Workshop, Cleveland, Ohio.

Goodale, M. A., & Milner, D. (2004). *Sight Unseen*. Oxford: Oxford University Press.

Grau, C. (2006). There Is No "I" in "Robots": Robots and Utilitarianism. *IEEE Intelligent Systems* 21(4), 52–55.

Greene, J., & Haidt, J. (2002). How (and Where) Does Moral Judgment Work? *Trends in Cognitive Sciences* 6(12), 517–523.

Greene, J. D., Nystrom, L. E., Engell, A. D., Darley, J. M., & Cohen, J. D. (2004). The Neural Bases of Cognitive Conflict and Control in Moral Judgment. *Neuron* 44, 389–400.

Greene, J. D., Sommerville, R. B., Nystrom, L. E., Darley, J. M., & Cohen, J. D. (2001). An fMRI Investigation of Emotional Engagement in Moral Judgment. *Science* 293, 2105–2108.

Gross, M. (2006, November 3). It's My (Virtual) World . . . *New York Times*.

Guarini, M. (2006). Particularism and Classification and Reclassification of Moral Cases. *IEEE Intelligent Systems* 21(4), 22–28.

Guth, W., Schmittberger, R., & Schwarze, B. (1982). An Experimental Analysis of Ultimatum Bargaining. *Journal of Economic Behavior and Organization* 3(4), 367–388.

Hahn, C. S., Fley, B., & Florian, M. (2005, April). *A Framework for the Design of Self-Regulation of Open Agent-Based Electronic Marketplace*. Paper presented at the Artificial Intelligence and the Simulation of Behavior '05 Convention, Social Intelligence and Interaction in Animals, Robots and Agents: Symposium on Normative Multi-Agent Systems, Hatfield, UK.

Haidt, J. (2001). The Emotional Dog and Its Rational Tail: A Social Intuitionist Approach to Moral Judgment. *Psychology Review* 108, 814–834.

Haidt, J. (2003). The Moral Emotions. In R. J. Davidson, K. R. Scherer, & H. H. Goldsmith (Eds.), *Handbook of Affective Sciences* (pp. 852–870). Oxford: Oxford University Press.

Haidt, J. (2007). The New Synthesis in Moral Psychology. *Science* 316, 998–1002.

Hall, J. S. (2000). *Ethics for Machines*. http://autogeny.org/ethics.html.

Hall, J. S. (2007). *Beyond AI: Creating the Conscience of the Machine*. Amherst, NY: Prometheus Books.

Hambling, D. (2007, September 10) Armed Robots Go into Action. *Wired Blog Network*. http://blog.wired.com/defense/2007/09/robosoldiers-hi.html.

Hamilton, E., & Cairns, H. (1961). *The Collected Dialogues of Plato, Including the Letters* (Cooper, L., Trans.). Princeton, NJ: Princeton University Press.

Hare, R. (1981). *Moral Thinking: Its Levels, Methods, and Point*. Oxford: Oxford University Press.

Harms, W. (1999). Biological Altruism in Hostile Environments. *Complexity* 5(2), 23–28.

Harms, W. (2000). The Evolution of Altruism in Hostile Environments. In L.D. Katz (Ed.), *Evolutionary Origins of Morality* (pp. 308–312). Exeter, UK: Imprint Academic.

Harnad, S. (2003). Can a Machine Be Conscious? How? *Journal of Consciousness Studies* 10 (4–5), 69–75.

Hauser, M. D. (2000). *Wild Minds*. New York: Holt.

Hauser, M. D. (2006). *Moral Minds: How Nature Designed Our Universal Sense of Right and Wrong*. New York: Ecco.

Hauser, M. D., Cushman, F., Young, L., Jin, R. K., & Mikhail, J. (2007). A Dissociation between Moral Judgment and Justification. *Mind and Language* 22(1), 1–21.

Heilman, K. M. (1997). The Neurobiology of Emotional Experience. *Journal of Neuropsychiatry and Clinical Neuroscience* 9, 439–448.

Henig, R. M. (2007, July 29). The Real Transformers. *New York Times Magazine*.

Hexmoor, H., Castelfranchi, C., & Falcone, R. (2003). *Agent Autonomy*. New York: Springer.

Hibbard, B. (2000). Super-Intelligent Machines. *Computer Graphics* 35(1), 11–13.

Hibbard, B. (2003). *Critique of the SIAI Guidelines on Friendly AI*. www.ssec.wisc.edu/~billh/g/SIAI_critique.html.

Hill, R. J. (1983). The Automation of Railways. *Physics in Technology*, 14, 37–47.

Hodges, A. (1992). *Alan Turing: The Enigma*. New York: Simon and Schuster.

Hoffman, M. (2000). *Empathy and Moral Development: Implications for Caring and Justice*: Cambridge, UK: Cambridge University Press.

Hofstadter, D. R., & Mitchell, M. (1995). The Copycat Project: A Model of Mental Fluidity and Analogy-Making. In K. J. Holyoak & J. Barnden (Eds.), *Advances in Connectionist and Neural Computation Theory*, Vol. 2: *Logical Connections* (pp. 205–267). Norwood, NJ: Ablex.

Holland, J. H. (1962). Outline for a Logical Theory of Adaptive Systems. *Journal of the Association for Computing Machinery* 9, 297–314.

Holland, J. H. (1975). *Adaptation in Natural and Artificial Systems*. Ann Arbor: University of Michigan.

Holland, J. H. (1992). Genetic Algorithms. *Scientific American* 267(1), 66–72.

Holland, O. (Ed.). (2003). Special issue on Machine Consciousness. *Journal of Consciousness Studies* 10 (4–5).

Holland, O. (Ed.) (2003). *Machine Consciousness*. Thorverton, UK: Imprint Academic.

Holland, O., & Goodman, R. (2003). Robots with Internal Models: A Route to Machine Consciousness. In O. Holland (Ed.), *Machine Consciousness* (pp. 77–110). Thorverton, UK: Imprint Academic.

Howell, S. R. (1999). *Neural Networks and Philosopy: Why Aristotle was a Connectionist*. www.psychology.mcmaster.ca/beckerlab/showell/aristotle.pdf.

Hume, D. (2000 [1739–40]). *A Treatise on Human Nature*. Oxford: Oxford University Press.

Irrgang, B. (2006). Ethical Acts in Robotics. *Ubiquity* 7(34), 241–250.

Isen, A. M. & Levin, P. F. (1972). The Effect of Feeling Good on Helping: Cookies and Kindness. *Personality and Social Psychology* 21, 382–388.

Ishiguro, H. (July, 2005). *Android Science: Towards a New Cross-Disciplinary Framework*. Paper presented at the CogSci-2005 Workshop: Towards Social Mechanisms of Android Science, Stresa, Italy.

ISO. (2006). ISO Robot Safety Standards, Standard No. 10218-1: 2006. International Organization for Standardization.

Jablonka, E., & Lamb, M. (2005). *Evolution in Four Dimensions: Genetic, Epigenetic, Behavioral, and Symbolic Variation in the History of Life.* Cambridge, MA: MIT Press.

Jackson, J. V. (1987). Idea for a Mind. *ACM Siggart Bulletin* 101, 23–26.

James, W. (1890). *The Principles of Psychology.* Cambridge, MA: Harvard University Press.

John, D. (1993). *Moral Reasons.* Oxford: Blackwell.

Johnson, D. (1985). *Computer Ethics.* New York: Prentice-Hall.

Johnson, M. (1993). *Moral Imagination: Implications of Cognitive Science for Ethics.* Chicago: University of Chicago Press.

Johnston, V. S. (1999). *Why We Feel: The Science of Human Emotions.* Reading, MA: Perseus Books.

Jonsen, A. R., & Toulmin, S. (1988). *The Abuse of Casuistry: A History of Moral Reasoning.* Berkeley: University of California Press.

Joy, B. (2000, April). Why the Future Doesn't Need Us. *Wired* 8(04). www.wired .com/wired/archive/8.04/joy_pr.html.

Kaelbling, L. P., Littman, M. L., & Moore, A. W. (1996). Reinforcement Learning: A Survey. *Journal of Artificial Intelligence Research* 4, 237–285.

Kahn, A. F. U. (1995). The Ethics of Autonomous Learning Systems. In K. Ford, C. Glymour, & P. Hayes (Eds.), *Android Epistemology* (pp. 243–252). Cambridge, MA: MIT Press.

Kahneman, D., Slovic, P., & Tversky, A. (1982). *Judgment under Uncertainty: Heuristics and Biases.* Cambridge, MA: Cambridge University Press.

Kanerva, P. (1988). *Sparse Distributed Memory.* Cambridge, MA: MIT Press.

Kant, E. (1996 [1785]). *Groundwork of the Metaphysics of Morals.* Cambridge, UK: Cambridge University Press.

Kara, D. (2005). *Sizing and Seizing the Robotics Opportunity.* www.robnexus.com/ roboticsmarket.htm.

Kassan, P. (2006). A.I. Gone Awry: The Futile Quest for Artificial Intelligence. *Skeptic* 12(2), 30–39.

Katz, L. (Ed.). (2000). *Evolutionary Origins of Morality: Cross-Disciplinary Perspectives.* Thorverton, UK: Imprint Academic.

Kennedy, C. (2004). Agents for Trustworthy Ethical Assistance. In I. Smit, W. Wallach, & G. Lasker (Eds.), *Sixteenth International Conference on Systems Research, Informatics and Cybernetics: Symposium on Cognitive, Emotive and Ethical Aspects of Decision Making in Humans and in Artificial Intelligence* (Vol. III, pp. 15–20). Windsor, Ontario, Canada: International Institute for Advanced Studies in Systems Research and Cybernetics.

Kennedy, C. M. (2000, April). *Reducing Indifference: Steps towards Autonomous Agents with Human Concerns.* Paper presented at the Convention of the Society for Artificial Intelligence and Simulated Behavior, Symposium on AI, Ethics and (Quasi-) Human Rights, Birmingham, UK.

Knutton, M. (2002, June). The Future Lies in Driverless Metros. *International Railway Journal.* http://findarticles.com/p/articles/mi_moBQQ/is_6_ 42/88099079.

Kohlberg, L. (1969). Stage and Sequence: The Cognitive-Developmental Approach to Socialization. In D. A. Gosli (Ed.), *Handbook of Socialization Theory and Research* (pp. 347–480). Chicago: Rand-McNally.

Kohlberg, L. (1981). *Essays on Moral Development*, Vol. 1: *The Philosophy of Moral Development*. San Francisco: Harper & Row.

Kohlberg, L. (1984). *Essays on Moral Development*, Vol. 2: *The Psychology of Moral Development*. San Francisco: Harper & Row.

Kolcaba, R. (2001). Angelic Machines: A Philosophical Dialogue. *Ethics and Information Technology* 2(1), 11–17.

Kraus, S. (2001). *Strategic Negotiation in Multiagent Environments*. Cambridge, MA: MIT Press.

Krazit, T. (2006, May 24). My Friend the Robot. *CNET News*.

Kuflik, A. (2001). Computers in Control: Rational Transfer of Authority or Irresponsible Abdication of Autonomy? *Ethics and Information Technology* 1(3), 173–184.

Kurzweil, R. (1999). *The Age of Spiritual Machines: When Computers Exceed Human Intelligence*. New York: Viking Press.

Kurzweil, R. (2000, October 23). Promise and Peril. *Interactive Week*.

Kurzweil, R. (2005). *The Singularity Is Near: When Humans Transcend Biology*. New York: Viking.

LaChat, M. R. (2003). Moral Stages in the Evolution of the Artificial Superego: A Cost-Benefits Trajectory. In I. Smit, W. Wallach, & G. Lasker (Eds.), *Fifteenth International Conference on Systems Research, Informatics and Cybernetics: Symposium on Cognitive, Emotive and Ethical Aspects of Decision Making in Humans and in Artificial Intelligence* (Vol. II, pp. 18–24). Windsor, Ontario, Canada: International Institute for Advanced Studies in Systems Research and Cybernetics.

LaChat, M. R. (2004). "Playing God" and the Construction of Artificial Persons. In I. Smit, W. Wallach, & G. Lasker (Eds.), *Sixteenth International Conference on Systems Research, Informatics and Cybernetics* (Vol. III, pp. 39–44). Windsor, Ontario, Canada: International Institute for Advanced Studies in Systems Research and Cybernetics.

Lakoff, G. (1987). *Women, Fire, and Dangerous Things—What Categories Reveal about the Mind*. Chicago: University of Chicago Press.

Lakoff, G. (1995). Metaphor, Morality, and Politics, Or, Why Conservatives Have Left Liberals in the Dust. *Social Research* 62(2), 177–214.

Lakoff, G., & Johnson, M. (1980). *Metaphors We Live By*. Chicago: University of Chicago Press.

Lang, C. (2002). *Ethics for Artificial Intelligences*. Paper presented at Wisconsin State-Wide Technology Symposium "Promise or Peril? Reflecting on Computer Technology: Educational, Psychological, and Ethical Implications," Madison, Wisconsin.

Latané, B. D., Darley, J. M. (1970). *The Unresponsive Bystander: Why Doesn't He Help?* New York: Appleton-Century Crofts.

Lazarus, R. (1991). *Emotion and Adaptation*. Oxford: Oxford University Press.

LeDoux, J. (1996). *The Emotional Brain: The Mysterious Underpinnings of Emotional Life.* New York: Simon & Schuster.

Lehman-Wilzig, S. (1981, December). Frankenstein Unbound: Towards a Legal Definition of Artificial Intelligence. *Futures*, 442–457.

Lenggenhager, B., Tadi, T., Metzinger, T., & Blanke, O. (2007). Video Ergo Sum. *Science* 317, 1096–1099.

Levy, D. (2007). *Love and Sex with Robots: The Evolution of Human-Robot Relationships.* New York: HarperCollins.

Lewis, J. (2005). Robots of Arabia. *Wired* 13(11), 188–195.

Libet, B. (1999). Do We Have Free Will? *Journal of Consciousness Studies* 6, 47–57.

Libet, B., Gleason, C. A., Wright, E. W., & Pearl, D. K. (1983). Time of Conscious Intention to Act in Relation to Onset of Cerebral Activity (Readiness-Potential): The Unconscioous Initiation of a Freely Voluntary Act. *Brain* 106, 623–642.

Lisetti, C., et al. (2003). Developing Multimodal Intelligent Affective Interfaces for Tele–Home Health Care. *International Journal of Human-Computer Studies* 59(1–2), 245–255.

Logical Endings: Computers May Soon Be Better Than Kin at Predicting the Wishes of the Dying. (2007, March 15). *Economist*, p. 63.

Longnian, L., et al. (2007). Neural Encoding of the Concept of Nest in the Mouse Brain. *Proceedings of the National Academy of Sciences* 10, 1073.

Looks, M., Goertzel, B., & Pennachin, C. (2004). Novamente: An Integrative Architecture for General Intelligence. In N. Cassimatis & P. Winston (Co-chairs), *AAAI Symposium: "Achieving Human-Level Intelligence via Integrated Systems and Research."* Alexandria, VA: AAAI Press.

Lorenz, E. (December, 1972). Predictability: Does the Flap of a Butterfly's Wings in Brazil Set Off a Tornado in Texas? Paper presented to the American Association for the Advancement of Science. Washington, DC.

MacDorman, K. F. (2006, July). *Subjective Ratings of Robot Video Clips for Human Likeness, Familiarity, and Eeriness: An Exploration of the Uncanny Valley.* Paper presented at the International Conference of the Cognitive Science/CogSci-2006 Long Symposium: Toward Social Mechanisms of Android Science, Vancouver, Canada.

Maes, P. (1989). How to Do the Right Thing. *Connection Science* 1, 291–323.

Maes, P. (1991). A Bottom-Up Mechanism for Behavior Selection in an Artificial Creature. In J. Meyer & S. W. Wilson (Eds.), *Proceedings of the First International Conference on Simulation of Adaptive Behavior: From Animals to Animats* (pp. 238–246). Cambridge, MA: MIT Press.

Malinowski, B. (1944). *A Scientific Theory of Culture.* Raleigh: University of North Carolina Press.

Maner, W. (2002). Heuristic Methods for Computer Ethics. In J. H. Moor & T. W. Bynum (Eds.), *Cyberphilosophy: The Intersection of Philosophy and Computing* (pp. 339–365). Malden, MA: Blackwell.

Markowitsch, H. J. (2000). Neuroanatomy of Memory. In E. Tulving & F. I. M. Craik (Eds.), *The Oxford Handbook of Memory* (pp. 465–484). Oxford: Oxford University Press.

Marks, P. (2006, September 21). Robot Infantry Get Ready for the Battlefield. *New Scientist*.

Marshall, J. (August, 2002). *Metacat: A Self-Watching Cognitive Architecture for Analogy-Making*. Paper presented at the twenty-fourth annual conference of the Cognitive Science Society, Fairfax, VA.

Martin, J. (2000). *After the Internet: Alien Intelligence*. Washington, DC: Capital Press.

Massimini, M., Ferrarelli, F., Huber, R., Esser, S. K., Singh, H., & Tononi, G. (2005). Breakdown of Cortical Effective Connectivity during Sleep. *Science* 309, 2228–2232.

Maturana, H. R., & Varela, F. J. (1980). *Autopoiesis and Cognition: The Realization of the Living*. New York: Springer.

May, L., Freidman, M., & Clark, A. (Eds.). (1996). *Mind and Morals: Essays on Ethics and Cognitive Science*. Cambridge, MA: MIT Press.

McCarthy, J. (1995). *Making Robots Conscious of Their Mental States*. www.formal.stanford.edu/jmc/consciousness/consciousness.html.

McCauley, L., & Franklin, S. (2002). A Large-Scale Multi-Agent System for Navy Personnel Distribution. *Connection Science* 14, 371–385.

McDermott, D. (1988). We've Been Framed: Or, Why AI Is Innocent of the Frame Problem. In Z. W. Pylyshyn (Ed.), *The Robot's Dilemma: The Frame Problem in Artificial Intelligence* (pp. 113–122). Norwood, NJ: Ablex.

McDermott, D. (2008, July 12). *Why Ethics is a High Hurdle for AI*. Paper presented at *2008 North American Conference on Computing and Philosophy*. Bloomington, Indiana.

McGinn, C. (1999). *The Mysterious Flame: Conscious Minds in a Material World*. New York: Basic Books.

McKeever, S., & Ridge, M. (2005). The Many Moral Particularisms. *Canadian Journal of Philosophy* 35(1), 83–106.

McLaren, B. (2003, November). Extensionally Defining Principles of Machine Ethics: An AI Model. *Artificial Intelligence Journal* 150, 145–181.

McLaren, B. (2006). Computational Models of Ethical Reasoning: Challenges, Initial Steps, and Future Directions. *IEEE Intelligent Systems* 21(4), 29–37.

McLaren, B., & Ashley, K. D. (1995). Case-Based Comparative Evaluation in Truth-Teller. In E. Lawrence (Ed.), *Seventeenth Annual Conference of the Cognitive Science Society* (pp. 72–77). San Diego, CA.

McNally, P., & Inayatullah, S. (1988) The Rights of Robots: Technology, Culture and Law in the Twenty-first Century. *Metafuture.org/Articles/TheRightsofRobots.htm*.

Meador, K. J., Ray, P. G., Echauz, J. R., Loring, D. W., & Vachtsevanos, G. J. (2002). Gamma Coherence and Conscious Perception. *Neurology* 59, 847–854.

Merker, B. (2005). The Liabilities of Mobility: A Selection Pressure for the Transition to Consciousness in Animal Evolution. *Consciousness and Cognition* 14, 89–114.

Metzinger, T. (2004). *Being No One: The Self-Model Theory of Subjectivity*. Cambridge, MA: MIT Press.

Mikhail, J. (2000). *Rawls' Linguistic Analogy: A Study of the "Generative Grammar" Model of Moral Theory Described by John Rawls in "A Theory of Justice."* Ithaca, NY: Cornell University Press.

Mikhail, J., Sorentino, C., & Spelke, E. (1998). *Toward a Universal Moral Grammar.* Paper presented at the twentieth annual conference of the Cognitive Science Society, Mahwah, NJ.

Mill, J. S. (1998 [1864]). *Utilitarianism.* Oxford: Oxford University Press.

Miller, G. (1956). The Magical Number Seven, Plus or Minus Two: Some Limits on Our Capacity for Processing Information. *Psychology Review* 63(2), 81–97.

Minsky, M. (1985). *The Society of Mind.* New York: Simon & Schuster.

Minsky, M. (2006). *The Emotion Machine.* New York: Simon & Schuster.

Mitchell, T. (1997). *Machine Learning.* Boston: McGraw-Hill.

Moor, J. H. (1979). Are There Decisions Computers Should Never Make? *Nature and System* 1(4), 217–229.

Moor, J. H. (1995). Is Ethics Computable? *Metaphilosophy* 26(1–2), 1–21.

Moor, J. H. (2001). The Future of Computer Ethics: You Ain't Seen Nothing Yet! *Ethics and Information Technology* 3(2).

Moor, J. H. (2001). The Status and Future of the Turing Test. *Minds and Machines* 11, 77–93.

Moor, J. H. (2006). The Nature, Importance, and Difficulty of Machine Ethics. *IEEE Intelligent Systems* 21(4), 18–21.

Moravec, H. (1988). *Mind Children: The Future of Robot and Human Intelligence.* Cambridge, MA: Harvard University Press.

Moravec, H. (2000). *Robot: Mere Machine to Transcendent Mind.* Oxford: Oxford University Press.

More, M. (2000). *Embrace, Don't Relinquish, the Future.* www.kurzweilai.net/articles/art0106.html?printable=1.

Morgenstern, O., & von Neumann, J. (1944). *Theory of Games and Economic Behavior.* New York: Wiley.

Mori, M. (1970). Bukimi no tani (The Uncanny Valley). *Energy* 7(4), 33–35.

Mowbray, M. (2002). Ethics for Bots. In I. Smit & G. Lasker (Eds.), *Sixteenth International Conference on Systems Research, Informatics and Cybernetics: Symposium on Cognitive, Emotive and Ethical Aspects of Decision Making in Humans and in Artificial Intelligence* (Vol. I, pp. 24–28). Windsor, Ontario, Canada: International Institute for Advanced Studies in Systems Research and Cybernetics.

Mulcahy, N. J., & Call, J. (2006). Apes Save Tools for Future Use. *Science* 312, 1038–1040.

Murakami, Y. (2004, September). *Utilitarian Deontic Logic.* Paper presented at Advances in Modal Logic Fifth International Conference, Manchester, UK.

Muramatsu, R., & Hanoch, Y. (2004). Emotions as a Mechanism for Boundedly Rational Agents: The Fast and Frugal Way. *Journal of Economic Psychology* 26(2), 201–221.

Nadel, L. (1992). Multiple Memory Systems: What and Why. *Journal of Cognitive Neuroscience* 4, 179–188.

Nadel, L., & Moscovitch, M. (1997). Memory Consolidation, Retrograde Amnesia and the Hippocampal Complex. *Current Opinions in Neurobiology* 7, 217–227.

Nagel, T. (1974). What Is It Like to Be a Bat? *Philosophical Review* 83(4), 435–450.

National Society of Professional Engineers. (1996). *The NSPE Code of Ethics.* www .onlineethics.diamax.com/CMS/profpractice/ethcodes/13411/9972.aspx.

Negatu, A., D'Mello, S. K., & Franklin, S. (2007). Cognitively Inspired Anticipatory Adaptation and Associated Learning Mechanisms for Autonomous Agents. In M. V. Butz, O. Sigaud, G. Pezzulo, & G. Baldassarre (Eds.), *ABiALS-2006—Anticipatory Behavior in Adaptive Learning Systems* (pp. 108–127). Rome: Springer.

Negatu, A., & Franklin, S. (2002). An Action Selection Mechanism for "Conscious" Software Agents. *Cognitive Science Quarterly* 2, 363–386.

Negatu, A., McCauley, T. L., & Franklin, S. (In Review). Automatization for Software Agents.

Nehaniv, C. L., & Dautenhahn, K. (2007). *Imitation and Social Learning in Robots, Humans and Animals: Behavioral, Social and Communicative Dimensions.* Cambridge, UK: Cambridge University Press.

Newell, A., & Simon, H. A. (1976). Computer Science as Empirical Inquiry: Symbols and Search. *Communications of the ACM* 19(3), 113–126.

Newman, S. D., Carpenter, P. A., Varma, S., & Just, M. A. (2003). Frontal and Parietal Participation in Problem Solving in the Tower of London: fMRI and Computational Modeling of Planning and High-Level Perception. *Neuropsychologia* 41, 1668–1682.

Nichols, S. (2004). *Sentimental Rules: On the Natural Foundations of Moral Judgment.* Oxford: Oxford University Press.

Nissenbaum, H. (1996). Accountability in a Computerized Society. *Science and Engineering Ethics* 2, 25–42.

Nissenbaum, H. (2001). How Computer Systems Embody Values. *Computer* 34(3), 118–119.

Nolfi, N., & Floreano, D. (2000). *Evolutionary Robotics: The Biology, Intelligence, and Technology of Self-Organizing Machines.* Cambridge, MA: MIT Press.

Norman, D. (2004). *Emotional Design.* New York: Basic Books.

Norvig, P. (2007, September 9). *The History and Future of Technological Change.* Transcript of a talk presented at the Singularity Summit 2007: AI and the Future of Humanity. San Francisco, CA.

Ornstein, R. (1986). *Multimind.* Boston: Houghton Mifflin.

Ortony, A., Clore, G., & Collins, A. (1988). *The Cognitive Structure of Emotions.* Cambridge, UK: Cambridge University Press.

Oyama, S. (1985). *The Ontology of Information.* Cambridge, UK: Cambridge University Press.

Panksepp, J. (1998). *Affective Neuroscience: The Foundations of Human and Animal Emotions.* Oxford: Oxford University Press.

Pascal, B. (2004 [1670]). *Pensées.* Whitefish, MT: Kessinger.

Penrose, R. (1989). *The Emperor's New Mind: Concerning Computers, Minds, and the Laws of Physics.* Oxford: Oxford University Press.

Perkowitz, S. (2005). *Digital People: From Bionic Humans to Androids*. Washington, DC: Joseph Henry Press.

Pettit, P. (2003). *Akrasia, Collective and Individual*. In S. Stroud & C. Tappolet (Eds.), *Weakness of Will and Practical Irrationality* (pp. 68–97). Oxford: Oxford University Press.

Piaget, J. (1932). *The Moral Judgment of the Child*. London: Routledge & Kegan Paul.

Piaget, J. (1972). *Judgment and Reasoning in the Child*. Totowa, NJ: Littlefield, Adams.

Picard, R. (1997). *Affective Computing*. Cambridge, MA: MIT Press.

Picard, R. W., & Klein, J. (2002). Computers that Recognise and Respond to User Emotion: Theoretical and Practical Implications. *Interacting with Computers* 14(2), 141–169.

Pickering, J. (2000, April). *Agents and Ethics*. Paper presented at the Convention of the Society for Artificial Intelligence and Simulated Behavior, Symposium on AI, Ethics and (Quasi-) Human Rights, Birmingham, UK.

Pollack, J. B. (2005). Ethics for the Robot Age: Should Bots Carry Weapons? Should They Win Patents? Questions We Must Answer as Automation Advances. *Wired* 13(1). www.wired.com/wired/archive/13.01/view.html.

Pollack, J. B. (2006). Mindless Intelligence. *IEEE Intelligent Systems* 21(3), 50–56.

Powers, T. (2006). Prospects for a Kantian Machine. *IEEE Intelligent Systems* 21(4), 46–51.

Premack, D. W., & Woodruff, G. (1978). Does the Chimpanzee Have a Theory of Mind? *Behavioral and Brain Science* 1, 515–526.

Prinz, J. (2004). *Gut Reactions: A Perceptual Theory of Emotions*. Oxford: Oxford University Press.

Pinz, J. (2006). The Emotional Basis of Moral Judgments. *Philosophical Explorations* 9(1).

Ramamurthy, U., D'Mello, S. K., & Franklin, S. (2004). *2004 Institute of Electrical Engineers International Conference on Systems, Man and Cybernetics*, 6 (pp. 5858–5863). The Hague: Institute of Electrical Electronics Engineers.

Ramamurthy, U., D'Mello, S. K., & Franklin, S. (2005, June). *Role of Consciousness in Episodic Memory Processes*. Poster presented at the ninth conference of the Association for the Scientific Study of Consciousness. Pasadena, CA.

Rao, R. P. N., & Fuentes, O. (1998). Hierarchical Learning of Navigational Behaviors in an Autonomous Robot Using a Predictive Sparse Distributed Memory. *Machine Learning* 31(1–3), 87–113.

Rawls, J. (1999). *A Theory of Justice*. Cambridge, MA: Harvard University Press.

Ray, T. (1991). An Approach to the Synthesis of Life. In C. G. Langton, C. Taylor, J. D. Farmer, & S. Rasmussen (Eds.), *Artificial Life II* (pp. 371–408). Santa Fe, NM: Westview Press.

Ray, T. (2002). Kurzweil's Turing Fallacy. In J. Richards & G. Gilder (Eds.), *Are We Spiritual Machines? Ray Kurzweil vs. the Critics of Strong A.I.* (pp. 116–127). Seattle: Discovery Institute.

Richards, J. W., & Gilder, G. (Eds.). (2002). *Are We Spiritual Machines? Ray Kurzweil vs. the Critics of Strong A.I.* Seattle: Discovery Institute.

Reeves, B., & Nass, C. (1996). *The Media Equation: How People Treat Computers, Television, and New Media.* Cambridge, MA: Cambridge University Press.

Reynolds, C., & Picard, R. (2004, April). *Affective sensors, privacy, and ethical contracts.* Paper presented at Conference on Human Factors in Computing Systems. Vienna, Austria.

Robbins, R. W., & Wallace, W. A. (2007). Decision Support for Ethical Problem Solving: A Multi-Agent Approach. *Decision Support Systems* 43(4), 1571–1587.

Roco, M., & Bainbridge, W. (2002). Conference report *Converging Technologies for Improving Human Performance—Nanotechnology, Biotechnology, Information Technology, and Cognitive Science.* Arlington, VA: NSF/DoC.

Rose, J., & Turkett, W. (2002). *Emergent Planning with Philosophical Agents.* Paper presented at the Third International Workshop on Planning and Scheduling for Space, Houston, TX.

Ross, W. D. (1930). *The Right and the Good.* Oxford: Clarendon Press.

Rothstein, J. (2006, May 23). Soldiers Bond with Battlefield Robots: Lessons Learned in Iraq May Show Up in Future Homeland "Avatars." MSNBC/Reuters. Originally retrieved from www.msnbc.msn.com/id/12939612 and archived at http://web.archive.org/web/20060613225745/http://www.msnbc.msn.com/id/12939612.

Rothstein, J. (2006, May 23). Soldiers Bond with iRobot Machine. Reuters, San Diego. www.boston.com/news/nation/articles/2006/05/23/soldiers_bond_with_irobot_machine_ceo_dreams_big/?rss_id=Boston.com+%2F+News.

Rozin, P., Haidt, J. & McCauley, C. (2000). Disgust. In M. Lewis & J. M.Haviland-Jones (Eds.), *Handbook of Emotions* (2nd ed.) (pp. 637–653). New York: Guilford Press.

Russell, S., & Norvig, P. (1995). *Artificial Intelligence: A Modern Approach.* Upper Saddle River, NJ: Prentice Hall.

Rzepka, R., & Araki, K. (2005). What Could Statistics Do for Ethics? The Idea of Common Sense Processing Based Safety Value. In M. Anderson, S. L. Anderson, & C. Armen (Cochairs), *Machine Ethics: Papers From The AAAI Fall Symposium.* (pp. 85–87). Arlington, VA: AAAI Press.

Saletan, W. (2007, May 11). Chess Bump: The Triumphant Teamwork of Humans and Computers. *Slate.* www.slate.com/id/2166000.

Salovey, P., & Mayer, J. D. (1990). Emotional Intelligence. *Imagination, Cognition, and Personality* 9, 185–211.

Satpute, A. B., & Lieberman, M. D. (2006). Integrating Automatic and Controlled Processes into Neurocognitive Models of Social Cognition. *Brain Research* 1079, 86–97.

Sawyer, R. J. (2007). Robot Ethics. *Science* 318, 1037.

Scassellati, B. (2001). *Foundations for a Theory of Mind for a Humanoid Robot.* Ph. D. Thesis submitted to the Department of Electrical Engineering and Computer Science. MIT, Cambridge, Massachusetts.

Schactman, N. (2007, August 16). Armed Robots Pushed to Police. *Wired Blog Network* http://blog.wired.com/defense/2007/08/armed-robots-so.html.

Schactman, N. (2007, Ocotober 18). Robot Cannon Kills 9, Wounds 14. *Wired Blog Network.* http://blog.wired.com/defense/2007/10/robot-cannon-ki.html.

Schactman, N. (2007, October 17). Roomba-Maker Unveils Kill-Bot. *Wired Blog Network.* http://blog.wired.com/defense/2007/10/roomba-maker-un.html.

Scheutz, M. (2004). Useful Roles of Emotions in Artificial Agents: A Case Study from Artificial Life. In *Proceedings of AAAI 2004* (pp. 42–48). San Jose, CA: AAAI Press.

Scheutz, M. C., & Crowell, C. (2007, April 14). *The Burden of Embodied Autonomy: Some Reflections on the Social and Ethical Implications of Autonomous Robots.* Paper presented at the Workshop on Roboethics at the International Conference on Robotics and Automation, Rome.

Scholl, B., & Tremoulet, P. (2000). Perceptual Causality and Animacy. *Trends in Cognitive Science* 4(8), 299–309.

Searing, D. (1998). *HARPS Ethical Analysis Methodology.* www.cs.bgsu.edu/maner/heuristics/-1998Searing.htm.

Searle, J. R. (1980). Minds, Brains, and Programs. *Behavioral and Brain Sciences* 3(3), 417–458.

Seville, H., & Field, D. G. (2000, April). *What Can AI Do for Ethics?* Paper presented at the convention for The Society for the Study of Artificial Intelligence and the Simulation of Behavior 2000, Birmingham, UK.

Shalowitz, D. I., Garrett-Myer, E., & Wendler, D. (2007). How Should Treatment Decisions Be Made for Incapacitated Patients, and Why? *Public Library of Science Medicine* 4(3), e35.

Shanahan, M. (2005, April). *Consciousness, Emotion, and Imagination: A Brain-Inspired Architecture for Conscious Robots.* Paper presented at the Artificial Intelligence and the Simulation of Behavior '05 Convention, Social Intelligence and Interaction in Animals, Robots and Agents: Symposium on Next Generation Approaches to Machine Consciousness, Hatfield, UK.

Shanahan, M. (2007, July). *Is There an Ethics of Artificial Consciousness?* Paper presented at the Hungary Cognitive Science Foundation conference, Towards a Science of Consciousness, Budapest.

Shanahan, M. P. (2005). Consciousness, Emotion, and Imagination: A Brain-Inspired Architecture for Cognitive Robotics, *Proceedings of the Artificial Intelligence and the Simulation of Behavior 2005 Symposium on Next Generation Approaches to Machine Consciousness* (pp. 26–35). www.aisb.org.uk/publications/proceedings/aisb05/7_MachConsc_Final.pdf.

Shanahan, M. P. (2006). A Cognitive Architecture that Combines Internal Simulation with a Global Workspace. *Consciousness and Cognition,* 15, 433–449.

Shanahan, M. S. (2007). A Spiking Neuron Model of Cortical Broadcast and Competition. *Consciousness and Cognition* 17(1), 288–303.

Shnayerson, M. (2004, January 1). The Code Warrior. *Vanity Fair.*

Sidgwick, H. (1874). *The Methods of Ethics.* London: Macmillan.

Sieghart, P., & Dawson, J. (1987). Computer-aided medical ethics. *Journal of Medical Ethics* 13(4). 185–188.

Sigman, M., & Dehaene, S. (2006). Dynamics of the Central Bottleneck: Dual-Task and Task Uncertainty. *Public Library of Science Biology* 4(7), e220.

Simon, H. A. (1967). Motivation and emotional controls of cognition. *Psychological Review* 74, 29–39.

Simon, H. A. (1982). *Models of Bounded Rationality*. Cambridge, MA: MIT Press.

Singh, S., & Thayer, S. (2001). *ARMS (Autonomous Robots for Military Systems): A Survey of Collaborative Robotics Core Technologies and Their Military Applications*. Pittsburgh, PA: Robotics Institute, Carnegie Mellon University.

Singularity_Institute. (2001). *SIAI Guidelines on Friendly AI*. www.singinst.org/ourresearch/publications/guidelines.html.

Skyrms, B. (1996). *Evolution of the Social Contract*. Cambridge, UK: Cambridge University Press.

Skyrms, B. (2000). Game Theory, Rationality and Evolution of the Social Contract. In L. Katz (Ed.), *Evolutionary Origins of Morality* (pp. 269–285). Thorverton, UK: Imprint Academic.

Skyrms, B. (2003). *The Stag Hunt and the Evolution of the Social Contract*. Cambridge, UK: Cambridge University Press.

Sloman, A. (1998). *Damasio, Descartes, Alarms and Meta-Management*. In *Proceedings of the Symposium on Cognitive Agents: Modeling Human Cognition*. San Diego, CA: Institute of Electrical Electronics Engineers.

Sloman, A. (1999). What Sort of Architecture Is Required for a Human-like Agent? In M. Wooldridge & A. S. Rao (Eds.), *Foundations of Rational Agency* (pp. 35–52). New York: Springer.

Sloman, A., & Chrisley, R. (2003). Virtual Machines and Consciousness. In O. Holland (Ed.), *Machine Consciousness* (pp. 133–172). Thorverton, UK: Imprint Academic.

Sloman, A. R., Chrisley, R., & Scheutz, M. (2005). The Architectural Basis of Affective States and Processes. In J. M. Fellous & Arbib, M. A. (Eds.), *Who Needs Emotions? The Brain Meets the Robot* (pp. 203–244). Oxford: Oxford University Press.

Slovic, P. (1987). Perception of Risk. *Science* 236, 280–285.

Smit, I. (2002). *Equations, Emotions, and Ethics: A Journey Between Theory and Practice*. In I. Smit & G. Lasker (Eds.), *Fourteenth International Conference on Systems Research, Informatics and Cybernetics: Symposium on Cognitive, Emotive and Ethical Aspects of Decision Making and Human Action* (Vol. I, pp. 1–6). Windsor, Ontario, Canada: International Institute for Advanced Studies in Systems Research and Cybernetics.

Smit, I. (2003). *Robots, Quo Vadis?* In I. Smit, W. Wallach, & G. Lasker (Eds.), *Fifteenth International Conference on Systems Research, Informatics and Cybernetics: Symposium on Cognitive, Emotive and Ethical Aspects of Decision Making in Humans and in Artificial Intelligence* (Vol. II, pp. 6–11). Windsor, Ontario, Canada: International Institute for Advanced Studies in Systems Research and Cybernetics.

Smith, J. D., & Washburn, D. A. (2005). Uncertainty Monitoring and Metacognition by Animals. *Current Directions in Psychological Science*, 14, 19–24.

Snapper, J. W. (1985). Responsibility for Computer-Based Errors. *Metaphilosophy* 16, 289–295.

Soskis, B. (2005, January/February). Man and the Machines. *Legal Affairs*. www .legalaffairs.org/issues/January-February-2005/feature_sokis_janfeb05 .msp.

Sousa, R. (1987). *The Rationality of Emotion*. Cambridge, MA: MIT Press.

Sparrow, R. (2002). The March of the Robot Dogs. *Ethics and Information Technology* 4(4), 305–318.

Sparrow, R. (2006). In the Hands of Machines? The Future of Aged Care. *Minds and Machines* 16, 141–161.

Sparrow, R. (2007). Killer Robots. *Applied Philosophy* 24(1), 62–77.

Stahl, B. C. (2002). Can a Computer Adhere to the Categorical Imperative? A Contemplation of the Limits of Transcendental Ethics in IT. In I. Smit & G. Lasker (Eds.), *Fourteenth International Conference on Systems Research, Informatics and Cybernetics: Symposium on Cognitive, Emotive and Ethical Aspects of Decision Making in Humans and in Artificial Intelligence* (Vol. I, pp. 13–18). Windsor, Ontario, Canada: International Institute for Advanced Studies in Systems Research and Cybernetics.

Stahl, B. C. (2004). Information, Ethics, and Computers: The Problem of Autonomous Moral Agents. *Minds and Machines* 14(1), 67–83.

Stickgold, R., & Walker, M. P. (2005). Memory Consolidation and Reconsolidation: What Is the Role of Sleep? *Trends in Neuroscience* 28, 408–415.

Stiehl, D., Lieberman, J., Breazeal, C., Basel, L., Lalla, L., & Wolf, M. (2005). The Design of the Huggable: A Therapeutic Robotic Companion for Relational, Affective Touch. In T. Bickmore (Ed.), *AAAI Fall Symposium in Caring Machines: AI in Eldercare*. Washington, DC: AAAI Press.

Stross, C. (2006). *Accelerando*. New York: Ace.

Stuart, S. (1994 [slightly rev. 2003]). Artificial Intelligence and Artificial Life— Should Artificial Systems Have Rights? www.gla.ac.uk/departments/ philosophy/Personnel/susan/NewNightmares.pdf.

Tarsitano, M. (2006). Route Selection by a Jumping Spider (Portia Labiata) during the Locomotory Phase of a Detour. *Animal Behavior* 72, 1437–1442.

Taylor, C. (1989). *Sources of the Self*. Cambridge, MA: Harvard University Press.

Transport for London. (2004). *Central Line facts*. Original web page retrieved from http://tube.tfl.gov.uk/content/faq/lines/central.asp10/18/2004; archived at the Internet Archive http://web.archive.org/web/*hh_/tube.tfl.gov.uk/content/ faq/lines/central.asp.

Thompson, H. S. (1999). Computational Systems, Responsibility and Moral Sensibility. *Technology in Society* 21(4), 409–415.

Torrance, S. (2000, April). *Towards an Ethics for Epersons*. Paper presented at the Symposium on AI, Ethics and (Quasi-) Human Rights, Birmingham, UK.

Torrance, S. (2003). Artificial Intelligence and Artificial Consciousness: Continuum or Divide? In I. Smit, W. Wallach, & G. Lasker (Eds.), *Fifteenth International Conference on Systems Research, Informatics and Cybernetics: Symposium on Cognitive, Emotive and Ethical Aspects of Decision Making in*

Humans and in Artificial Intelligence (Vol. II, pp. 25–30). Windsor, Ontario, Canada: International Institute for Advanced Studies in Systems Research and Cybernetics.

Torrance, S. (2004). Us and Them: Living with Self-Aware Systems. In I. Smit, W. Wallach, & G. Lasker (Eds.), *Sixteenth International Conference on Systems Research, Informatics and Cybernetics: Symposium on Cognitive, Emotive and Ethical Aspects of Decision Making in Humans and in Artificial Intelligence* (Vol. III, pp. 7–14). Windsor, Ontario, Canada: International Institute for Advanced Studies in Systems Research and Cybernetics.

Tulving, E. (1983). *Elements of Episodic Memory*. Oxford: Clarendon Press.

Turing, A. (1950). Computing Machinery and Intelligence. *Mind and Language* 59, 434–460.

Turkle, S. (1984). *The Second Self: Computers and the Human Spirit*. New York: Simon & Schuster.

Tversky, A., & Kahneman, D. (1974). Judgment under Uncertainty: Heuristics and Biases. *Science* 185, 1124–1131.

Tyrell, T. (1994). An Evaluation of Maes's Bottom-Up Mechanism for Behavior Selection. *Adaptive Behavior* 2(4), 307–348.

Uchida, N., Kepecs, A., & Mainen, Z. F. (2006). Seeing at a Glance, Smelling in a Whiff: Rapid Forms of Perceptual Decision Making. *Nature Reviews Neuroscience* 7, 485–491.

US Plans "Robot Troops" for Iraq. (2005, January 23). *BBC News*.

van den Hoven, J., & Lokhorst, G. (2002). Deontic Logic and Computer-Supported Computer Ethics. In J. H. Moor & T. W. Bynum (Eds.), *Cyberphilosophy: The Intersection of Computing and Philosophy* (pp. 280–289). Malden, MA: Blackwell.

Van der Loos, H. F. M. (2007, March). *Ethics by Design: A Conceptual Approach to Personal and Service Robot Systems*. Paper presented at the Institute of Electrical Electronics Engineers '07 Workshop on Roboethics, Rome.

Van der Loos, H. F. M., Lees, D. S., & Leifer, L. J. (1992, June). *Safety Considerations for Rehabilitative and Human-Service Robot Systems*. Paper presented at the Fifteenth Annual Conference of the Rehabilitation Engeneering and Assistive Technology Society of North America, Toronto.

Varela, F. J., Thompson, E., & Rosch, E. (1991). *The Embodied Mind*. Cambridge, MA: MIT Press.

Vauclair, J., Fagot, J., & Hopkins, W. D. (1993). Rotation of Mental Images in Baboons When the Visual Input Is Directed to the Left Cerebral Hemisphere. *Psychological Science* 4, 99–103.

Veruggio, G. (2005, April). The Birth of Roboethics. Paper presented at the Institute of Electrical and Electronics Engineers International Conference on Robotics and Automation 2005 Workshop on Roboethics, Barcelona.

Veruggio, G. (2006, June). *EURON Roboethics Roadmap*. Paper presented at the EURON Roboethics Atelier, Genoa.

Veruggio, G., & Operto, F. (2006). Roboethics: A Bottom-Up Interdisciplinary Discourse in the Field of Applied Ethics in Robotics. *International Review of Information Ethics* 6, 2–8.

Vidnyánszky, Z., & Sohn, W. (2003). Attentional Learning: Learning to bias Sensory Competition [Abstract]. *Journal of Vision* 3, 174a.

Vinge, V. (1983, January). First Word. *OMNI*.

Vinge, V. (1993, Winter). The Coming Technological Singularity: How to Survive in the Post-Human Era. *Whole Earth Review, 77*.

von Foerster, H. (1992). Ethics and Second-Order Cybernetics. *Cybernetics and Human Knowing* 1(1), 40–46.

Wallach, W. (2003). *Robot Morals and Human Ethics*. In I. Smit, W. Wallach, & G. Lasker (Eds.), *Fifteenth International Conference on Systems Research, Informatics and Cybernetics: Symposium on Cognitive, Emotive and Ethical Aspects of Decision Making in Humans and in Artificial Intelligence* (Vol. II, pp. 1–5). Windsor, Ontario, Canada: International Institute for Advanced Studies in Systems Research and Cybernetics.

Wallach, W. (2004). *Artificial Morality: Bounded Rationality, Bounded Morality and Emotions*. In I. Smit, W. Wallach, & G. Lasker (Eds.), *Sixteenth International Conference on Systems Research, Informatics and Cybernetics: Symposium on Cognitive, Emotive and Ethical Aspects of Decision Making in Humans and in Artificial Intelligence* (Vol. III, pp. 1–6). Windsor, Ontario, Canada: International Institute for Advanced Studies in Systems Research and Cybernetics.

Wallach, W. (2007, September 8). *The Road to Singularity: Comedic Complexity, Technological Thresholds, and Bioethical Broad Jumps*. Transcript of a presentation at the Singularity Summit 2007: AI and the Future of Humanity. San Francisco.

Wallach, W. (2008). Implementing Moral Decision Making Faculties in Computers and Robots. *AI and Society* 22(4), 463–475.

Wallach, W., Allen, C., & Smit, I. (2008). Machine Morality: Bottom-Up and Top-Down Approaches for Modelling Human Moral Faculties. *AI and Society* 22(4), 565–582.

Warwick, K. (2003). Cyborg Morals, Cyborg Values, Cyborg Ethics. *Ethics and Information Technology* 5, 131–137.

Warwick, K. (2004). *I Cyborg*. London: Century.

Watt, D. F. (1998). Affect and the Limbic System: Some Hard Problems. *Journal of Neuropsychiatry and Clinical Neuroscience* 10, 113–116.

Weckert, J. (1997). Intelligent Machines, Dehumanisation and Professional Responsibility. In J. van den Hoven (Ed.), *Computer Ethics: Philosophical Enquiry* (pp. 179–192). Rotterdam: Erasmus University Press.

Weckert, J. (2005). *Trusting Agents*. In P. Brey, F. Grodzinsky, & L. Introna (Eds.), *Ethics of New Information Technology: Proceedings of the Sixth International Conference of Computer Ethics: Philosophical Enquiry* (pp. 407–412). Enschede, The Netherlands: Center for Telematics and Information Technology.

Weiner, T. (2005, February 16). New Model Army Soldier Rolls Closer to Battle. *New York Times*.

Weinman, J. (2001). *Autonomous Agents: Motivations, Ethics, and Responsibility*. Manuscript originally retrieved from www.weinman.cc/ethics.phtml archived at http://web.archive.org/web/*/http://www.weinman.cc/ethics .phtml.

Werdenich, D., & Huber, L. (2006). A Case of Quick Problem Solving in Birds: String Pulling in Keas, Nestor Notabilis. *Animal Behaviour* 71, 855–863.

Wertheim, M. (1999). *The Pearly Gates of Cyberspace*. New York: Norton.

Whitbeck, C. (1995). Teaching Ethics to Scientists and Engineers: Moral Agents and Moral Problems. *Science and Engineering Ethics* 1(3), 299–308.

Whitby, B. R. (1990, November). *Problems in the Computer Representation of Moral Reasoning*. Paper presented at the Second National Conference on Law, Computers and Artificial Intelligence. Exeter University, UK.

Whitby, B. R. (1991). AI and the Law: Proceed with Caution. In M. Bennun (Ed.), *Law, Computer Science and Artificial Intelligence* (pp. 1–14). New York: Ellis Horwood.

Whitby, B. R. (1996). *Reflections on Artificial Intelligence: The Social, Legal, and Moral Dimensions*. Exeter, UK: Intellect Books.

Whitby, B. R., & Oliver, K. (2000). *How to Avoid a Robot Takeover: Political and Ethical Choices in the Design and Introduction of Intelligent Artifacts*. Paper presented at the Convention of the Society for Artificial Intelligence and Simulated Behavior, Symposium on AI, Ethics and (Quasi-) Human Rights. Birmingham, UK.

Wiegel, V., van den Hoven, J., & Lokhorst, G. (2005). Privacy, Deontic Epistemic Action Logic and Software Agents. In *Sixth International Conference on Computer Ethics: Ethics of New Information Technology* (pp. 419–434). Enschede, The Netherlands: Center for Telematics and Information Technology.

Wilcox, S., & Jackson, R. (2002). Jumping Spider Tricksters: Deceit, Predation, and Cognition. In M. Bekoff, C. Allen, & G. M. Burghardt (Eds.), *The Cognitive Animal* (pp. 27–33). Cambridge, MA: MIT Press.

Williams, B. (1985). *Ethics and the Limits of Philosophy*. Cambridge, MA: Harvard University Press.

Willis, J., & Todorov, A. (2006). First Impressions: Making Up Your Mind after a 100-Ms Exposure to a Face. *Psychological Science* 17, 592–599.

Wilson, E. O. (1975). *Sociobiology: The New Synthesis*. Cambridge, MA: Harvard University Press.

World Health Organisation. (2002) *Injury: A leading cause of the global burden of disease, 2000*. Geneva: World Health Organisation.

Wu, X., Chen, X., Li, Z., Han, S., & Zhang, D. (2007). Binding of Verbal and Spatial Information in Human Working Memory Involves Large-Scale Neural Synchronization at Theta Frequency. *Neuroimage* 35(4), 1654–1662.

Yaeger, L., & Sporns, O. (2006). Evolution of Neural Structure and Complexity in a Computational Ecology. In *Artificial Life X*. Bloomington, IN: MIT Press.

Yudkowsky, E. (2001). *What Is Friendly AI?* www.kurzweilai.net/meme/frame.html?main=/articles/art0172.html.

Yudkowsky, E. (2001). *Creating Friendly AI*. www.singinst.org/upload/CFAI.html.

Yudkowsky, E. (Forthcoming). Artificial Intelligence as a Positive and Negative Factor in Global Risk. In M. Rees, N. Bostrom, & M. Cirkovic (Eds.), *Global Catastrophic Risks* Oxford: Oxford University Press.

Zhang, Z., Dasgupta, D., & Franklin, S. (1998). Metacognition in Software Agents Using Classifier Systems. In *Proceedings of the Fifteenth National Conference on Artificial Intelligence* (pp. 83–88). Menlo Park, CA: AAAI Press.

Zhu, J., & Thagard, P. (2002). Emotion and Action. *Philosophical Psychology* 15, 19–36.

INDEX

J. Craig Venter Institute, 55
Jablonka, Eva, 227
James, William, 145–146, 176, 232
Japan Robot Association (JARA), 49
JARA. *See* Japan Robot Association
Johnson, Deborah, 221
Johnson, Mark, 232
Joy, Bill, 229

Kahn, Peter, 40–41, 45, 222
Kant, Immanuel, 70, 78, 84, 95–96, 201
Kara, Dan, 220
Kennedy, Catriona, 168, 231
Key restraints of computational
    systems, 111
Khepera robots, 157–159, 158*f*
Killing machine morals and ethics,
    20–21, 20*f*, 74, 171–172
Kismet (robot), 28*f*, 29–30, 44, 108,
    160–161
Knobe, Joshua, 200, 226
Knutton, Mike, 220
Koch, Christof, 67
Kohlberg, Lawrence, 108–109, 228
Krazit, Tom, 223
Kronrod, Aleksandr, 220
Kurzweil, Ray, 57, 189, 232

LaChat, Michael Ray, 194, 232
Lahnstein, Mercedes, 225
Lamb, Marion, 227
Lang, Christopher, 62, 109–110, 224
Law enforcement robots, 32
Lazarus, Richard, 145, 230
Learning-based approach to AMAs,
    109–110, 195
Learning intelligent distribution
    agent (LIDA)
    attention codelets in, 176–177,
        183, 232
    challenges to, 180–181
    cognitive cycle of, 175*f*
    conscious information processing in,
        174–175, 175*f*, 179, 182
    and GWT, 176, 186
    human moral decision-making,
        177–179
    as IDA with learning, 174
    learning approach to, 184–185
    as modular system, 186
    moral decisions of, 173
    perceptual memory, 180
    planning implementation for,
        183–184

with ToM, 186–187
and utilitarianism, 179
Learning machines in bottom-up
    approach, 106–111, 179–181
LeDoux, Joseph, 230
Lee, Rabinder, 225
Legal questions in futurist concerns, 191
Lehman-Wilzig, Sam, 204
Von Leibniz, Gottried Wilhelm, 83
Leonardo (robot), 161–162
Levy, David, 49
Lewis, Michael, 230
Liability issues in robotic engineering,
    15–16, 45, 197–199, 208
LIDA. *See* Learning intelligent
    distribution agent
Lisetti, Christine, 230
Logically moral vaporware, 125–129
Lokhorst, Gert-Jan, 229
Lovelace, Ada, 100, 227
LUDWIG (humanoid robot), 231

Machine Consciousness, 68, 169,
    205, 225
Machine guns, robotic, 6, 20, 47
Machine morality. *See* Bottom-up
    approach to morality; Robots as
    moral agents; Top-down morality
Marriage, humans to robots, 49, 210
Massachusetts Institute of Technology
    (MIT)
    Affective Computing Laboratory, 3,
        23, 43, 152
    Artificial Intelligence
        Laboratory, 64
    Cognitive Machines Group, 112
    Humanoid Robotics Group, 44
    Robotic Life Group, 150–151, 161
Maturana, Humberto, 231
Mayer, John, 144, 230
McCauley, Clark, 230
McDermott, Drew, 34–35, 222
McGinn, Colin, 67, 225
McLaren, Bruce, 127, 129–130
MedEthEx, medical ethics expert
    system, 27, 29, 97, 127–129, 229
Metanet network, 132
Methodist Theological School, 194
Metzinger, Thomas, 205, 209, 232
Military robots, 73
Mill, John Stuart, 70, 78, 87
Minsky, Marvin, 156, 232
MIT. *See* Massachusetts Institute of
    Technology

Model of User's Emotions (MOUE),
154–155, 230
Modular computer systems, 186
Module assembling, bottom-up
approach, 111–114
Monkeys, 228
Moor, James, 33–36, 103, 221, 229
Moore's law, 189
Moor's categories of ethical agents,
33–36, 103
Moral grammar, 105–106, 111, 228*f*
Moral reasoning and beyond. *See
also* Decision-making by moral
machines; Reasoning capacity
affective computing, 141, 152–155
cognitive or somatic theories,
145–150
computational challenges, 145–150
embodied robots, 167–169
emotional intelligence, 141, 143–145
emotions and, 139, 150–152
feelings *vs.* emotions, 140–141
human *vs.* robot interaction,
160–163
multiagent environments, 165–167
the OCC, 155–156
"satisficing," 149–150
sensory technologies, 150–152
suprarational faculties, 140–143, 150
and ToM, 163–165
Moral Turing Test (MTT), 70, 206–207
Morals and morality. *See also* Bottom-up
approach to morality; Decision-
making by moral machines;
Engineering morality; Functional
morality; Reasoning capacity;
Robots as moral agents; Top-down
morality
accountability *vs.* responsibility,
201, 207
algorithms translated to, 71, 84, 88
bottom line *vs.*, 31
commandment model of, 84
connectionist approaches to AI,
132–133
developmental approach, 77, 99
dilemmas in, 75, 94, 181–183
distributed concept of, 203
good samaritan experiments,
178, 185
logically moral vaporware, 125–129
particularism in, 122–123, 132,
228–229
philosophy of, 6, 8, 84, 91, 215

political correctness *vs.*, 78–79
psychological considerations of, 8,
11, 77, 140, 173, 178
Moravec, Hans, 189, 232
Morgenstern, Oskar, 101, 227
Mori, Masahiro, 44
Movements, robots imitating human,
44, 64, 112, 141, 154, 164
MTT. *See* Moral Turing Test
Multiagent systems
environments for, 165–167
ethical software approaches to, 125
platform implementation for,
135–137
values of, 104
Multibots, vaporware, 133–134
Multimodal approach to robots,
63, 154–155

Nagel, Thomas, 225
Nanotechnology
cyborgs as outgrowth of, 33, 165
ethical challenges posed by, 192
as unpredictable, 38, 190, 211, 213
Nash, John, 101
National Institutes of Health (NIH), 42
National Society of Professional
Engineers (NSPE), 25, 131
Nature *vs.* nurture, developmental
process, 99
NERD. *See* Norms Evolving in Response
to Dilemmas
Neumann, John von, 101
Neural networks. *See also*
Consciousness
affective touch classes, 151
connectionist approaches to, 107,
119, 121–123, 132, 194
feedback connections, 132
Neuroethics program, 222
Neuroprosthetics research, 33, 190
Neuropsychology field in morality,
8, 173
Newell, Allen, 56, 90, 224
Nichols, Shaun, 230
Nico (robot), 161, 164
Nissenbaum, Helen, 39, 198, 221–222
Nonmaleficence principle,
bioethics, 127
Norms Evolving in Response to
Dilemmas (NERD), 133
Norvig, Peter, 22, 193–194, 207, 221
NSPE. *See* National Society of
Professional Engineers

Nuclear power technology, 51–52
Nuclear weapons, 45

OCC. *See* Ortony, Clore and Collins
Omniscient computers, 86–91
Ontological question, careworthy
    technology, 55, 80
Operational morality, 26, 29, 34
Organic morality, bottom-up
    approach, 99–101
Ortony, Andrew, 230
Ortony, Clore and Collins (OCC),
    emotion model, 155–156, 230
Oversight mechanisms, futurist
    concerns, 212

Packard, Norman, 224
Packbot (robot), 20, 47–48, 64, 223
Pain as sensory technology, 90, 92,
    151–152, 194, 196, 209
Panksepp, Jaak, 147
Particularism principle for morality,
    122–123, 132, 228–229
Perceptual memory in LIDA model,
    180, 182
Pettit, Philip, 93, 226
Phenomenal self model (PSM), 205
Philosophy and Phenomenological Research
    (Eells, Fitelson, Sober), 227
Philosophy/philosophers. *See also*
    Consciousness; Emotions in robots;
    Engineering morality
  in AI design, 74, 76–77, 118, 202
  of building ethical agents, 34–35,
    168, 185
  Chinese room argument, 57–58, 63
  CogAff decision-making model,
    156, 173
  experimental field of, 136, 200
  good samaritan experiments,
    178, 185
  Kant's theory, 95
  moral considerations of, 6, 8, 84,
    91, 215
  neural correlates of consciousness, 67
  on technological dependence, 37–39
  trolley cases in, 13–16, 220
  Turing test as solution, 70
Picard, Rosalind, 23, 152–153, 221, 230
Pleasure forms, top-down morality, 49,
    87, 89, 150, 156, 209
Politics/political problems. *See also*
    Future concerns for robotics; Risk
    assessment for robotics

correctness *vs.* morality, 78–79
  sexual related, 210
  with technology, 14, 199–200,
    207–208, 211–212
  with weapon robots, 21, 52
Pollack, Jordan, 192
Power blackouts by computer networks,
    18, 21–22, 31
Powers, Thomas, 226
Precautionary principle in future
    dangers, 52, 211
Preference rankings, robots, 61
Premack, David, 231
Prima facie duties
  in MedEthEx, 97, 127–128
  principles for, 85, 94, 96
Principlism theory in bioethics, 127
Prinz, Jesse, 144, 230
Prisoner's dilemma in game theory,
    101–102
Propensities, bottom-up approach,
    179–181
Protolife (robotics development
    company), 55
PSM. *See* Phenomenal self model
Psychology/psychologists. *See also*
    Cognitive capacities and theories;
    Emotions in robots
  evolutionary field of, 101
  infant developmental, 107, 160–161,
    163–165
  moral considerations in, 11, 77,
    140, 178
  neuropsychology field, 8, 173
  social robotic development and, 43,
    48, 96, 190, 196
  teaching tools for, 109
  trolley cases, investigation by,
    13–16, 220
Public welfare *vs.* technology, 25, 38
Punishment of AMAs, 109, 196, 208

QRIO (toy), 43

Rawls, John, 105, 228
Ray, Thomas, 104–105, 228
Reasoning capacity. *See also* Cognitive
    capacities and theories; Ethics
    and ethical considerations; Moral
    reasoning and beyond; Morals and
    morality
  casuistic approach to, 127, 129
  emotional link in, 143, 147, 156–157,
    168–169

Truth-teller system, 130
Varela, Francisco, 231
Varner, Gary, 225
Venter, Craig, 223–224
Veruggio, Gianmarco, 212–213
Vinge, Vernor, 224
Viruses in computers, 18–19
"Volitional" decision-making, 176, 232
Von Neumann, John, 227

Waal, Frans de, 228
Warrior X700 (robot), 20
Wayback Machine (internet archive
    search), 19–20, 221
Weapon robots
    ARMS as, 223
    as border guards, 3
    ethical issues of, 73, 171
    in law enforcement, 32
    machine guns, 6, 20, 47
    nuclear submarines, 45
    political problems with, 21, 52

safety problems with, 48–49
soldiers as, 47–48, 195
SWORDS (robot), 20, 47
for warfare, 21, 47, 73
Weiner, Tim, 221, 223
Wendler, David, 42
Whitbeck, Caroline, 75, 226
Whitby, Blay, 35
Wiegel, Vincent, 136, 229
Williams, Bernard, 88, 226, 228
Wilson, Daniel, 192
Wilson, E. O., 101, 227
Woodruff, Guy, 231
World Health Organization (WHO), 52
World Transhumanist
    Association, 194

Yaeger, Larry, 228
Yudkovsky, Eliezer, 192

Zeroth Law, Asimov, 48, 91, 219
Zinser, Jason, 225